Technical Analysis

FT Press

FINANCIAL TIMES

In an increasingly competitive world, it is quality
of thinking that gives an edge—an idea that opens new
doors, a technique that solves a problem, or an insight
that simply helps make sense of it all.

We work with leading authors in the various arenas
of business and finance to bring cutting-edge thinking
and best-learning practices to a global market.

It is our goal to create world-class print publications
and electronic products that give readers
knowledge and understanding that can then be
applied, whether studying or at work.

To find out more about our business
products, you can visit us at www.ftpress.com.

Technical Analysis

Power Tools for Active Investors

Gerald Appel

Library of Congress Number: 2004116766

Publisher: Tim Moore
Executive Editor: Jim Boyd
Editorial Assistant: Kate E. Stephenson
Development Editor: Russ Hall
Marketing Manager: Martin Litkowski
International Marketing Manager: Tim Galligan
Cover Designer: Sandra Schroeder
Managing Editor: Gina Kanouse
Senior Project Editor: Sarah Kearns
Copy Editor: Krista Hansing
Indexer: Angie Bess
Compositor: Tolman Creek Design
Manufacturing Buyer: Dan Uhrig

© 2005 Pearson Education, Inc.

Publishing as FT Press

Upper Saddle River, NJ 07458

FT Press offers excellent discounts on this book when ordered in quantity for bulk purchases or special sales. For more information, please contact: U.S. Corporate and Government Sales, 1-800-382-3419, corpsales@pearsontechgroup.com. For sales outside the U.S., please contact International Sales at international@pearsoned.com.

Company and product names mentioned herein are the trademarks or registered trademarks of their respective owners.

Printed in the United States of America

Fifth Printing: September 2007

ISBN 0-13-147902-4

Pearson Education LTD.
Pearson Education Australia PTY, Limited
Pearson Education Singapore, Pte. Ltd.
Pearson Education North Asia Ltd.
Pearson Education Canada, Ltd.
Pearson Educación de Mexico, S.A. de C.V.
Pearson Education—Japan
Pearson Education Malaysia, Pte. Ltd.

To my grandchildren—Emily, Caroline, and Alexandra. May children all the world over enjoy a bright and peaceful future.

Contents

Foreword

This is a feast for a serious trader—for a professional looking to improve his or her performance or a beginner trying to avoid some of the more painful collisions with reality. I wish I had this book years ago, and I enjoy reading it today, finding pearls of wisdom to improve my trading.

Jerry is one of the world's top-performing money managers whose dazzling mind produces more fresh ideas in a month than most people have in a lifetime. He has, since 1973, been the editor of a technical newsletter, *Systems and Forecasts*, published by his firm, Signalert Corporation, is an important money manager, and the author of several books. He became famous in the era of computerized technical analysis as the inventor of MACD. Moving Average Convergence-Divergence is now included in most trading programs.

This book taps into the results of a lifetime of research and money management. Jerry gives you market mood indicators to identify high- and low-risk investment climates, backing them up with gain/pain ratios. He lays bare powerful signals from moving averages and rate of change indicators. He takes one of the most obscure areas of technical analysis—chart reading—and reduces it to a set of clear and lucid rules.

All traders and investors study price movements, but only the best pay attention to time. Jerry teaches you to ride market cycles, supplementing them with powerful T-formations. He explains why he believes the real market is reflected in market breadth, such as New High—New Low Index. His chapter on volume and volatility makes it clear why market tops are "calm before the storm" and market bottoms "storm before calm." These and other simple but profound concepts will change the way you trade.

The chapters on MACD and moving average trading bands take you to the heart of the master's method. I first heard Jerry speak of them around 1990, and those ideas continue to influence my trading to this day. Jerry distills his vast market expertise into a set of what he calls Power Tools.

I recently visited Jerry and asked why he wrote this book. He laughed, "I enjoy seeing my picture on book jackets.... It feels good to get your ideas out into the world, leave a little of your imprint around. I have never lost anything by giving ideas away. If people find it useful, it makes me feel good."

The only thing you have to bring to reading this book is a commitment to market work. What you need to succeed is right here, on the table in front of you. It will be curious to see how many people actually take this knowledge and work with it to become successful traders and investors.

Dr. Alexander Elder
Haciendas El Choco
Dominican Republic
January 2005

Acknowledgments

I would like to acknowledge the myriad and endless research, graphics, and editorial contributions to this work made by staff members of Signalert Corporation, in particular (in alphabetical order) my son, Dr. Marvin Appel; my brother, Arthur Appel; Joon Choi; Bonnie Gortler; Glenn Gortler; and Roni Nelson, without whose contributions this book would not have been possible.

I would like to acknowledge as well the myriad of technical analysts and students of the stock market from whom I have learned over the years and from whom I continue to learn. Although there have been too many to specify, my appreciation is, nonetheless, sincere and considerable.

And last, but absolutely not least....

My first book, *Winning Market Systems*, written 34 years ago, in 1971, was dedicated to my wife, Judy, as "the best investment I have ever made." At this time, 34 years later and after 48 years of marriage, I make the same dedication, only more so. Judy has not been simply important to my life. She has been my life....

Gerald Appel

About the Author

Gerald Appel has, since 1973, published *Systems and Forecasts*, a leading technical analysis publication. Appel is legendary for his work in technical analysis and market timing, including the creation of Moving Average Convergence-Divergence (MACD), one of the field's most widely used tools. His numerous books include, among others, *Winning Market Systems: 83 Ways to Beat the Market, Stock Market Trading Systems* (with Fred Hitschler), *New Directions in Technical Analysis* (with Dr. Martin Zweig), *The Big Move,* and *Time-Trend III.* His company, Signalert Corporation, and affiliates, currently manages more than $550,000,000 in investor capital. Appel has trained thousands of traders through his world-renowned video and audio tapes, seminars, and workbooks. He recently taught a series of four-day international master classes on investing and trading strategies in partnership with Dr. Alex Elder. As Appel puts it, "I have never lost anything by giving ideas away. If people find it useful, it makes me feel good."

Introduction

This book, *Technical Analysis*, is meant for every investor who has been hurt trusting his brokerage firm, trusting his friendly mutual fund manager, or trusting the latest hot guru. It is meant for every investor who has ever wished for the skills required to deal with an increasingly volatile and uncertain stock market. It is meant for every investor willing to take responsibility for the outcome of his own investments. It is meant for every investor ready to take at least some of the time and to put forth at least some of the effort required for the quest.

The stock market tends to condition investors to make the wrong decisions at the wrong times. For instance, the stock market explosion of the late 1920s convinced investors that the only path for stocks was up, and that the prospects of stocks rising indefinitely justified even the high levels of margin leverage that could be employed at the time.

Investors plowed in, the stock market collapsed, and, thereafter, the public remained fearful of stocks for 20 years, although the stock market actually reached its lows during 1931 and 1932. In the mid-1990s, the Standard & Poor's 500 Index was king and index mutual funds were the royal coach. Between 1996 and 1998, huge inflows of capital were injected into Standard & Poor's 500–based index mutual funds, such as those sponsored by Vanguard. The largest inflows took place just before a serious intermediate market decline in mid-1998. The market advance that followed that decline was headed not by the Standard & Poor's 500 sector of the stock market, but by speculative areas of the Nasdaq Composite: technology sectors (Internet issues and the like) that, in some cases, sold for hundreds of dollars per share, even though many companies had no earnings whatsoever. And then came the crash, in March of 2000. The Nasdaq Composite ultimately declined by more than 77%.

So, investors returned to the sanctity of total return, value, earnings, and dividends, not the worst strategy during the bear market that took place between 2000 and 2002, but definitely not the best of strategies when the new bull market more clearly emerged during the spring of 2003. The play returned to technology and the Internet, with growth back in and total return back out. (During the first nine months of 2004, however, technology issues once again lost market leadership to value- and income-oriented market sectors.)

The point, of course, is that the typical investor follows and does not lead trends, is late rather than early, and is a crowd-follower rather than a self-director. According to Dalbar, Inc., a financial services research firm, the average equity fund investor realized an annualized return of 5.32% between 1984 and 2000, while the

Standard & Poor's 500 Index rose at a rate of 16.3% per annum. Matters become even worse when comparisons are updated through July 2003. The average investor was ahead by only 2.6% per year for the 1984–2003 period, compared to annualized returns of 12.2% for the Standard & Poor's 500 Index.

This book has been prepared to help investors achieve better than average performance—considerably better, we believe.

The structure of *Technical Analysis* has been designed to provide information and investment tools, some of which can be put to work immediately, by both sophisticated and relatively unsophisticated stock market investors. I will share with you, right at the start, my favorite techniques for picking mutual funds and ETFs (securities that trade on the stock exchange and act similarly to market index mutual funds but provide greater investment flexibility at lower ongoing internal management fees, though, possibly, with some initial commission expense, which is often involved with mutual funds as well).

We move from there to some of the basic tools stock market technicians use to track and predict market behavior. A certain amount of statistical calculations is required in applying some of the "practical power tools" you will be learning—nothing truly complex. I have placed a strong emphasis on the "practical" in "practical power tools." The KISS (Keep It Simple, Stupid) principle is observed throughout the book—at least, to the best of my ability.

For example, in Chapter 1, "The No-Frills Investment Strategy," I show you two indicators that, together, should require no more than five or ten minutes for you to post and maintain each week—that's right, each week, not each day. These have a fine history of helping investors discriminate between favorable and unfavorable market climates. Nothing in the stock market can ever be guaranteed for the future, of course, but you will see how powerful these two simple indicators have been during more than three decades of stock market history in supplementing your selections for market investment with straightforward but surprisingly effective market-timing strategies.

Even if you go no further, you will have already acquired a useful arsenal of tools for improved investment results. By this time, you might well have become ready for additional, more involved technical tools that I have found over the decades to be more than useful in my own investment decisions. These include, for example, T-formations, special time-based patterns of market movement that frequently provide advance notice of when market turning points are likely to occur. In a subsequent chapter, you learn about the application of moving average trading channels, a technique for employing certain patterns of past market behavior to predict likely patterns for the future.

Finally, you get my personal take on Moving Average Convergence-Divergence (MACD), an indicator that I invented in the late 1970s and, since then, has become one of the most widely followed of market-forecasting tools employed by technical analysts, private and professional. You will learn how to maintain the MACD indicator and how to interpret it for time frames ranging from 15 minutes (for day trading) to many years (for long-term investing).

Each of these indicators alone can be quite powerful, particularly as you develop the facility for combining various elements of your trading strategy for disciplined decision-making, higher returns, and less risk. Synergy helps the cause. I will show you many ways to achieve this synergy.

All in all, *Technical Analysis* is about the best stock-market timing tools that I have learned in nearly 40 years of studying, trading in, and writing about the stock market. These are real tools, practical tools, tools that my staff and I employ every day in tracking the stock market and investing our own and our clients' capital. These are tools that you, yourself, can begin to employ almost immediately.

There will be some additional interesting side trips and excursions along the way, but I think that we will conclude the description of our itinerary at this point. The time has come to begin the journey....

The No-Frills Investment Strategy

Part I: Picking the Right Investment Vehicles

Successful investing involves two basic areas of decision: what do you buy and sell, and when do you buy and sell. We'll be moving along into the "whens" in chapters to come, as we develop a broad array of market timing techniques. Before we move into timing, however, we will consider some principles and procedures that should prove helpful in selecting vehicles in which to invest.

It's not how much you make that counts; it's how much you manage not to lose.

Let's start by considering just a few numbers. The Nasdaq Composite Index reached an all-time high on March 6, 2000, closing that day at 5048.60. The ensuing bear market took the index down to a low of 1,114.40 on October 9, 2002—a loss of 77.9%. Prices advanced from that point. By December 3, 2003, the Composite had risen to 1960.20—that's 75.9% above the lows of October 2002. And where did the buy-and-hold investor stand at that point? Down—very much down still, by 61.2% from the March 2000 close!

The moral: To make up any losses taken in the stock market, you have to achieve greater percentage gains than such losses entail. It does not matter whether the losses or the gains come first.

For example, if you lose 20% of the value of your assets, you have to make 25% on the remainder to break even. (If you start with $100,000 and lose 20%, you have $80,000. To bring that $80,000 back to $100,000, you have to show a gain of $20,000 which represents 25% of the $80,000 you have left in your account.)

If you lose one-third, or 33.33%, of your assets, you will have to make 50% on your remaining assets to break even. If you make 50% first, a loss of 33.33% will bring you back to your starting level.

If you lose 25%, you will need to gain 33.33% to bring you back to your starting level.

If you lose 50%, you will need to make 100% to restore your original capital.

If you lose 77.9%, you will need to make 352.5% on the assets left to break even.

I think you get the idea by now. Capital preservation is, by and large, more important for successful long-term investment than securing an occasional large profit. We will, of course, be reviewing a number of timing tools that are designed to provide more efficient entries and exits into the stock market, thereby reducing risk and improving the odds of maintaining and growing your capital assets. Let's begin, however, with strategies for portfolio selection, which should be very useful supplements to your market-timing arsenal.

Risk: Reward Comparisons Between More Volatile and Less Volatile Equity Mutual Fund Portfolios

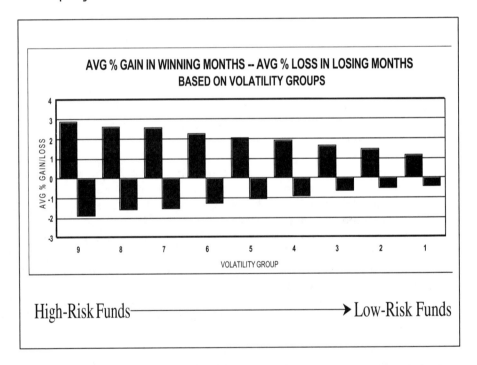

Chart 1.1   Average Percent Gain in Winning Months and Average Percent Loss in Losing Months, Based on Volatility Groups

This chart shows the average gain during months in which the average mutual fund rose in price (winning months) compared to months in which the average mutual fund declined (losing months). Mutual funds are ranked by volatility, the amount of daily and/or longer-term

price fluctuation that takes place in that fund, usually compared to the Standard & Poor's 500 Index as a benchmark. Group 9 represents the most volatile group of funds; Group 1 represents the least volatile segment. The period represented by this study was December 1983 to October 2003. The more volatile the group, typically the greater the gain during winning months, the greater the losses during losing months.

Calculations and conclusions presented in this chapter and in other areas where performance data is shown are based, unless otherwise mentioned, on research carried forth at Signalert Corporation, an investment advisory of which the author is sole principal and president. In this particular case, research encompassed mutual fund data going back to 1983, involving, among other processes, simulations of the strategies described for as many as 3,000 different mutual funds, with the number increasing over the years as more mutual funds have been created.

Chart 1.1 shows the relationships between average percentage gains during rising months for mutual funds of various volatility levels (range of price fluctuations) and the average percentage loss during declining market months, 1983 to 2003. For example, the most volatile segment of the mutual fund universe employed in this study (Group 9) gained just less than 3% during months that the average fund in that group advanced, and incurred an average loss of just less than 2% during months that the average fund in that group declined. As a comparison, funds in Group 1, the least volatile segment of this mutual fund universe, advanced by approximately 1.2% on average during rising months for that group and declined by approximately 4/10 of 1% during months that the average fund in that group showed a decline.

Chart 1.1 shows us that, basically, when more volatile mutual funds—and, by implication, portfolios of individual stocks that show above-average volatility—are good, they can be very good, indeed. However, when such portfolios are bad, they can be very bad, indeed. Are the gains worth the risks? That's a logical question that brings us to a second chart.

Gain/Pain Ratios

We have seen that the more aggressive the portfolio, the larger the average gain is likely to be during rising market periods. We have also seen that more aggressive portfolios are likely to lose more during declining market periods. That's logical enough—nothing for nothing. But what are the gain/pain ratios involved?

Well, Chart 1.2 shows that, on a relative basis, more volatile mutual funds involve greater pain to gain, lower profit/loss ratios than less volatile portfolios. For example, Group 9, the most volatile portfolio segment, makes about 3% during winning months for every 2% lost during declining months, a gain/loss ratio of essentially 1.5. Group 1, the least volatile group, has had a gain/loss ratio of approximately 2.7. You make 2.7% per winning month for every percent of assets lost during losing months. The amount of extra gain achieved by more volatile funds is offset by the disproportionate risk assumed in the maintenance of such portfolios.

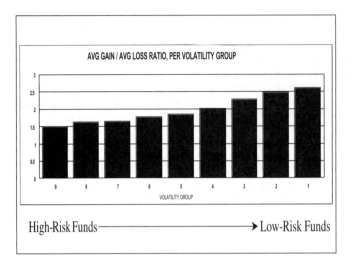

Chart 1.2   Average Gain/Average Loss, by Volatility Group

This chart shows the ratio of the average gain per winning month to the average loss per losing month, by volatility group. For example, Group 9, the highest-volatility group, shows a gain/loss ratio of 1.5. Winning months were, on average, 1.5 times the size of losing months. Group 2, the second-least-volatile group, shows a gain/loss ratio of 2.5. Winning months, on average, were 2.5 times the size of losing months. The period here was 1983 to 2003.

You might notice that relationships between volatility and risk are very constant and linear. The greater the volatility, the lesser the gain/loss ratio, the greater the risk—a relationship frequently lost to investors during periods when speculative interest in high-volatility stocks runs high.

Drawdown: The Measure of Ultimate Risk

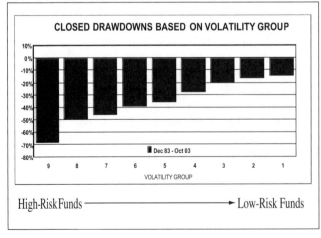

Chart 1.3   Closed Drawdowns by Volatility

Drawdown represents the maximum loss taken from a peak in portfolio value to a subsequent low before a new peak in value is achieved. The highest-volatility group, Group 9, incurred losses of as much as 68% during the 1983–2003 period, whereas the lowest-volatility group, Group 1, had a maximum drawdown of just 15%.

Drawdown, the amount by which your portfolio declines from a peak reading to its lowest value before attaining a new peak, is one of the truer measures of the risks you are taking in your investment program.

For example, let us suppose that you had become attracted to those highly volatile mutual funds that often lead the stock market during speculative investment periods, and therefore accumulated a portfolio of aggressive mutual funds that advanced between late 1998 and the spring of 2000 by approximately 120%, bringing an initial investment of $100,000 to $220,000. So far, so good. This portfolio, however, however, declines by 70% during the 2000–2003 bear market to a value of $66,000. Although losses of this magnitude to general mutual fund portfolios previously had not taken place since the 1974 bear market, they have taken place during certain historical periods and must be considered a reflection of the level of risk assumed by aggressive investors. Moreover, this potential risk level might have to be increased if asset values for this portfolio and similar portfolios were to decline to new lows before achieving new peaks, which had not yet taken place during the first months of 2004.

Protracted gains in the stock market tend to lead investors to presume that stock prices will rise forever; buy-and-hold strategies become the strategy of choice. Interest focuses on gain. Potential pain is overlooked. (Conversely, long periods of market decline tend to lead investors to minimize the potential of stock ownership. The emphasis becomes the avoidance of pain; the achievement of gain seems hopeless.)

Drawdowns—and risk potential—decline dramatically as portfolio volatility decreases, although risks to capital are still probably higher than most investors realize, even in lower-volatility areas of the marketplace. For example, maximum drawdowns between 1983 and 2003 were roughly 16% for Group 2, the second-least-volatile group of mutual funds, rising to 20% in Group 3, a group of relatively low volatility. Mutual funds of average volatility, Group 5, showed drawdowns of 35%.

In evaluating mutual funds or a selection of individual stocks or ETFs for your portfolio, you should secure the past history of these components to assess maximum past risk levels. ETFs (exchange traded funds) are securities, backed by related baskets of stocks, which are created to reflect the price movement of certain stock market indices and/or stock market sectors. For example, there are ETFs called SPYDRS that reflect the price movement of the Standard & Poor's 500 Index, rising and falling in tandem with the index. Another ETF, the QQQs, reflects the Nasdaq 100 Index. There are ETFs that reflect a portfolio of high-yielding issues in the Dow Industrial Average, a real estate trust portfolio, and even an ETF that reflects a portfolio of 10-year Treasury bonds. In many ways, ETFs are similar to index- or sector-based mutual funds, have the advantages of unlimited trading at any time of the day, as well as lower internal expenses than mutual funds. There are certain disadvantages, however, mainly associated with bid-ask spreads, which add to transaction costs as well as occasional periods of limited liquidity.

You can fine-tune the total risk of your total portfolio by balancing its components to include lower-risk as well as higher-risk segments. For example, a mutual fund portfolio consisting 50% of intermediate bond funds (past maximum drawdown 10%) and 50% Group 8 mutual funds (past maximum drawdown 50%) would represent a total portfolio with a risk level of approximately 30%, probably as much, if not more, risk than the typical investor should assume.

The End Result: Less Is More

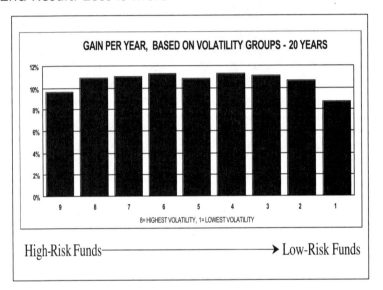

Chart 1.4   Twenty Years of Results, Based on Volatility Group

All things considered, investors gain little, if anything, by placing investments in higher-risk holdings. Lower-volatility groups have provided essentially the same investment results over the long run as higher-volatility groups, but with much less risk.

Chart 1.4 pretty much tells the story. With the exception of mutual funds in Group 1 (which includes many hybrid stock, bond funds), equity and balanced mutual funds of relatively low volatility produced essentially the same returns over the 1983–2003 decade as mutual funds of higher volatility. Generally, the highest average returns were secured with mutual funds of approximately average volatility, where the curve of returns appears to peak. However, differentials in return between Groups 2–3 and Groups 4–6 might or might not justify the increases in risk that are involved in stepping up from the very low-volatility groups to those at the average level.

To sum up, for buy-and-hold strategies, higher volatility has historically produced little, if any, improvement in return for investors, despite the greater risks involved. These actual results run counter to the general perception that investors can secure higher rates of return by accepting higher levels of risk, an assumption that might be correct for accurate and nimble market traders during certain periods but, in fact, is not the case for the majority of investors, who are most likely to position in aggressive market vehicles at the wrong rather than the right times.

Lower-volatility mutual funds typically produce higher rates of return and less drawdown, something to think about.

In as much as accurate timing can reduce the risks of trading in higher-velocity equities, active investors can employ more volatile investment vehicles if they manage portfolios in a disciplined manner with efficient timing tools. Relative returns compared to lower-volatility vehicles improve. Aggressive investors with strong market-timing skills and discipline might find it worthwhile to include a certain proportion of high-velocity investment vehicles in their portfolios—a certain proportion, perhaps up to 25%, but not a majority proportion for most.

Again, we will continue to consider tools that will improve your market timing. However, before we move into that area, I will show you one of the very best strategies I know to maintain investment portfolios that are likely to outperform the average stock, mutual fund, or market index.

Changing Your Bets While the Race Is Still Underway

Let's suppose you have a choice.

You go to the racetrack to bet on the fourth race, research the history of the horses, evaluate the racing conditions, check out the jockeys, evaluate the odds, and finally buy your tickets. Your selection starts well enough but, by the first turn, starts to fade, falling back into the pack, never to re-emerge; your betting capital disappears with the horse. The rules of the track, of course, do allow you to bet on more than one horse. The more horses you bet on, the greater your chances are that one will come through or at least place or show, but then there are all those losers....

Then you find a track that offers another way to play. You may start by betting on any horse you choose, but at the first turn, you are allowed to transfer the initial bet—even transfer your bet to the horse leading at the time. If the horse is still leading at the second turn, you will probably want to hold your bet. If the horse falters, however, you are allowed to shift your bet again, even to the horse that has just taken the lead. Same at the third turn. Same at the final turn. You can stay with the leaders, if you like, or, if your horse falls back into the pack, you can move the bet to the new leading horse until the race comes to an end. (I have, of course, taken some liberties with the analogies, to make a point.)

Which way do you think you'd prefer? Betting and holding through thick and thin, and, perhaps, through your horse running out of steam? Or shifting bets at each turn so your money starts each turn riding on a leading horse?

The first track is a little like the stock market, whose managers seem always to be telling investors what to buy, sometimes when to buy, but rarely, if ever, when to change horses. Buy-and-hold strategies do have their benefits, particularly over the very long term. It is possible, after all, for all stock market investors to make money in the end, which is not true for all bettors at the track.

The second track, however, is more likely to give an edge to the player. Strong horses tend to remain strong, especially when you don't have to ride them to the finish line if they begin to lose serious ground. That brings us to relative strength investing.

Relative Strength Investing

The basic principles of relative strength investing are as follows:

- Identify the leaders.
- Buy the leaders.
- Hold the leaders for as long as they lead.
- When the leaders slow down, sell them and buy new leaders.

Simple enough?

Let's get more specific.

For investors of average to below average risk tolerance, start by securing a database or two of a large number of mutual funds. I prefer a database of at least 1,000 mutual funds—preferably more, but for the purposes of a single investor instead of a capital manager, a few hundred is almost certainly sufficient.

You need quarterly data, so almost any source that tracks mutual funds and provides quarterly performance data serves your purpose. *Barron's the Dow Jones Business and Financial Weekly*, for example, provides good coverage. Other sources can be found on the Web.

For example, in the Finance areas of Yahoo.com and MSN.com, you can find charts and information regarding mutual funds. A number of investment advisory newsletters provide performance and other information regarding mutual funds. Newsletters that provide recommendations and data specific to the sort of investment approach I am suggesting include my own newsletter, *Systems and Forecasts*, and the newsletter *No-Load Fund X*. You can find information regarding these publications at www.Signalert.com and www.NoloadfundX.com, respectively.

Conservative investors should eliminate from the array of funds covered those that are normally more volatile than the Standard & Poor's 500 Index. Such funds often provide excellent returns during strong and speculative market climates, but you will probably secure better balances between risk and reward if you concentrate your selections on mutual funds that are, at most, just somewhat above (preferably approximately equal to or below) the Standard & Poor's 500 Index in volatility. Your portfolio, when fully invested, will probably include holdings that are, on average, approximately 80–85% as volatile (risky) as the Standard & Poor's 500 Index. Actual risk is likely to be reduced below these ratios as a result of the exceptional relative strength of your holdings. (More on this comes shortly.)

When you have isolated a universe of mutual funds whose volatility is more or less equal to or less than the Standard & Poor's 500 Index—for example, the Dodge and Cox Balanced Fund and First Eagle Sogen—determine from the performance tables which funds have shown performance results over the past three months that rank in the upper 10% (top decile) of all the mutual funds of similar volatility in your database. These are funds that have shown the greatest percentage gain for the period.

Buy a selection of at least two—preferably four or five—funds in the top decile of the mutual fund universe that consists of funds of equal or less volatility than the Standard & Poor's 500 Index. Some level of diversification is significant. Even a portfolio of as little as two mutual funds provides considerable increase in safety compared to a single-fund portfolio. Look for funds that charge no loads for purchase and involve no redemption fees for holding periods of at least 90 days.

Review your portfolios every three months, as new quarterly data becomes available. If any funds have fallen from the top decile, sell those funds and replace them with funds that remain or have just entered into the top decile in performance. Maintain current holdings that retain their positions in the top 10% of performance of all mutual funds of that volatility group.

Funds should be ranked against their own volatility peers. During rising market periods, funds of higher volatility tend to outperform funds of lower volatility simply because higher-volatility mutual funds and stocks tend to move more quickly than funds and stocks of lower volatility. Conversely, higher-volatility positions tend, on average, to decline more quickly in price than lower-volatility vehicles. We are seeking funds that produce the best returns for varied market climates, including both advancing and declining market periods. You can secure volatility ratings of mutual funds from a variety of sources, including Steele Mutual Fund Expert (see www.mutualfundexpert.com), an excellent reference for mutual fund information.

If you follow this procedure, you will regularly rebalance and reapportion your mutual fund holdings so that, at the start of every quarter, you will hold a portfolio of mutual funds that have been leading their peer universe in strength. Your portfolio will consist of mutual funds with the highest relative performance, horses that are leading the pack at every turn of the course.

Testing the Relative Strength Investment Strategy: A 14-Year Performance Record of Relative Strength Investing

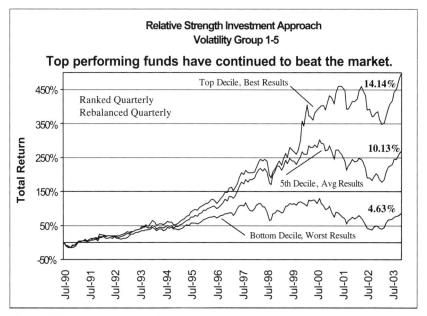

Chart 1.5   Performance of the Relative Strength Investment Approach (1990–2003)

Chart 1.5 shows the performance of ten performance deciles of mutual funds from 1990 to 2003. The assumption is made that, at the start of each quarter, assets are rebalanced so that investments are made only in funds that are ranked in the top 10% of performance for the previous quarter among mutual funds whose volatilities were equal to or less than the volatility of the Standard & Poor's 500 Index. The initial universe in 1990 was approximately 500 funds, increasing over the years to more than 3,000 by 2003. Performance was very consistent with rankings. This chart is based upon hypothetical research.

Chart 1.5 shows the results of a hypothetical back-test of this procedure of maintaining a portfolio of mutual funds of average to below-average volatility, reranking in performance each quarter, reallocating your holdings at that time by selling positions that have fallen from the top 10% in performance, and selecting and replacing such positions from those funds that have remained or recently entered into the upper decile.

Again, it goes without saying that this program should be carried out with no-load mutual funds that charge redemption fees only if assets are held less than 90 days. Brokerage firms such as Schwab and T. D. Waterhouse, as well as many others, provide platforms of no-load mutual funds from which you can make selections. Our research universe included equity, balanced, and sector mutual funds. Your own universe can be similarly created.

Rebalancing can take place more frequently than at 90-day intervals, if you prefer. For example, somewhat higher rates of return appear to accrue when ranking and rebalancing procedures take place at monthly rather than quarterly intervals. However, more frequent portfolio rotations result in increased trading expenses and probable increases in mutual fund redemption fees, all of which could well offset the advantages gained by more frequent portfolio reallocation. A program of rebalancing at intervals of more than three months is also likely to provide considerable benefit, although returns are likely to diminish in comparison to quarterly rebalancing as a result.

There is another significant reason to reduce trading frequency. As a result of scandals during 2003 and 2004 that took place related to mutual fund timing, mutual fund management companies and the distribution network of mutual funds became more sensitive to frequent trading by active market timers as a source of possible fund disruption. Close monitoring of active investors has become the norm, with frequent traders banned from investing in certain funds. In this regard, it is probably more prudent from your own public relations standpoint not to wear out your welcome with excessive trading.

ETFs may be traded with no restrictions, apart from trading expenses, which do mount with frequent trading and are something to definitely consider. Our own research, however, suggests that although the program of relative strength rebalancing just described is likely to improve on random selection of ETFs, the strategy appears to perform better when it is applied to mutual funds. ETFs seem more likely to show rapid gains or losses in inconsistent patterns than mutual funds and, as a group, tend to be more concentrated and volatile than lower-volatility mutual funds. That said, research carried forth by Signalert Corporation and research discussed in the newsletter *Formula Research* confirms the validity of applying relative strength rebalancing strategies to at least certain ETFs. For the most part, the use of mutual funds is recommended.

Incidentally, significant benefits might be achieved by rebalancing your portfolios at intervals of as long as one year. At the start of each year, you purchase mutual funds that were in the top decile of performance the year previous, hold them for a full year, and then rebalance at the start of the next year. Annual rebalancing does not appear to produce quite as high rates of pretax return as rebalancing quarterly, but given reductions in possible transaction costs and more favorable tax treatment, net gains could well prove to be the equal of quarterly rebalancing.

Results of Quarterly Reranking and Quarterly Rebalancing (1990–2003)

As you can see in Chart 1.5, an almost perfect linear relationship develops if you maintain your portfolio in funds of the different deciles and rebalance at the start of each quarter. The top decile is highest in performance; the lowest decile at the start of each quarter produces the lowest rates of return.

Here are the results in tabular form.

Investment Results of Quarterly Rebalancing (June 1990–October 2003) for Mutual Funds with Volatility Ranks 1–5 (Below or Equal to the S&P 500 Index)

Performance Decile	$100 Becomes	Gain Per Annum	Maximum Drawdown*
First decile	$596.31	+14.1%	20.3%
Second decile	556.85	+13.6	24.0
Third decile	508.53	+12.8	27.4
Fourth decile	427.32	+11.4	27.4
Fifth decile	368.06	+10.1	31.6
Sixth decile	327.59	+9.2	34.8
Seventh decile	337.09	+9.4	35.6
Eighth decile	303.17	+8.6	37.0
Ninth decile	275.22	+7.8	35.0
Tenth decile	184.31	+4.6	40.1

* Maximum drawdown is the largest decline in the value of your portfolio from its highest peak level before the attainment of a new peak value. Although it cannot be said that past maximum drawdown represents maximum risk, it can be said that past maximum drawdown certainly does represent minimum portfolio risk.

Buy-and-Hold Results: The Standard & Poor's 500 Benchmark

By comparison, the Standard & Poor's 500 Index, on a buy-and-hold basis, produced a total return (including dividends but not investment expenses) of 10.8% per annum during this period, with a maximum drawdown (the greatest reduction of capital before your portfolio reaches a new high in value) of 44.7%. The Vanguard Standard & Poor's 500 Index fund achieved an annual rate of return of 10.7%, with a maximum drawdown of 44.8%. These returns fell between the fourth and fifth deciles of the funds in our study on a buy-and-hold basis, just about what would be expected, given the lower comparative volatility of the mutual fund universe employed.

A program of investment in the highest-ranked decile of low- to average-volatility mutual funds, reallocated quarterly, produced an annual return of 14.1%, compared to 10.8% for buying and holding the S&P 500 Index. Moreover, and possibly more significant, the maximum drawdown of this first-decile portfolio was just 20.2%, compared to 44.7% for the Standard & Poor's 500 Index. More return. Less risk. More gain. Less pain.

If your account is housed at a brokerage house, you will almost certainly be able to trade in ETFs as well as mutual funds. You might establish an ETF universe for relative strength rotation, or you might include ETFs in the universe you rank each quarter, treating each ETF as though it were a mutual fund. Again, ETFs tend to be somewhat less stable in their movement than many mutual funds but, as more are developed, might prove to be worthwhile adjuncts to mutual funds.

Increasing the Risk: Maintaining a Portfolio of Somewhat More Aggressive Mutual Funds

The suggestion has been made that there is little to be gained by investing in more volatile equities (or their equivalents) rather than less volatile equities. To test this hypothesis, a study was undertaken in which the quarterly ranking and rebalancing procedure was carried forth, but this time with a portfolio of mutual funds ranked 1–7 in volatility instead of 1–5. Because the "5" group represents mutual funds that are roughly equal to the Standard & Poor's 500 Index in volatility, including the 6 and 7 volatility groups brings the total portfolio universe to roughly the equivalent of the S & P 500 Index in volatility, whereas the total 1–5 universe carries less volatility than the Standard & Poor's 500 Index.

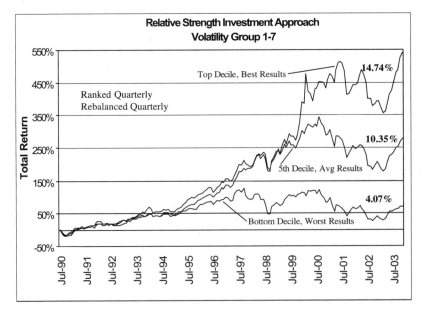

Chart 1.6   Performance of the Relative Strength Investment Approach (1990–2003), Including Groups 6 and 7 in Addition to Groups 1–5

Rates of return for the better-performing deciles are slightly greater than rates of return for the leading deciles in the lower-volatility Group 1–5 portfolio, but risks were clearly increased for this higher-volatility universe of mutual funds. Returns were very consistent, again, with decile rank: The higher the decile group was at the start of each quarter, the better the performance.

Chart 1.6 shows the results of the study, which employs a 1–7 volatility universe instead of a less volatile 1–5 universe. Let's move right along to a tabular listing of the study results.

Investment Results of Quarterly Rebalancing (June 1990–October 2003) for Mutual Funds with Volatility Ranks 1–7 (Below to Above the S&P 500 Index)

Performance Decile	$100 Becomes	Gain Per Annum	Maximum Drawdown
First decile	$640.05	+14.7%	25.7%
Second decile	598.58	+14.2	26.1
Third decile	546.91	+13.4	27.0
Fourth decile	436.13	+11.5	33.1
Fifth decile	377.81	+10.4	37.3
Sixth decile	338.25	+9.5	39.3
Seventh decile	338.48	+9.5	39.3
Eighth decile	303.26	+8.6	39.3
Ninth decile	262.72	+7.4	38.6
Tenth decile	171.37	+4.2	44.2

The Standard & Poor's 500 Index advanced at an annual rate of 10.8% (including dividends) during this period, with a maximum drawdown of 44.7%.

Observations

Increasing the volatility range of the mutual fund universe from 1–5 to 1–7 resulted in a slight improvement in the best-performing decile (+14.7 gain per annum, compared to 14.1% for the lower-volatility group). However, maximum drawdowns for the highest-performing group increased from 20.3% to 25.7%. The average gain/risk level for the best-performing decile in the 1–5 group came to .69 (14.3% average gain, 20.2% maximum drawdown), whereas the average gain/risk level for the best performing decile in the 1–7 group came to .57 (14.7% average gain, 25.7% maximum drawdown).

Conclusion: There is little, if anything, to be gained in the long run by taking the risks associated with more aggressive stock portfolios.

Upping the Ante: The Effects of Applying the Concepts of Relative Strength Selection to a Still More Volatile Portfolio of Mutual Funds

Let's try the procedure just one more time, this time with a universe of mutual funds that includes the most volatile sectors in the equity spectrum. This universe includes all the high-rolling areas of the stock market—gold, the internets, small caps, technology, whatever—as well as lower-volatility funds, encompassing the complete spectrum of mutual funds rated by volatility as 1–9.

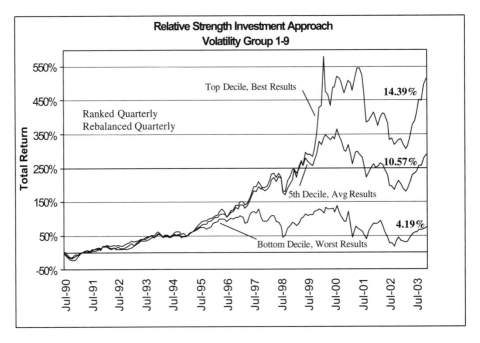

Chart 1.7   Performance of the Relative Strength Investment Approach (1990–2003), Including All Mutual Fund Groups, Rated as 1–9

Rates of return for the best deciles in the 1–9 universe remained in the area of returns secured from lower-volatility mutual fund universes 1–5 and 1–7. However, risks increased considerably, as you can see by the drawdowns reflected on the chart. The first-performance decile for the previous quarter proved, again, to be the best for the subsequent quarter, although the lead over the second-best-performing decile the previous quarter was not great.

Let's review, just one more time, a tabular table.

Investment Results of Quarterly Rebalancing (June 1990–October 2003) Mutual Funds with Volatility Ranks 1–9 (Virtually All Equity-Oriented Mutual Funds, Including Those Considerably More Volatile Than the Standard & Poor's 500 Index)

Performance Decile	$100 Becomes	Gain Per Annum	Maximum Drawdown
First decile	$614.44	+14.4	40.2
Second decile	605.24	+14.3	34.2
Third decile	539.98	+13.3	31.5
Fourth decile	454.66	+11.9	38.6
Fifth decile	388.29	+10.6	39.9
Sixth decile	335.07	+9.4	41.8
Seventh decile	330.19	+9.3	42.2
Eighth decile	296.95	+8.4	43.7
Ninth decile	267.68	+7.6	43.1
Tenth decile	173.97	+4.2	50.1

General Observations

Again, we see a very linear relationship between fund performance in a previous quarter and its performance in subsequent periods. Within the highest-velocity mutual fund group, the second decile runs very closely in strength to the first decile. I have found this to be the case in studies I have conducted of other ways to employ past relative strength to predict future market performance. It seems that, among the most volatile mutual fund areas, more consistent performance is sometimes attained from second and third decile holdings than by first, although, in this study, the first decile produced the best rates of return.

The average gain/maximum drawdown ratio for even the strongest (first decile) area of the 1–9 group of mutual funds is low, at 0.36 (14.39 rate of return, 40.18% maximum drawdown). The gains can be there, but the pains can be considerable, indeed, for investors who live in the fast lane.

Although portfolios are rebalanced at quarterly intervals, this does not mean that you will have to replace your entire portfolio each quarter. On average, holdings are likely to be maintained through two quarterly cycles, or for six months in total. Conclusion: Increasing the volatility of your mutual fund portfolio does not add to profitability in any significant manner, even though risk levels do increase. As a general rule, your emphasis should remain with funds of average or below-average volatility.

A Quick Review of Relative Strength Investing

Here is the three-step procedure for managing your mutual fund portfolio:

- **Step 1:** Secure access to data sources that will provide you with at least quarterly price data and volatility ratings of a universe of at least 500 (preferably somewhat more) mutual funds. (Suggestions have been provided.)

- **Step 2:** Open an investment account with a diversified portfolio of mutual funds whose performance the previous quarter lay in the top 10% of the mutual funds in your trading universe and whose volatility is equal to or less than the Standard & Poor's 500 Index, or, at the most, no greater than the average fund in your total universe.

- **Step 3:** At the start of each new quarter, eliminate those funds in your portfolio that have fallen from the first performance decile, replacing them with funds that are currently in the top performance decile.

This account is probably best carried forth at a brokerage house that provides a broad platform of mutual funds into which investments may be placed. Schwab and T. D. Waterhouse, for example, provide both the requisite service and the requisite mutual fund platform. Other brokerage firms might do so as well.

Summing Up

To sum up, we have reviewed a strategy for maintaining mutual fund portfolios that has been effective since at least 1990 (almost certainly longer), a strategy that produces returns that well exceed buy-and-hold strategies while significantly reducing risk.

These strategies appear to be effective with a variety of investments, including mutual funds, ETFs, and probably (although I have not personally tested for this) individual stocks as well. Generally, mutual funds seem somewhat more suited for this approach than ETFs, which tend, on average, to be more volatile than the best-performing mutual fund universe (1–5).

You have learned a significant strategy for outperforming buy-and-hold strategies in the stock market, a strategy based upon relative-strength mutual fund selection, not upon market timing.

Let's move along to the next chapter and to two simply maintained indicators that can help you decide when to buy.

Two Quick-and-Dirty Stock Market Mood Indicators

Identifying High- and Low-Risk Investment Climates

As we know, all stocks, mutual funds, and related investments are not equal. In Chapter 1, "The No-Frills Investment Strategy," we considered a strategy for identifying investments that are likely to prove more equal than the general population. Similarly, not all investment climates are equal. During some periods, stocks seem to rise effortlessly; during other periods, gains, if any, are more labored and intermittent. In this chapter, you will learn two readily applied strategies for segregating climates that are generally more favorable for stocks from climates that are, on average, really not much better than neutral climates and that represent periods when severe stock market declines are most likely to take place.

Let's consider possible alternatives. In the first, you invest in the stock market at all times, a strategy that has worked out well enough over the very long run. Stocks, on average, have had a century-long tendency to produce annual rates of total return of roughly 10% per year. However, you would have had to live through some serious bear markets—1929–1932, 1969–1970, 1973–1974, and 2000–2002—not to mention numerous other periods in between when stocks underwent serious intermediate and major term declines. In the second scenario, you invest only when certain investment models indicate that market moods are benevolent and the probabilities are more favorable than average that stocks will advance in price.

If you invest only when market climates are most favorable, you might still secure average returns in the order of 10% per year (actually a conservative estimate if we go by past history). However, you likely will be invested, on balance, mainly only during periods that stocks tend to advance. For the periods that you are invested—approximately 50% of the time, give or take—your capital produces returns not at a rate of 10% per annum while invested, but at a rate of about 20%, depending on the market index assumed. During the periods that you are out of stocks, your capital is not at risk and you usually can secure interest rate returns that generally exceed stock market dividend payouts, to augment returns secured when your capital is in the stock market.

I will show you two stock market indicators that, over more than three decades of history, have done a fine (not a perfect, but, nonetheless, a fine) job of defining the best periods during which to invest in the stock market. These indicators can be maintained and tracked just once each week; probably not more than 15 minutes or so is required—maybe even less. Moreover, the information that you require is widely available. You will not have to ferret out difficult-to-locate data from arcane sources.

As we move along into this work, we review tools associated with technical analysis (the art or science of predicting the future course of the stock market by ana-lyzing current and past action of the stock market itself). These tools, such as mov-ing averages and rate of change measurements, are useful in defining trends in the stock market as well as price momentum. Don't worry if you are unfamiliar with these terms; definitions and explanations are forthcoming.

Finally, we review tactics that combine the use of market mood indicators with stock-selection strategies to see whether you can improve on the results of your powerful mutual fund selection techniques by combining them with market deci-sions based upon market mood indicators.

Enough introduction. The time has arrived to cut to the chase.

The Nasdaq/New York Stock Exchange Index Relative Strength Indicator

Here's the basic premise.... Although the New York Stock Exchange is the oldest and best known of the stock market trading centers, trading takes place in signifi-cant amounts in other areas: the Nasdaq, or over-the-counter, market; the American Stock Exchange; third markets, where off-the-floor trades take place; various options exchanges; other regional stock exchanges; and so forth.

The New York Stock Exchange Index and the Nasdaq Composite Index each now includes more than 3,500 separate stocks, traded on the New York Stock Exchange floor and within dealer networks, respectively. The New York Stock Exchange is often referred to as the "senior" exchange, partly because it has been the longest established and partly because companies listed on that exchange tend to be among the largest and most established corporations in the country.

Nasdaq, which has lower standards for listing than the New York Stock Exchange, used to be thought of as an area for only smaller, speculative companies. Although stocks of that type continue to be found in this trading sector, more recently, major companies such as Microsoft and Intel, among others, have chosen to remain on Nasdaq rather than seek a listing on the New York Stock Exchange. Some companies consider jointly listing on both Nasdaq and the New York Stock Exchange. Some of the most exciting and fastest-growing technology, health-related companies, and Internet corporations are now traded in the over-the-counter markets. Although the number of Nasdaq's larger companies listed is increasing, Nasdaq-listed companies, as a group, tend to be more speculative, more technology oriented, and smaller in size than those listed on the New York Stock Exchange. The total daily trading volume on Nasdaq, however, now regularly surpasses the daily trading volume on the New York Stock Exchange.

The Nasdaq Composite Index and the New York Stock Exchange Index tend to be closely correlated in the direction, if not the extent, of their price movement—not perfectly correlated, but essentially so. Given the higher volatility of the Nasdaq Composite Index, its tendency to rise and fall at greater velocities than New York Stock Exchange–oriented indices, such as the Standard & Poor's 500 Index or the New York Stock Exchange Index, we can readily understand that during most periods of market advance, the Nasdaq Composite Index (an average of all stocks on Nasdaq, weighted by corporate capitalization so that larger companies count for more than smaller companies) is likely to outperform the less volatile New York Stock Exchange Index (a capitalization-weighted index of all listed stocks on the New York Stock Exchange), if for no reason other than its generally higher velocity of price movement.

The Nasdaq Composite Index tends to rise and fall at rates that are between 1.5 and twice that of the New York Stock Exchange Index. The Standard & Poor's 500 Index, which includes issues that are listed on Nasdaq as well as the New York Stock Exchange, is more volatile than the New York Stock Exchange Index and less so than the Nasdaq Composite Index.

Similarly, the Nasdaq Composite Index is likely to decline more rapidly than the New York Stock Exchange Index during declining market periods, again as a result of its greater volatility, if for no other reason.

Volatility aside, relative strength relationships between the Nasdaq Composite Index and the New York Stock Exchange Index are often affected by the nature of public sentiment regarding the stock market. When investors are optimistic about the economy and stocks, they are more likely to place capital into speculative growth companies and to take risks with smaller, emerging corporations and technologies. When investors are relatively pessimistic regarding the economy and stocks, they are more likely to concentrate investments into more established, stable, defensive corporations and to seek out dividend return as well as capital appreciation.

For whatever the reason, and there are no doubt many, it has generally been the case historically that the stock market produces greater gains during periods when the Nasdaq Composite Index leads the New York Stock Exchange Index in relative strength. That's true not just of the Nasdaq Composite Index. The New York Stock Exchange Index, the Dow Industrials, and the Standard & Poor's 500 Index all tend to perform best during periods when the Nasdaq Composite Index leads the New York Stock Exchange Index in relative strength. This is not to say that conditions are necessarily bearish when the NYSE Index leads in strength. Market action has typically been neutral when the NYSE Index outperforms the Nasdaq Composite Index. There are winning periods when the NYSE leads in relative strength. However, these also tend to be the periods when most serious market declines take place. Investments made during periods when the NYSE Index leads the Nasdaq Composite Index in strength are likely, on balance, to more or less just break even.

The Maintenance and Interpretation of the Nasdaq/NYSE Index Relative Strength Indicator

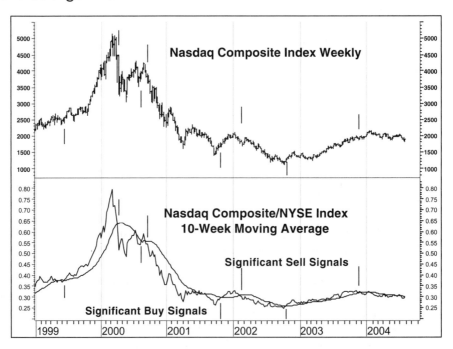

Chart 2.1 The Nasdaq/NYSE Index Relative Strength Indicator

This chart shows the Nasdaq/NYSE Index relative strength line, along with its ten-week moving average. Nasdaq lagged the New York Stock Exchange in relative strength during much of the 2000–2002 bear market, assumed the lead during the fourth quarter of 2002, and pretty much maintained its leadership throughout 2003, reflecting the strength that developed in the stock market that year. The Nasdaq/NYSE Index relative strength line trends upward during periods when the Nasdaq leads in relative strength and trends downward during periods when the NYSE Index leads.

Here are the steps involved in creating the Nasdaq/NYSE Index Relative Strength Indicator. These are carried out at the conclusion of each trading week. Once established, the status of this indicator remains in effect for a full week, until the next calculation takes place.

Step 1: Secure the weekly closing levels of the Nasdaq Composite and the New York Stock Exchange Index. These are readily available in financial sections of the Web, in *Barron's,* and in the financial pages of virtually any major newspaper.

Step 2: Divide the weekly closing level of the Nasdaq Composite by the closing level of the New York Stock Exchange Index. You might want to post entries as a table similar to the table, "Weekly Postings.....", below. For example, if the Nasdaq Composite closes the week at 1865.59 and the New York Stock Exchange Index closes the week at 5851.14, the weekly relative strength ratio (Nasdaq/NYSE Index) would be .3188 (1,865.59 ÷ 5,851.14 = .3188).

Step 3: Each week, calculate the average of the most recent ten weekly relative strength ratios. To do this, add the most recent ten weekly ratios and divide the total by ten. On the eleventh week, drop the eleventh weekly ratio back and add the latest new weekly ratio, so that you are always totaling and then averaging the most recent ten weeks of data. This is called a moving average.

Step 4: Compare the most recent reading of the Nasdaq/NYSE Index relative strength ratio to the ten-week average of this ratio. If the Nasdaq/NYSE Index relative strength ratio stands above its ten-week moving average, consider the Nasdaq Composite to be leading the New York Index in relative strength. This will have bullish implications (buy). If the Nasdaq/NYSE Index relative strength ratio stands below its ten-week moving average, consider the Nasdaq to be lagging the New York Stock Exchange in relative strength, which will have less bullish implications (neutral).

Here is how the data stream would have looked at the conclusion of the week for January 2, 2004.

Weekly Postings, Nasdaq/NYSE Index Relative Strength Ratio

Date	Nasdaq Composite	NYSE Index	Ratio Nasdaq/ NYSE	Ten-Week Weekly Ratios	Leading Index
10/24/03	1865.59	5851.14	.3188		
10/31/03	1932.21	5959.01	.3243		
11/07/03	1970.74	5989.17	.3291		

Continued

Weekly Postings, Nasdaq/NYSE Index Relative Strength Ratio *(Continued)*

Date	Nasdaq Composite	NYSE Index	Ratio Nasdaq/ NYSE	Ten-Week Weekly Ratios	Leading Index
11/14/03	1930.26	6010.73	.3211		
11/21/03	1893.88	5942.32	.3187		
11/28/03	1960.26	6073.02	.3228		
12/05/03	1937.82	6122.89	.3165		
12/12/03	1949.00	6196.29	.3145		
12/19/03	1951.02	6284.30	.3105		
12/26/03	1973.14	6364.36	.3100	.3186	NYSE
01/02/04	2006.68	6451.26	.3111	.3179	NYSE

The first ten weeks of this data stream end on December 26, 2003, the first date on which a ten-week moving average can be computed because ten weeks of data are required for a ten-week average. Because the Nasdaq/NYSE Index relative strength ratio on that date (.3100) was below the ten-week average (.3186), relative strength readings favored the NYSE Index.

As a general rule, again, both Nasdaq and indices associated with issues traded on the New York Stock Exchange perform best when Nasdaq leads in relative strength. This does not mean that stocks never rise when Nasdaq lags. That frequently does take place. It does mean that the *probabilities* of market advance increase considerably when the Nasdaq Composite Index leads the New York Stock Exchange Index in relative strength.

Let's examine some numbers in this regard.

Table 2.1 *Investing Based Upon the Relative Strength of Nasdaq Versus the New York Stock Exchange Index*

(Stock positions held only when the Nasdaq leads—at other times, in risk-free income positions.)

Transactions are assumed to take place at the closing levels of the weeks when relative strength reversals take place.

Period of study: April 8, 1971, to December 12, 2003

	Nasdaq Composite	Standard & Poor's 500 Index	NYSE Index
Number of trades	130	130	130
Trades per year	4	4	4
Percentage of trades profitable	54.6%	64.6%	69.2%
Average percent gain of winners	9.2%	4.9%	4.5%

Continued

Table 2.1 *Investing Based Upon the Relative Strength of Nasdaq Versus the New York Stock Exchange Index* (Continued)

	Nasdaq Composite	Standard & Poor's 500 Index	NYSE Index
Average percent loss of losers	3.6%	3.1%	3.4%
Average percent change, all trades	+3.4%	+2.1%	+2.1%
Total percent gained	443.6%	266.5%	267.2%
Total gain per annum (trading)	12.0%	7.7%	7.7%
Total gain, buy and hold	9.2%	7.4%	7.4%
Percentage of time invested	54.9%	54.9%	54.9%
Gain per annum while invested	23.0%	14.5%	14.5%
Maximum closed drawdown, trading	32.2%	21.5%	21.6%
Maximum open drawdown, trading	39.7%	24.2%	23.7%
Buy and hold, open drawdown	77.4%	48.0%	49.7%

These tabulations do not include the effects of interest received while in cash which, historically, have usually exceeded dividend payouts from stocks while invested.

Observations

The similarity in performance between the Standard & Poor's 500 Index and the New York Stock Exchange Index is quite striking:

- **Frequency of trading:** This is a significant parameter for any timing model because trades do tend to involve expenses such as those involved with slippages and commissions. If you wanted to be invested only when the mood model is in a favorable position, you would be making four round-trip trades per year, suitable for investments that involve minimal or no commission rates—perhaps no-load mutual funds, a large number of which accept that frequency of trading. This frequency is probably acceptable for most investors, particularly for tax-sheltered accounts for which there are unlikely to be adverse tax consequences.

- **Percentage of profitable trades:** These are 54.6% for Nasdaq, 64.6% for the Standard & Poor's 500 Index, and 69.2% for the New York Stock Exchange Index. All rate well for timing indicators that signal with this frequency.

- **Percentage gains and losses of winning and losing trades:** Profitable trades are larger in the extent of gain than unprofitable trades in the extent of loss. Win/loss ratios are favorable in terms of size as well as frequency.

- **Total gain per year, using the Nasdaq/NYSE ratio, compared to buy-and-hold returns:** Portfolios trading in the Nasdaq Composite Index would have grown at a rate of 12.0% per annum, while growth on a buy-and-hold basis would have been just 9.2%. These results do not include the effects of transaction costs and tax consequences, but they also do not reflect income that would have accrued during the 45% of each year (average) that capital was out of the stock market. Greater gains were achieved on average per year using the model and being invested just less than 55% of the time, compared to gains secured by being fully invested 100% of the time.

- **Rate of gains while invested, compared to rate of gains, buy and hold:** The Nasdaq Composite Index advanced at a rate of 23% per annum during the periods when the relative strength ratio between the Nasdaq and NYSE Index was favorable. Its rate of gain, if always invested, was just 9.2% per year. Its rate of gain when the ratio favored the NYSE Index was moderately negative on balance. The Composite has shown negative returns during periods when the NYSE Index leads Nasdaq in relative strength.

  The Standard & Poor's 500 Index advanced at a rate of 14.5% per year during periods in the study when Nasdaq led in relative strength, declined slightly on balance at other times. The New York Stock Exchange Index showed almost identical results.

- **Drawdowns:** Maximum drawdowns (losses in account values from peak to low) were 39.7% for the Nasdaq Composite, 24.2% for the Standard & Poor's 500 Index, and 23.7% for the New York Stock Exchange Index if stocks were held only during periods when the Nasdaq Composite led the NYSE Index in relative strength.

  Maximum drawdowns were much higher for buy-and-hold investors: 77.4% for the Nasdaq Composite, 48.0% for the Standard & Poor's 500 Index, and 49.7% for the New York Stock Exchange Index.

If you had been invested in the Nasdaq Composite Index only when the Nasdaq Relative Strength Model was in a favorable position, by mid-2004, you would have recaptured most of the 2000–2002 market decline, with your equity curve (cumulative growth of equity value) almost but not quite reaching its peak levels of 2000. If you had remained fully invested in the Nasdaq Composite Index at all times, your equity would have remained more than 60% below its year 2000 peak.

To summarize, the Nasdaq/NYSE Index has produced higher annual returns than buy-and-hold approaches, although it was invested only a bit more than half the time—much higher rates of return while invested with reductions in risk. The indicator can be employed as a standalone buy/sell decision-maker for investors who have only limited time or inclination to track the stock market. However, it is probably best employed as a key element in your decisions for how fully invested you want to be at any given time, with larger long positions maintained during periods when the Nasdaq/NYSE Index relative strength ratio indicator favors the Nasdaq Composite Index. Lesser, perhaps less volatile positions would be taken when relative strength favors the New York Stock Exchange Index.

Measuring the Market Mood with the Intermediate Monetary Filter

The relationship between the direction of stock price movement and trends in interest rates has been long recognized. As a general rule, stocks tend to rise in price during periods that interest rates decline and to make relatively little progress, on balance, during periods that interest rates advance. Chart 2.2 illustrates these relationships.

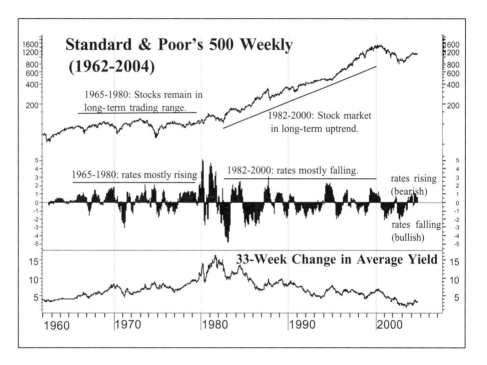

Chart 2.2 Major Trends in the Stock Market Versus Major Trends in Interest Rates

A number of bear markets have come to an end as interest rates peaked—for example, in 1970, 1974, 1982, and 1990, but not the 2000–2002 bear market. You can see the correlations between secular long-term trends in the stock market and secular long-term trends in interest rates.

The links between the direction and levels of interest rates and the performance of the stock market, again, are well known ("Don't fight the Fed"). Although correlations are, again, not quite perfect, as a general rule, stocks do best when interest rates are stable to declining, and worst when interest rates are unstable and rising.

This is not surprising if you consider the positive impacts of relatively low interest rates on the economy and on the stock market. Low interest rates, for example, lead to reduced mortgage payments, which support the pricing of homes and commercial real estate, which leads to increased building, which benefits all those industries connected to home and office building and adds to homeowners' sense of well-being, which leads them to spend more on goods and services, and so on.

Low interest rates also support business investment, the purchase of inventory, installment sales to the public, and so forth—all of which are favorable for business conditions.

Finally, low interest rates reduce the competitiveness of long-term bonds, shorter-term money market funds, and bank certificates of deposit in comparison to the stock market. This encourages the concentration of investments into equities and, thereby, directly and indirectly into new and established companies.

All of this is no secret, of course. Meetings of the Federal Reserve Board are closely monitored in the financial press for indications of policy changes that might affect the levels of interest rates. The Fed has been quite sensitive to the potential effects of monetary policies upon the stock market, in recent decades moving rapidly to lower short-term interest rates (which are under its control) whenever the stock market runs into serious trouble. For example, the Fed lowered rates almost immediately following the market crash of 1987 and during the market correction of 1990, lowered rates a dozen times during the 2000–2002 bear market, and maintained low rates during the market recovery of 2003.

The 2000–2002 bear market was very severe and persistent, developing from a speculative bubble that took place during the late 1990s. There were, for a time, threats of actual deflation in the economy, the worst sort of economic environment for the stock market. Whereas two or three reductions in interest rates are usually sufficient to end market declines, 12, in conjunction with tax reductions on the federal level, were required to stimulate an economic recovery, in general, and a recovery in the stock market, in particular.

All that said, and pretty generally agreed upon, the investor is still left with the tasks of objectively and systematically defining, identifying, and separating favorable monetary climates (interest rates trending down) from unfavorable monetary climates (interest rates rising). We review one basic strategy for accomplishing these purposes that you can employ on a weekly basis to define the monetary mood, perhaps at the same time that you are calculating your Nasdaq/NYSE Index relative strength ratios. As before, we discuss first the method of calculation and then the results of applying the method. Finally, we examine the results of using the Monetary Model in conjunction with the Nasdaq/NYSE Index Relative Strength Model.

The Monetary Model

The Ingredients

Just two items of data are required to maintain the Monetary Model. These are the yields each week provided by two intermediate U.S. government notes: the three-year Treasury note and the five-year Treasury note.

These yields are widely available in the financial press and over the Web. The *Barron's* financial weekly newspaper carries them in its "Market Laboratory" section, which also contains data related to various stock market indices, as well as market breadth and prices of individual securities and mutual funds.

The January 5, 2004, issue of *Barron's* reported the following data for the week ending January 2, 2004.

Adjustable Mortgage Base Rates

	January 2, 2004	December 26, 2003	December 27, 2002
3-year Treasury notes	2.40	2.38	2.08
5-year Treasury notes	3.22	3.20	2.89
Average weekly yield	2.81	2.79	2.485

(We employ the average of the yields of three- and five-year notes in our indicator.)

It appears that, on a near-term basis, interest rates are fairly stable, with just a hint of pressure: The most recent weekly yields are just a touch higher than the previous week's. However, longer-term trends suggest that interest rates are rising because rates are above prevailing rates from one year ago.

The Calculation and Rules of the Intermediate Monetary Filter

The procedures are quite simple and basic:

1. Secure the weekly readings of yields of the three-year notes and yields of the five-year notes. Average the two together, as done earlier, for an average weekly yield.

2. Maintain a posting of this average yield on a weekly basis. You will need at least 34 weeks of data for your indicator.

3. When you have secured 34 weeks of data (in some way—possibly by checking back issues of *Barron's* at a library), simply compare the latest reading of the yield average with the reading of the yield average 33 weeks earlier. If yields are lower than they were 33 weeks ago, we consider interest rate trends to be down and favorable. If the average is higher than 33 weeks ago, we consider interest rate trends to be rising and unfavorable.

4. If rate trends are favorable, we consider the stock market to be in a favorable position, as far as interest rates are concerned. Prices are likely to advance at above-average rates when this condition exists. When interest rate trends are negative, the stock market generally shows neutral rates of return—sometimes advancing, sometimes not. If a serious market decline is to take place, odds are, it will take place during periods when rates are rising rather than falling; however, a good part of the 2000–2003 bear market was an exception to this rule.

The Three- to Five-Year Note Yield Indicator, Sample Data Stream

Week Ending	Yield, 3-Year Note	Yield, 5-Year Note	Average	33-Week Change
1) 5/16/2003	1.76%	2.52%	2.14%	
2) 5/23/2003	1.65	2.35	2.00	*Continued*

The Three- to Five-Year Note Yield Indicator, Sample Data Stream   *(Continued)*

Week Ending	Yield, 3-Year Note	Yield, 5-Year Note	Average	33-Week Change
3) 5/30/2003	1.60	2.32	1.96	
4) 6/06/2003	1.53	2.27	1.90	
5) 6/13/2003	1.39	2.13	1.76	
6) 6/20/2003	1.52	2.27	1.90	
7) 6/27/2003	1.59	2.36	1.98	
8) 7/03/2003	1.67	2.49	2.08	
9) 7/11/2003	1.74	2.60	2.17	
10) 7/18/2003	1.90	2.82	2.36	
11) 7/25/2003	2.07	3.08	2.58	
12) 8/01/2003	2.27	3.31	2.79	
13) 8/08/2003	2.32	3.24	2.78	
14) 8/15/2003	2.41	3.35	2.88	
15) 8/22/2003	2.47	3.39	2.93	
16) 8/29/2003	2.55	3.49	3.02	
17) 9/05/2003	2.51	3.51	3.01	
18) 9/12/2003	2.25	3.23	2.74	
19) 9/19/2003	2.16	3.10	2.63	
20) 9/26/2003	2.15	3.07	2.61	
21) 10/03/2003	2.02	2.94	2.48	
22) 10/10/2003	2.17	3.13	2.65	
23) 10/17/2003	2.36	3.32	2.8	
24) 10/24/2003	2.36	3.24	2.80	
25) 10/31/2003	2.33	3.22	2.78	
26) 11/07/2003	2.49	3.37	2.93	
27) 11/14/2003	2.51	3.36	2.94	
28) 11/21/2003	2.35	3.16	2.76	
29) 11/28/2003	2.47	3.27	2.87	
30) 12/05/2003	2.58	3.40	2.99	
31) 12/12/2003	2.45	3.27	2.86	
32) 12/19/2003	2.38	3.20	2.79	*Continued*

The Three- to Five-Year Note Yield Indicator, Sample Data Stream   (Continued)

Week Ending	Yield, 3-Year Note	Yield, 5-Year Note	Average	33-Week Change
33) 12/26/2003	2.38	3.22	2.80	
34) 1/02/2004	2.40	3.28	2.84	+.70 A
35) 1/09/2004	2.36	3.24	2.80	+.80 B

Week 34 (2.84) – Week 1 (2.14) = +.70. B) Week 35 (2.80) – Week 2 (2.00) = +.80.

Interpretation: Yields are higher than they were 33 weeks ago. The monetary indicator was not lending support to the stock market in early 2003.

Here are the results of trading with use of the Monetary Filter Model.

Trading the Nasdaq Composite with the Nasdaq Composite/NYSE Index Relative Strength Indicator, the Monetary Filter Indicator, and a Combined Use of the Two, in the Market Only When Both Mood Indicators Are Favorable (Period April 8, 1971–December 12, 2003)

	Nasdaq/NYSE Index Relative Strength	Monetary Filter	In the Market Only When Both Favorable
Trades	130	36	88
Trades per year	4	1.1	2.7
Percent profitable	54.6%	63.9%	61.4%
Average % gain, winning trades	9.2	24.3	7.7
Average % loss, losing trades	3.6	6.4	3.2
Average % change, all trades	3.4	13.2	3.5
Gain per annum	12.0%	10.6%	8.7%
Annualized gain while invested	23.0%	20.8%	30.4%
% of time invested	54.9%	52.7%	31.4%
Maximum closed drawdown	32.2%	52.6%	28.3%
Maximum open drawdown	39.7%	66.4%	34.0%
Buy-and-hold gain per annum	9.2%	9.2%	9.2%
Buy-and-hold open drawdown	77.4%	77.4%	77.4%

Observations

The Three- to Five-Year Yield Indicator produced final investment returns that approached those produced by the Nasdaq/NYSE Index Relative Strength Indicator, but on many fewer trades. Average gains and losses were both higher using the Yield Indicator, as were drawdowns, but the percentage of winning trades was higher.

This indicator involves many fewer trades (36 compared to 130) and fewer expenses than the Nasdaq/NYSE Index Relative Strength Model, the potential impacts of which are not reflected in the previous table. The rate of return while invested for the three- to five-year note indicator was 20.8%, similar to the 23.0% rate of return achieved via the Nasdaq/NYSE Index Relative Strength Indicator.

Combining the Two Indicators

A strategy of being invested in the stock market only when both indicators—monetary and relative strength—are favorable would have had investors in the stock market between 1971 and 2003 only 31.4% of the time, during which invested periods capital would have appreciated at a rate of 30.4% per annum, with full-year gains averaging 8.7% per year (just less than the 9.2% achieved by buy-and-hold strategies).

These figures do not reflect additional income that might have come from interest while being in cash 68.6% of the time. Drawdowns and risk have been considerably reduced while this strategy has been in effect.

Point and Counterpoint

Stock market timing indicators, particularly those that produce trades on a relatively infrequent basis, do not produce even performance. During some periods, they perform extremely well in comparison to buy-and-hold strategies. During other periods, they might not. Investors should be alert to changes in parameters that occur from time to time. For example, until the 1990s, it was widely accepted that the stock market was likely to be in danger when dividend yields from the Standard & Poor's 500 Index declined to less than 3% and/or when price/earnings ratios (the ratio of stock price divided by the amount of corporate profit per share of stock) rose to above 22. By the time the bull market peaked in early 2000, dividend yields had fallen to the area of just above 1%. The price/earnings ratio had risen to as high as 46.

These changes in what were market-acceptable measures of stock value took place largely because of the very low levels of prevailing interest rates, which, as we have seen, support stock prices. Many other changes in the parameters of technical and fundamental indicators have taken place over the years as a result of much heavier volume in the stock market, a pronounced increase in the number of issues listed on the various exchanges and over the counter, online computer trading, and discount brokerage commissions. All of these have led to more rapid and extensive intraday market movement and less consistent day-to-day market directional fluctuation.

For these and other reasons, it is usually best to employ more than one or two (but not too many) indicators to track the stock market.

With this in mind, we might review a decade-to-decade performance summary of the Three- to Five-Year Note Yield Indicator.

Decade-by-Decade Performance, the Nasdaq Composite
Three- to Five-Year Note Yield Indicator Versus Buy and Hold

Decade	Gain Per Annum Yield Indicator	Number of Years	Open Drawdown	Gain Per Buy and Hold	Open Drawdown
1971–1979	+9.95%	8.8	−12.8%	+ 4.7%	−59.4%
1980–1989	+16.19%	10.1	−15.7%	+11.6%	−35.7%
1990–1999	+15.85%	10.1	−25.7%	+24.3%	−32.3%
2000–2003	−12.06%	3.9	−66.4%	−16.9%	−77.4%

Observations

Investing in accordance with signals generated by the Three- to Five-Year Note Yield Indicator produced returns superior to buy-and-hold investing during three of the four periods measured. Drawdowns were reduced by using the indicator during all of the periods measured, although they were not nearly as well contained during the 2000–2003 bear market as they had been during previous bear market periods, including the very serious 1973–1974 bear market and the period of the 1987 market crash.

The high drawdowns that developed during 2000–2003 reflected, again, the failure of the stock market and the economy to respond to reductions in interest rates during that period. During this market cycle, the bear market was the result not of rising rates and rising inflation, but rather largely of fears of deflation and a negative environment for stocks, even with declining interest rates. (The stock market's ideal climate is one that features moderate and controlled inflation, but some inflation nonetheless.)

As a historical note, during the early 1930s, Treasury bills actually provided a slightly negative rate of interest. If you lent money to the U.S. government, it was understood in advance that it would pay you less than the loan signified by the Treasury bills. With banks failing, investors were willing to pay something to the Treasury for holding their capital for them.

A Final Long-Term Statistic

We tested the Three- to Five-Year Yield Indicator for a longer period, August 1962 to January 2004. During periods when interest rates were falling, 49% of the time, the Standard & Poor's 500 Index advanced at an average rate of 8.5% per year, with a maximum drawdown of 36%. During the 51% of the time that interest rates were advancing, the Standard & Poor's 500 Index declined at a rate of 1% per year, with a maximum drawdown of 48%. (The Nasdaq Composite did not exist before 1971.)

On a buy-and-hold basis, the Standard & Poor's 500 Index advanced by 7.3% per year (dividends were excluded in all of these calculations). All net gains, on balance, were achieved during periods when the interest rate climates were favorable, with small losses occurring on balance at other times. Again, you would historically have made more, risked less, and been invested only about 50% of the time if you had been making use of this single indicator alone.

Summing Up

Chapter 1 reviewed techniques for selecting stock market investments, some underlying principles of mutual fund selection, and a specific procedure by which you are very likely to outperform the typical mutual fund and the stock market indices in general.

This chapter examined two fully objective weekly indicators that have had long-term histories of outperforming the stock market when they were invested, while reducing risks associated with buy-and-hold strategies.

If you go no further, you have already probably acquired the means to improve both your stock and mutual fund selection results and your general market timing. Your task is to apply what you have learned.

We now proceed to more nuanced tools for reading and interpreting patterns of stock price movement.

3

Moving Averages and Rates of Change: Tracking Trend and Momentum

In the last chapter, you learned a method of constructing and maintaining moving averages. The method described there applies to the construction of what is called a simple moving average, a moving average that gives equal weight to all the data points included in that average. Other forms of moving averages assign greater weight to more recent data points so that the average is more influenced by recent data. This chapter provides additional information regarding the construction and application of moving averages.

The Purpose of Moving Averages

Moving averages are used to smooth out the "noise" of shorter-term price fluctuations so as to more readily be able to identify and define significant underlying trends.

For example, Chart 3.1 shows the Nasdaq 100 Index along with three simple moving averages, a ten-day moving average that reflects short-term trends in the market, a 50-day (if plotted weekly, a 10-week) moving average that reflects intermediate market trends, and a 200-day (or 40-week) average that reflects major trends in the stock market. (Moving averages can employ monthly entries for very major term trends or, conversely, can be plotted even at one-minute intervals for very short-term, intra-day, day-trading purposes.)

Chart 3.1 The Nasdaq 100 Index with Moving Averages Reflecting Its Long-, Intermediate-, and Short-Term Trends

Chart 3.1 shows the Nasdaq 100 Index with three moving averages, reflecting different time frames. The 200-day moving average reflects a longer-term trend in the stock market—in this case, clearly up. The 50-day or approximately 10-week moving average reflects intermediate-term trends in the stock market during this period, also clearly up. The ten-day moving average reflects short-term trends in the stock market that, on this chart, show a bullish bias in their patterns but are not consistently rising.

Chart 3.1 starts as the 2000–2002 bear market was moving toward completion, reaching its bear market lows and completing its transition into the emerging bull market that developed during 2003. The ten-day moving average was penetrated by daily price movement in mid-March that year, turning sharply upward. You can see how turns in the ten-day average took place, reflecting changing trends in daily price movement.

Let's review this ten-day moving average more carefully. The slopes of moving average thrusts indicate the underlying strength of market trends. Examine the upturn in the ten-day moving average that took place in mid-February 2003 and continued into March. The slope and length of this upturn were moderate, as was the subsequent downturn into mid-March.

Now look at the upturn in the ten-day moving average that took place starting in mid-March: This had very different characteristics. The slope of the March advance was much more vertical, indicating greater initial momentum, a sign of increasing market strength. The length of the initial upthrust lengthened, another positive indication. The subsequent retracement into April took place at a lesser slope. The advancing leg had more vitality than the declining leg, which was of lesser duration.

Let's consider now the moving average pulses that developed in mid-April, late May, and early July. The April to late May advancing pulse was relatively long in its consistent advance, which developed at a strongly rising angle. The May to June pulse was shorter (signifying lessening upside momentum or strength). The June to July pulse showed further reductions in its length and steepness of thrust, reflecting still diminishing upside momentum.

As a rule, a series of diminishing upside pulses during a market advance suggests that a market correction lies ahead. A series of increasing upside pulses suggests that further advances are likely.

You might want to review the series of pulses between August and November for further examples of these concepts. You might also want to notice the series of higher highs and higher lows in the ten-day moving average, clearly signifying an uptrend in motion.

The Intermediate-Term Moving Average

The ten-day moving average during the period in Chart 3.1 was clearly tracing out patterns that, between March and October, signified a strong market climate. However, market indications produced by moving average patterns became somewhat more ambiguous as October moved into early December. Upside pulses weakened, and a more neutral pattern developed.

Although short-term patterns were becoming more neutral, intermediate trends remained strongly uptrended, as you can see from the 50-day moving average, which based during March and April, turned upward thereafter, and rose steadily through the end of the year.

When intermediate trends are strong, the strategy of choice is usually to buy when prices fall to or below the shorter-term moving averages. Such patterns frequently provide fine entry points within favorable, strongly rising stock market cycles. The rules are reversed during more bearish periods. When intermediate-term market trends are clearly in decline, selling opportunities frequently develop when daily stock prices or market indices approach or penetrate shorter-term moving averages from below.

The Long-Term 200-Day Moving Average

The 200-day moving average reflects longer-term market trends. As you can see, it naturally responds more slowly than the 50-day moving average to changes in the direction of market movements. The 200-day average turned upward in April 2003 and continued upward throughout the year, with the slope of its advance accelerating and reflecting ongoing market strength. Again, accelerating slopes suggest extensions of trends in motion. Decelerating trends imply that current trends might be approaching reversal. The 200-day moving average did lose momentum early in 2004, reflecting the weakening stock market that year.

Be sure to check the lengths of pulses and the slope of moving averages that you are tracking. The longer the pulse is, the more vertical the slope is and the greater the odds there are of a continuation in trend. As pulses and slopes moderate, the odds of an imminent market reversal increase.

Using Weekly-Based Longer-Term Moving Averages

Chart 3.2 The New York Stock Exchange Index Weekly Chart, 30-Week Moving Average

This chart shows the New York Stock Exchange Index of 1995–1997, along with its 30-week moving average. The symbols B and S indicate periods during which upside penetrations of the 30-week moving average proved significant, and periods during which downside penetrations proved significant. These marked penetrations were followed by above-average advances and declines respectively.

Chart 3.2, the New York Stock Exchange Index, is based on weekly price closings and employs a weekly-based 30-week moving average, calculated at the ends of weeks based upon weekly closing price levels. This was a strongly trended period for the stock market, marked by upward action during the late 1990s into 2000, sharply downtrended action thereafter until late 2002, and then a renewal of sharp advances during 2003. To the extent that longer-term trends were more pronounced than usual during this period, the significance of whether prices stood above or below the 30-week moving average was probably greater than normal.

Do you remember the rule regarding diminishing market pulses? You might want to review the long-term buying pulses, reflected by the moving average on the chart. The longest and strongest rising pulse took place between 1996 and mid-1998. This was followed by a sharp decline and then by a second significant upswing between mid-1998 and mid-1999, the pulse of which was *not* as strong as the 1996–1998 advance.

The final upside pulse between late 1999 and early 2000 took place at a more moderate slope than both of the previous two pulses, confirming a weakening of upside momentum in the New York Stock Exchange Index. Price levels and the moving average flattened quickly, a harbinger of the weakness to come. These are the same patterns that are present in Chart 3.1, the daily price action of the Nasdaq 100 Index.

In both periods, the series of pulses involved were completed in three waves. This three-wave pattern, which occurs frequently, appears to be associated with The Elliott Wave Theory, an approach to studying wave movements and their predictive significance that has a wide following among stock market technicians. We will return to the significance of pulse waves when we examine moving average trading channels, which I consider to be a very powerful market timing tool.

Moving Averages and Very Long-Term Moving Averages

Moving averages, as we have seen, may be applied to shorter-term, intermediate-term, and very long-term price movements. You may also apply them, if you are a very active trader, to intra-day market data for day trading purposes. Such data may be plotted on hourly, 30-minute, 15-minute, and even 5-minute bases, but at this time we are considering longer term applications.

Chart 3.3 is a monthly chart of the Standard & Poor's 500 Index, posted with a 30-month moving average. You should note two items. First, consider the significance of the moving average in providing areas of support for the stock market. During positive market periods, price declines frequently come to an end in the area of key intermediate- and major-term moving averages. Second, note that the accelerating rise in the moving average creates a rising parabolic curve. Such formations usually occur only during very speculative periods (for example, consider the price of gold in 1980) and are generally followed by long-lasting and serious market declines. As you can see, the highs of 2000 had still not been surpassed by early 2004. The peak in gold prices that developed during 1980 has to date remained unchallenged for nearly a quarter of a century.

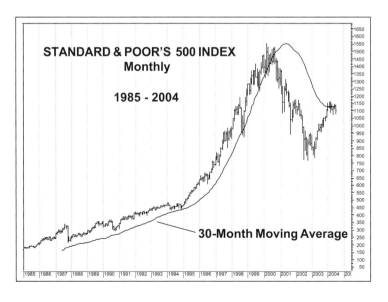

Chart 3.3   The Standard & Poor's 500 Index, 1986–2003 30-Month Moving Average

As illustrated in Chart 3.3, the stock market advanced in an accelerating, parabolic advance between 1986–2000, with the 30-month moving average line providing support throughout the rise. Market tops generally end in gradual decelerations, but sometimes advances are marked by parabolic acceleration, such advances often ending with a spikelike peak. Parabolic patterns of this nature usually take place during highly speculative periods, which are great fun for as long as they last, although they usually do end badly.

Moving Averages: Myths and Misconceptions

It is frequently said that the stock market is in a bullish position because prices lie above their 30-week moving averages or that it is bearish because prices lie below their 30-week moving averages. Sometimes 10-week or 20-week moving averages are referenced instead. There are some elements of truth to these generalizations, but strategies of buying and selling stocks based on crossings of moving averages tend to add only moderately, if at all, to buy-and-hold performance.

For example, consider two possible strategies. The first strategy involves buying the Dow Industrials when its daily close exceeds its 200-day moving average, and selling at the close of days when its close declines to below the 200-day moving average. The second strategy employs the same rules but is applied to crossings of the 100-day moving average.

Trading the Dow Industrials on Moving Average Crossings (January 5, 1970– January 13, 2004)

	200–Day Moving Average Model	100-Day Moving Average Model
Total round-trip trades	120	195
Profitable trades	26 (21.7%)	44 (22.6%)
Unprofitable trades	94 (78.3%)	151 (77.4%)
Average gain, winning trades	14.1%	18.7%
Average loss, losing trades	–1.2%	–1.1%
Percentage of time invested	68.6%	65.5%
Rate of gain per annum while invested	9.6%	9.1%
Gain per annum, including cash periods	6.6%	6.0%
Open drawdown	44.2%	48.1%
Buy and hold: Gain per annum +7.8%; open drawdown –45.1%		

* Gain per annum includes neither money market interest income while in cash, which has averaged approximately 2% per year, nor dividend payments. If these were included, gains per annum for the trading and buy-and-hold strategies would have been essentially equal.

As you can see, there has been very little benefit or disadvantage to trading the Dow Industrial Average based on penetrations of either the 100-day or the 200-day moving averages. The Dow has not been a particularly volatile or trendy market index. The Nasdaq Composite Index, more volatile and trendy, has generally proven in the past to be somewhat more compatible with this form of timing model, although less so in recent years because this market sector has lost a good deal of its autocorrelation, the tendency of rising market days to be followed by rising market days, and of market-declining days to be followed by market-declining days. Rising and falling days are now more likely to occur in random order than in decades past.

Results of buying on upside penetrations of moving averages and selling on downside penetrations seem to improve if exponential moving averages, which provide more weight to recent than distant past periods, are employed. The construction of exponential averages will be discussed in Chapter 6 when we review The Weekly Impulse Signal. A special application of moving averages, moving average trading bands, a means of predicting future market movement by past market action, has a chapter of its own (see Chapter 9, "Moving Average Trading Channels: Using Yesterday's Action to Call Tomorrow's Turns").

Using Moving Averages to Identify the Four Stages of the Market Cycle

Moving averages can be employed to define the four major stages of the typical market cycle (see Chart 3.4). This identification leads readily to logical portfolio strategies that accompany each stage.

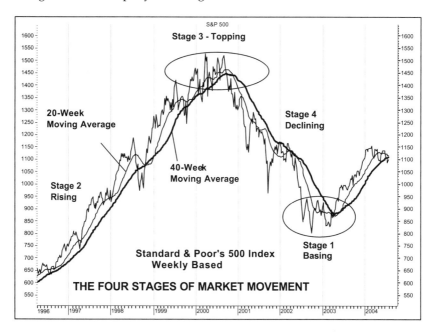

Chart 3.4 The Four Stages of the Market Cycle

Chart 3.4 shows the four stages of the market cycle: rising, topping, declining, and finally basing for the next Stage 2 advance. As you can see, during Stage 2 advances, prices mainly trend above the key moving averages. During Stage 4 declines, prices mainly trend below the key moving averages.

Stage 1

In this stage, the stock market makes a transition from a major bear market to a major bull market. This is a period of base building as the market prepares for advance. This stage encompasses a period that includes, at its beginning, the ending phase of bear markets or market declines that take place during shorter periods. These declines give way to neutral market action as stocks move from late-selling investors to perspicacious investors accumulating positions for the next upswing. In the final phases of Stage 1, the stock market usually begins to inch upward, market breadth readings (measures of the extent to which large numbers of stocks are participating in market advances or declines) improve, and fewer stocks fall to new 52-week lows, the lowest price for each stock over the last 52 weeks.

Patterns of Moving Averages During Stage 1

Shorter-term moving averages begin to show more favorable patterns as longer-term moving averages continue to decline. The downward slopes of all moving averages mediate.

Selling pulses show diminishing length, slope, and momentum. Prices, which have been trailing *below* key moving averages, begin to rally to and through their key moving averages, which themselves become more horizontal in their movement.

Accumulate investment positions during periods of short-term market weakness, in anticipation of a significant trend reversal. There is a good chance that you will be able to assemble your portfolio leisurely because major term Stage 1 basing formations often require weeks and sometimes even months for completion.

Stage 2

Price advances become confirmed by the ability of the stock market to penetrate initial resistance zones, price areas that previously rebuffed upside penetration. Investors become aware that a significant change in market tone is developing and begin to buy aggressively. This is the best of periods in which to own stocks.

Stage 2 often originates in a burst of strength as prices move upward and above the trading ranges that developed during Stage 1. This is the period during which it becomes widely recognized that a major trend change for the better is taking place and is also usually a period in which selling strategies are unlikely to produce much in the way of benefit.

Patterns of Moving Averages During Stage 2 Advances

Intermediate- and then longer-term moving averages join short-term moving averages in first reversing and then accelerating to the upside. Prices tend to find support at the level of their key moving averages, often moving averages of 25 days to 10 weeks in length. Penetrations to the downside of moving average lines are brief. Buying pulses are longer and at a sharper angle than selling pulses, as measured by the slopes and lengths of moving average waves.

Initiate long positions early in this phase, with plans to hold throughout the rising cycle, if possible. The major portion of your portfolio should be in place relatively early in this stage of the market cycle.

Stage 3

The market advance slows, with shares passing from earlier buyers to the hands of investors who are becoming invested late. This period is marked by distribution, when savvy investors dispose of holdings to less savvy latecomers.

Patterns of Moving Averages During Stage 3 Distribution Periods

The shorter-term and, later, intermediate- and longer-term moving averages lose upside momentum and flatten. Price declines carry prices as far beneath as above key moving averages. Uptrends give way to neutral price movement and to neutral patterns in moving average movement. Fewer stocks and industry groups demonstrate rising moving average trends.

In many ways, this is a difficult period for many investors. This is partly because of the insidious way Stage 2 advances often give way to Stage 3 distribution. In addition, many investors, actually more fearful of missing a profit than of taking a loss, are reluctant to concede that the happy bullish party might be coming to a close.

New purchases should be made selectively, with care. Selling strategies for existing holdings should be established, profits should be protected with stop-loss orders, and portfolios should be lightened by selling stocks that have fallen in relative strength. Rallies should be employed as opportunities for liquidation.

Stage 4

Bear markets are in effect. Market declines broaden and accelerate. Short-term and then longer-term moving averages turn down, with downtrends accelerating as bear markets progress. An increasing amount of price movement takes place beneath key moving averages. Rallies tend to stop at or just above declining moving averages. Market rallies do take place and are sometimes sharp but generally relatively brief.

This is the stage during which investors accrue the greatest losses. Stage 4 declines are often, but not always, marked by rising interest rates and usually start during periods in which economic news remains favorable. In its price action, the stock market tends to anticipate changing economic news by approximately nine months to one year, rising in anticipation of improving economic conditions and declining in anticipation of deteriorating conditions. In the former case, initial market advances are usually greeted with some skepticism. In the latter case, still favorable economic news leads investors to ignore warnings provided by the stock market itself.

For most investors, it is probably best simply to maintain cash positions. Serious market declines are usually associated with high interest rates, which can be secured with minimal or no risk. Aggressive and accurate traders, of course, might attempt to profit from short selling. For the most part, it is not advisable to attempt to ride through major market downtrends with fully invested positions. Although the very long-term trend of the stock market is up, serious bear markets that have reduced asset values by as much as 75% periodically take place.

The Rate of Change Indicator: How to Measure and Analyze the Momentum of the Stock Market

The Concept and Maintenance of the Rate of Change Indicator

Rate of change measurements measure *momentum*, which is the rate at which price changes are taking place. Consider a golf drive, for example. A well-hit ball leaves the tee quickly, rising and gaining altitude quickly. Momentum is very high. Although it might be difficult to estimate the carry of the drive in its initial rise from the tee, it is often possible to determine, from the initial rate of rise of the ball, that this is a well-hit drive, likely to carry for some considerable distance. Sooner or later, the rate of climb of the ball clearly diminishes and the ball loses momentum. At this time, an estimate of the final distance of the drive can be more readily made.

The important concept involved is that rates of rise diminish before declines actually get under way. The falling rate of change of the drive provides advance warning that the ball is soon going to fall to the ground.

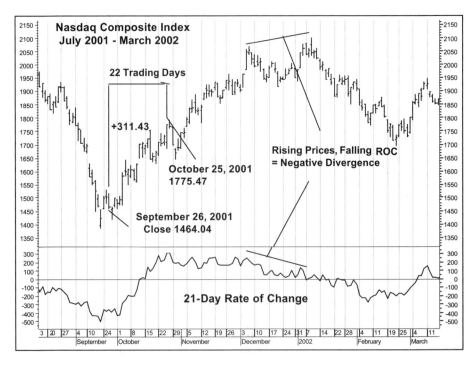

Chart 3.5 The Nasdaq Composite Index 2001–2002

Chart 3.5 illustrates the construction and application of the rate of change indicator. Two dates are marked on the chart: September 26, 2001, at which time the Nasdaq Composite closed at 1464.04, and October 25, 21 days later, at which time the Composite closed at 1775.47. The Composite gained 311.43 over these 21 days of trading; the 21-day rate of change of the indicator on October 25 was +311.43, the rate at which the Nasdaq Composite was advancing. For the most part, rate of change measurements kept pace with price movement between October and early December, with momentum matching price movement. However, rate of change readings fell off sharply as prices reached a new high in January 2002, a failure of momentum to confirm price gain, referred to as a negative divergence. Such patterns are often the precursor to serious market declines.

In its price movements, the stock market often demonstrates momentum characteristics that are very similar to the momentum characteristics of the golf drive.

For example, review Chart 3.5, which covers the period of September 2001 to March 2002. This was a bear market period, but spirited, if usually short-term, market rallies do take place during bear markets. Such an advance took place between late September and early December 2001, when the stock market "golf ball" reached an effective peak in momentum. Momentum had fallen off sharply by the time the "ball" reached its final zenith in early January 2002, giving investors ample warning that the advance was reaching essential completion.

In reviewing the chart, you might notice that the initial lift in prices from the late September lows was accompanied by sharply rising rate of change readings. Momentum did not peak until five weeks had passed since the onset of the market rise, tracking thereafter in a relatively high and level course until early December, when a downward trend in momentum readings diverged from a final high in price levels.

This pattern of price levels reaching new highs as momentum readings fail to do so is referred to as a negative divergence. The divergence carries bearish implications because of the decline in power suggested by the failure of momentum readings to keep up with market advances. A converse pattern, with price levels falling to new lows while momentum readings turn upwards, reflects declining downside momentum and is referred to as a positive divergence because of its bullish implications.

Of course, additional concepts are involved in the interpretation and use of rate of change readings—not to mention a neat short-term timing model based on such measurements. However, first matters first....

Constructing Rate of Change Measurements

Rate of change measurement was discussed in the last chapter when we covered the yield indicator, but there is no harm in a refresher course. Rate of change measurements can be made for any period of time and can be based on hourly, daily, weekly, or monthly data. In my own work, I frequently employ daily closing prices of key market indices or levels of the advance-decline line (a cumulative total of advances minus declines on the NYSE or on Nasdaq) as my data stream.

I have found ten-day rate of change readings to be helpful for shorter-term trading and 21-day to 25-day rate of change readings to be useful for intermediate-term trading. It is helpful to maintain both shorter- and longer-term rate of change measurements. Often changes in direction in the shorter-term readings presage subsequent changes in the direction of longer-term rate of change measurements.

Here is how your worksheet might look if you were maintaining a ten-day rate of change indicator stream of the Standard & Poor's 500 Index from January 30th into February 2004.

Date	Closing Level, S&P 500	10-Day Rate of Change
1 January 30	1131.13	
2 February 2	1135.26	
3 February 3	1136.03	
4 February 4	1126.52	
5 February 5	1128.59	
6 February 6	1142.76	
7 February 9	1139.81	
8 February 10	1145.54	
9 February 11	1157.76	
10 February 12	1152.11	
11 February 13	1145.81	+14.68 (Day 11, 1145.81 – Day 1, 1131.13)
12 February 17	1156.99	+21.73 (Day 12, 1156.99 – Day 2, 1135.26)

As you can see, a data stream of at least one unit more than your rate of change measurement is required for maintenance, so for a ten-day rate of change reading to be secured, at least eleven days of data must be maintained.

It is useful to plot both price and rate of change readings on the same chart sheet, to identify divergences, create trendlines, and so on. Daily rate of change lines can be rather jagged, so moving averages of daily measurements are often useful to smooth out patterns of the indicator.

Let's start this section with Chart 3.6, which illustrates a number of the major concepts employed in interpreting rate of change measurements.

Bull Market and Bear Market Rate of Change Patterns

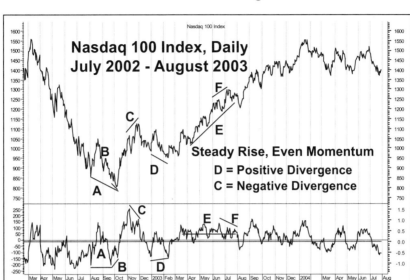

Chart 3.6 Nasdaq 100 Index, Daily, July 2002–August 2003

This chart shows the behavior of rate of change measurements during both bear and bull markets. As you can see, rate of change readings tend to be negative (below 0) during market declines and positive (above 0) during bull markets.

You would naturally expect stock prices to show generally negative rates of change during market declines and generally positive rates of change during market advances. This characteristic of rate of change lines is very apparent in the transition of the stock market from a major bearish trend to a major bullish trend between 2002 and 2003.

Market analysts often refer to the stock market as being "oversold" or "overbought." By this, they mean that the momentum of the market's change in price level has become unusually extended in a negative or positive direction, based upon normal parameters of the indicator employed. For example, in recent years, the ten-day rate of change of the NYSE advance-decline line has tended to range between +7,500 and –8,500. Forays beyond these boundaries represent overbought and oversold conditions, respectively. In theory, when measurements of momentum reach certain levels, the stock market is likely to reverse direction, in the same manner that a rubber band, when stretched, has a tendency to snap back to a state of equilibrium.

Popular as this generalization is—and it's usually accurate enough during neutral market periods—it becomes less reliable in its outcomes when the stock market is strongly trended. For example, the very negative readings in rate of change measurements that developed during the spring and early summer of 2002 portended a greater likelihood of continuing decline than of immediate recovery because readings had become just about as negative as they ever get. Extreme weakness suggests further weakness to come. Extreme strength suggests further strength to come. Market reversals rarely take place without at least some prior neutralization of rate of change measurements.

Adjusting Overbought and Oversold Rate of Change Levels for Market Trend

The levels at which momentum indicators can be considered "oversold" (with the market likely to try to firm, especially during a neutral or bullish period) and "overbought" (with the market likely to at least pause in its advance, especially during a bearish or neutral period) often vary depending upon the general market climate.

During bullish market periods, rate of change readings rarely reach the negative extremes that can exist for many weeks or even months during bear markets. When they do decline to their lower ranges, the stock market frequently recovers rapidly. During bearish market periods, rate of change readings tend not to track at levels as high as those during better market climates; the stock market more likely declines rapidly when readings reach relatively high levels for bear market periods. Referring to Chart 3.6 again, you can see examples of shifts in the parameters of rate of change indicator levels as the market's major trend changed direction from bearish to bullish.

When assessing whether momentum indicators suggest an imminent market reversal based on overbought or oversold levels, adjust your parameters based upon the market's current price trend, moving average direction, and rate of change parameters that are currently operative. These adjustments are, of course, somewhat subjective rather than completely objective.

For the most part, significant market advances do not start when rate of change and other momentum oscillators stand at their most negative or oversold readings. They tend to begin after momentum oscillators have already advanced from their most negatively extreme readings. For example, review Chart 3.6 again. The October 2002 advance did not start until the 21-day rate of change oscillator had already established a rising, double-bottom pattern, the second low point of which was considerably higher than the first.

The end of the November–December market advance (see Chart 3.6) did not start until the 21-day rate of change oscillator had already retreated from its peak levels, with a descending double-top formation created in the process.

The summer 2002 decline did not end until rate of change measurements established a pattern of rising lows (diminishing downside momentum). A positive divergence developed within Area A on the chart; the price level of the Nasdaq 100 Index fell to new lows, whereas its 21-day rate of change level did not. You can also see a minor-term but nonetheless significant secondary positive divergence in Area B, with prices declining to a final low while rate of change measurements became less negative.

The recovery from the lows of September 2002 developed in a classical fashion. The first step was a strong leg upward that carried prices above a resistance area (the peak in August) and momentum readings to high levels, more positive than at any time since March. However, the initial spike came to an end after approximately two months.

Was there a warning of the forthcoming two-month decline? Yes, indeed. Check out Area C on the chart, the area in which prices rose to new recovery peaks in November while rate of change levels declined, a classic negative divergence that foretold developing market weakness.

The decline in the stock market in Area D appeared to be developing from a bearish-looking head and shoulders market top formation (defined in Chapter 6, "Bottom Fishing, Top Spotting, Staying the Course: Power Tools That Combine Momentum Oscillators with Market Breadth Measurements for Improved Market Timing"), but the positive divergence (lower prices unconfirmed by rate of change patterns) that developed in January 2003 argued for a more favorable outcome, which did develop.

Looking Deeper into Levels of the Rate of Change Indicator

The rate of change oscillator conveys a good deal of information in and of itself, but it provides more information if the time is taken to study the market action that created the current reading.

More specifically, each day's new rate of change indicator level actually involves two variables: the current day's change in price level and direction of movement, and the level and direction of the price movement of the day that is being removed from the calculation being made.

If the day being removed was a day of market decline, rate of change measurements will turn upward even if today shows no gain in price, for as long as it shows lesser loss than the day being removed. Therefore, if weaker market periods are being eliminated from rate of change calculations, rate of change levels tend to rise easily, often before price trends turn upward. If today happens to be a rising day and the day eliminated from the calculation was a falling day, rate of change measurements might rise rapidly.

Conversely, if the days being removed from your calculations were days of market advance, it will be more difficult for your rate of change indicator to gain ground. During strong market periods, rate of change indicators are likely to track sideways, but at relatively high levels. It might appear at such times that negative divergences are taking place, but if you examine the data stream carefully, you might notice that the stock market is not really weakening at all and that, in fact, the ability of its rate of change readings to remain high is a sign of strength.

Let's go back to Chart 3.5. September was a period of sharply declining stock prices, so rate of change levels rose quickly in October, even prior to price gains of any significance. Not until the turn of the month into November were the days being eliminated in the calculations rising market days. Rate of change measurements remained flat, though high for several weeks. The inability of rate of change measurements to advance further was, in this instance, not a sign of market weakness, but rather simply a reflection of the ongoing strength that had been maintained over several weeks.

Relative strength readings (Chart 3.5) did not seriously begin to fail until the end of 2001, when, after a dip, prices rose to new highs while rate of change measurements clearly failed to do so. Prices and rate of change measurements declined simultaneously early in 2002, the decline preceded by the negative divergence that had developed between December 2001 and January 2002.

The first dip down in early December, accompanied by declines in the rate of change indicator, was not necessarily indicative of a more negative market climate. Even the strongest market advances have periods of consolidation. You might notice that at no time did rate of change levels decline below 0 during December. However, a negative divergence, with more bearish implications, did develop at year end.

What made this negative divergence more significant than the flattening of the rate of change indicator during October and November? Well, for one thing, rate of change readings were no longer tracking at high levels, declining to near the zero line. For another, patterns of price movement had changed, with price trends flattening. As a third consideration, there was very little time between the time that the rate of change failed to reach new peaks that would have confirmed new highs in price, and the rapid turndown in price levels from the early January peak.

Again, declines in rate of change readings and the presence of negative divergences are more significant if they are accompanied by some weakening in price trend. Double-top formations in price (two peaks spaced a few days to a few weeks apart) accompanied by declining double top formations in rate of change measurements can be quite bearish.

Conversely, rising patterns in rate of change measurements are more significant if they are confirmed by a demonstrated ability of the stock market to turn upward. Double-bottom stock market formations, spaced a few days to a few weeks apart, accompanied by rising rate of change readings often provide excellent entry points.

The Triple Momentum Nasdaq Index Trading Model

You will now learn about a simple-to-maintain timing model that is designed for use with investment vehicles that track closely with the Nasdaq Composite. This is a short-term, hit-and-run timing model that was invested only 45.9% of the time from 1972 to May 2004, yet it outperformed buy-and-hold strategies during 20 of the 32 years included in the study. Gains per winning trade were more than five times the size of losses taken during losing trades. More performance data is shown afterward, but first you should look at the logic and rules of the model.

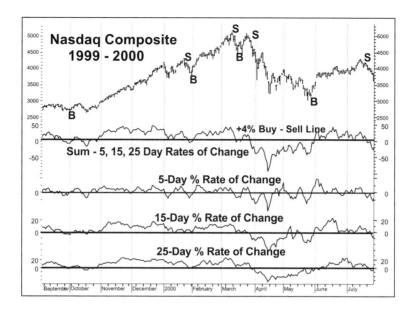

Chart 3.7 The Triple Momentum Timing Model (1999–2000)

This chart shows the Nasdaq Composite from late October 1999 through early October 2000. Below the price chart are three rate of change charts: the 5-, 15-, and 25-day rates of change of the Nasdaq Composite, expressed in percentage (not in point) changes in that index. At the top of those three charts is a chart that is created by summing the daily readings of the separate rate of change measurements. B signifies a buy date, and S signifies a sell date. You might notice that the shorter-term 5-day rate of change indicator leads the longer-term 15-day and 25-day rate of change indicators in changing direction before changes in price direction. (This chart is based upon hypothetical study. There can be no assurance of future performance.)

Maintenance Procedure

The procedure for maintaining this indicator is very straightforward.

You will need to maintain three daily rate of change measurements: a 5-day rate of change of the daily closing prices of the Nasdaq Composite, a 15-day rate of change measurement, and a 25-day rate of change measurement.

These are maintained as percentage changes, not as point changes. For example, if the closing price of the Nasdaq Composite today is 2000 and the closing level ten days previous is 1900, the ten-day rate of change would be +5.26%. (2000 − 1900 = 100; 100 ÷ 1900 = .0526; .0526 × 100 = +5.26%.)

At the close of each day, you add the percentage-based levels for the 5-day, 15-day, and 25-day rates of change measurements to get a composite rate of change, the Triple Momentum figure for the day. For example, if the 5-day rate of change level is +3.0%, the 15-day rate of change level is +4.5%, and the 25-day rate of change level is +6.0%, the composite Triple Momentum Level would come to +13.5%, or to +13.5. A reading of this nature, positive across all time frames, would suggest an uptrended stock market.

There is only one buy rule and only one sell rule: You buy when the Triple Momentum Level, the sum of the 5-, 15-, and 25-day rates of change, crosses from below to above 4%. You sell when the Triple Momentum Level, the sum of the 5-, 15-, and 25-day rates of change, crosses from above to below 4%.

Again, there are no further rules. The model is almost elegant in its simplicity. Here are the year-to-year results.

The Triple Momentum Timing Model (1972–2004)

Year	Buy and Hold, Nasdaq Composite	Triple Momentum
1972	+4.4%	+2.3%
1973	−31.1	+7.5
1974	−35.1	−0.3
1975	+29.8	+32.9
1976	+26.1	+23.6
1977	+7.3	+5.3
1978	+12.3	+26.2
1979	+28.1	+25.3
1980	+33.9	+43.2
1981	−3.2	+9.8
1982	+18.7	+43.8
1983	+19.9	+29.4
1984	−11.2	+3.6
1985	+31.4	+31.3
1986	+7.4	+10.7
1987	−5.3	+24.1
1988	+15.4	+11.6
1989	+19.3	+15.2
1990	−17.8	+10.8
1991	+56.8	+32.9
1992	+15.5	+17.9
1993	+14.8	+7.4
1994	- 3.2	+2.0
1995	+39.9	+27.0
1996	+22.7	+20.3
1997	+21.6	+26.3
1998	+39.6	+50.9
1999	+85.6	+43.5

Continued

The Triple Momentum Timing Model (1972–2004) (Continued)

Year	Buy and Hold, Nasdaq Composite	Triple Momentum
2000	−39.3	+8.6
2001	−21.1	+27.5
2002	−31.5	+4.9
2003	+50.0	+21.5
2004 (partial)	−2.3	+ 0.8

Summary of Performance Results

	Buy and Hold	Triple Momentum
Gain per annum	+9.0%	+19.8%
Open drawdown	−77.4%	−17.5%
Round-trip trades		288 (8.9 per year)
Percentage of trades profitable		54.4%
Percentage of time invested		45.9%
Rate of gain while invested, annualized	+9.0%	+ 43.1%
Average gain per profitable trade		+4.8%
Average loss per losing trade		−0.9%
Gain/loss per trade ratio		5.3
Total gain/loss ratio		6.2

Gains achieved by the Triple Momentum Timing Model were more than six times the amount of loss over this 32-year period. The model outperformed buy-and-hold by an average of 120% per year while being invested only 45.9% of the time. Interest income derived at other times is not included in these calculations, but, for that matter, neither are possible trading expenses or negative tax consequences that accrue from active as opposed to passive stock investment.

The question might naturally arise whether it is really necessary to employ three rates of change measurements in this system or whether just one might do the job as well. Actually, using three measurements seems to provide smoother results, with less trading and risk. For example, if the Nasdaq Composite was purchased on days that the 15-day rate of change alone rose from below to above 0 and sold on days that it fell below 0, the average annual gain would have been +18.3%, the maximum drawdown would have risen to −28.6%, the number of trades would have risen to 307, and the accuracy would have declined to 44.3%. Rates of return while invested would have fallen from 43.1% to 30.7%, and profit/loss ratios per trade would have declined from 5.3 to 4.1. Comparisons with other alternative single rate of change strategies seem to produce similar results.

This timing model has stood the test of time very well. Stock market technicians and timing model developers have found that, in many cases, there have been deteriorations in the performance of stock market timing models in recent decades. Models that worked well during the 1970s began to lose performance during the 1980s, lost more during the 1990s, and lost even more during the bear market of 2000–2002. Losses in efficiency have possibly resulted from rising daily market volatility over the years, increasing trading volume and day trading activity, a considerable reduction in day-to-day trendiness in the various stock market sectors, and probably other factors as well.

You might find it reassuring to observe that the Triple Momentum Timing Model has shown consistent performance relative to buy-and-hold strategies over the past three decades, outperforming buy-and-hold most years during the 1970s and the 1980s, and since 2000. During the 1990s, there were five years in which buy-and-hold strategies outperformed Triple Momentum, and five years in which the model outperformed buy-and-hold. In assessing the value of the model, you might want to recall that it is invested only 45.9% of the time.

Notes Regarding Research Structure

By their nature, research designs employed in creating this sort of timing model tend to involve processes that often produce results that have been optimized for the period of time covered by the research data and that are not equaled in real time going forward. A way to reduce, if not totally eliminate, these problems connected with optimization is to test a model in two or more stages. Parameters are set based on one period of time and then are applied to subsequent periods of time to see if the model continues to perform as well in a hypothetically established future as in the past.

The Triple Momentum Timing Model was created and tested in the following manner. First, parameters were established based upon the time period of September 1972 to December 31, 1988. These parameters were then applied to the remainder of the test period, January 1 1989 to May 5, 2004. Comparative results are shown here.

The Triple Momentum Timing Model Performance by Period

	Period Used for Creation September 1972–December 1988	Forward Testing Period January 1989–May 2004
Returns, buy and hold	+7.6%	+11.3%
Annual returns, trading	+19.7%	+19.6%
Number of trades	128 (7.8 per year)	162 (10.6 per year)
Percentage profitable trades	56.3%	51.9%
Percentage of time invested	43.4%	48.6%
Return while invested	45.3%	40.9%
Open drawdown	−6.9%	−17.5%
Average gain/average loss	8.0	4.1
Average gain per trade	+2.5%	+1.9%

Although there was a certain amount of deterioration in performance between the creation period (1972–1988) and the subsequent test period (1989–2004) of the Triple Momentum Timing Model, its performance actually remained relatively stable, given the increase in the daily volatility of the Nasdaq Composite during the 1989–2004 period and the wide and erratic swings up during 1999 and down during the bear market (not to mention the reduction in day-to-day trendiness that has taken place in the Nasdaq Composite since 1999). I have found in my research that very few timing models have maintained their performance in recent years, and that the Triple Momentum model has done far better than most.

Incidentally, research indicates that the principles of the Triple Momentum Model can be applied to other markets as well (for example, U.S. Treasury bonds). Back testing suggests that risks can be considerably reduced with minimal impact on profitability in this very difficult market to trade.

Rate of Change Patterns and the Four Stages of the Stock Market Cycle

Rate of change patterns can be employed in conjunction with moving averages to define the four stages of the stock market cycle. Rate of change readings usually change direction in advance of moving averages; the momentum of price movement generally reverses in advance of changes of price movement.

Charts 3.5 and 3.6 in this chapter provide examples of the behavior of rate of change measurements as significant market trends reverse. Moving averages can be made of daily rate of change measurements to smooth the often-jagged daily fluctuations of this indicator.

To sum up, moving averages, which reflect shorter and longer trends in the stock market, can help investors define the strength in the market by their direction, their slope, and the angle and length of their pulses upward and downward. Rate of change measurements, which define the momentum of market advances and decline, often provide advance warning of impending market reversals, as well as a measure of the strength of trends in effect. Both moving averages and rate of change measurements provide significant indications of the four stages of major and shorter-term market cycles.

4

More Than Just Pretty Pictures: Power Tool Chart Patterns

The practice of maintaining charts of the movement of the stock market and of stocks is probably as old as the stock market itself. Certainly, the development of computer-based trading programs, online market-tracking programs, and the various financial web sites (not to mention the old-line stock market advisory services) have made stock market charts increasingly familiar and available to countless investors.

It is beyond the scope of this book to investigate the myriad forms of charting, such as point and figure and candlestick, that chartists use, or to attempt to evaluate the efficacy of the many charting alternatives available to chart aficionados. It is safe to say that interpreting stock chart patterns is almost certainly more an art than a science, and chart patterns frequently, if not generally, lend themselves to subjective interpretation that is more apparent after the fact than beforehand. Such caveats notwithstanding, I have found certain chart patterns to be quite useful in their implications. Before we move into the specific area of charting, however, it's important to understand a very important principle for investing: synergy.

The Concept of Synergy

Synergy is defined as the mutually cooperating action of separate substances that together produce an effect greater than that of any component taken alone. The combined effect is greater than the sum of the two parts taken separately.

In spite of all the research that takes place regarding the movement of stock prices, in spite of all the data available to investors, and in spite of all the charts produced by all the computers traders use, the simple fact remains that there are no "perfect" stock market indicators—and probably not even any near-perfect indicators. Every so often, some indicator becomes popular, usually after only two or three successful predictions. For example, based on a just a few major market cycles that took place after World War II, it was assumed that bear markets "must" take place when dividend yields for stocks decline to below 3% or when price/earnings ratios rise to 21 or 22. These parameters, which indicated the bear markets of 1966, 1969, and 1970, for example, were again approached during the mid-1990s. However, this time around, the Standard & Poor's 500 Index did not see its bull market end until the year 2000, by which time its price/earnings ratio had risen to 46 and its dividend yield had declined to just a touch above 1%.

In any event, even if a perfect indicator were discovered, sooner or later its components would become known, with its effectiveness dissipating as investors began to follow it en masse. (Where would the sellers come from if every investor became a simultaneous buyer?) The simple fact is that, at best, market forecasting is a matter not of perfection, but of probabilities. A realistic set of goals is to be right more often than wrong, to develop the emotional willingness and technical ability to recognize quickly when we are wrong and to take appropriate action, even if that means accepting a stock market loss. (Generally, the best losses in the stock market are the losses quickly taken.)

Successful investors are not in the stock market at all times. They assess the probabilities of success as carefully as possible and take positions only when the odds are in their favor. One way to improve the odds is to employ the concept of synergy: The likelihood of a successful trade improves considerably if there are multiple indications in favor of the stock market action you are contemplating.

How do synergistic indicators compound the favorable probabilities? Well, suppose that there are a number of uncorrelated stock market indicators, each of which tends to be correct 60% of the time and incorrect 40% of the time. That's probably about as good a batting average as you are likely to see in a stock market timing indicator. (The indicators should be dissimilar to each other in their construction and concept. Otherwise, they might, in reality, simply be the same indicator in disguise.)

You normally trade on one indicator that produces a buy signal, which opt to follow. The probabilities of a successful trade are 60%—actually, pretty decent for a stock market trade, particularly if you have an effective exit strategy.

Instead, you change your strategy and begin to maintain two unrelated market indicators, each of which has a 60% success rate. You initiate a plan by which you will take positions only when both indicators produce confirming signals to support your contemplated market action. What effect is this likely to have on the odds of a successful trade? The probability of a profitable trade rises from 60% to 84%.

If you maintained three indicators, each of which has a 60% accuracy rate, taking positions only when all three suggest similar action, the odds of a successful trade rise even more, this time to 93.6%.

It follows, then, that you should make serious attempts to confirm buy signals with multiple indicators whenever possible and to look for confirming as well as nonconfirming indications before taking positions. I shall be emphasizing this concept as we move along.

Powerful Chart Formations

Chart 4.1 illustrates a fine technique for projecting the time and length of a market swing, given the presence of a certain pattern of previous price movement. This pattern involves changes in the angle of stock market movement, an analysis of which can provide excellent projections of not only where the stock market is likely to go, but how long it will take to get there. Incidentally, the concepts involved are applicable to day trading as well as to short-term and even longer-term position investment.

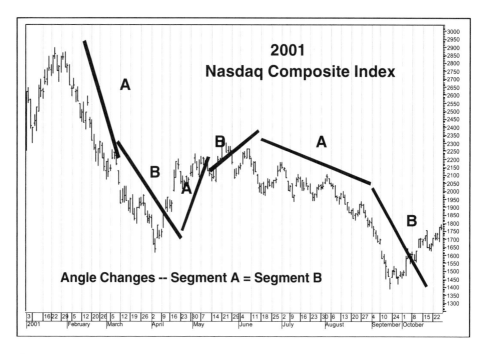

Chart 4.1   Using Angle Changes to Project Price Targets

Sometimes the stock market appears to be rising or falling at a particular angle, and then the angle of movement changes. If you measure the distance encompassed by the first angle segment (A) and then project that distance along the second angle segment (B) in the direction that it is moving, you can frequently secure an accurate projection of the length of the B segment, which frequently is the same length as the first A segment.

It sometimes happens—actually, with reasonable frequency, that the stock market starts a move along one angle of rise or fall. Sometimes the initial angle is steep; sometimes it is not. At some point, the angle or slope of the move clearly changes.

A steep rise or fall seems to change in its angle to a move with less velocity. Conversely, a gradual market advance or decline suddenly changes slope and becomes more acute, sometimes almost vertical.

When you recognize that this pattern is developing, which should be fairly early in the duration of the second segment of the move, it is possible to accurately project the length and duration of the remaining market swing. The first leg, along the first angle of the total advance or decline, is called segment A. The second leg is called segment B. As soon as you have recognized a change in direction of segment A, you measure that segment. Project the measurement you secure along segment B in the path that segment B is traveling, starting at the initiation point of segment B. That projection will provide not only the likely extent of segment B, but also the time frame in which the projection will be achieved.

eg Example 1

In Chart 4.1, the stock market started downward at the start of 2001 and declined at a rather sharp rate until a "pennant" formation, with sideways movement, took place. (This sort of pennant formation generally takes place at the 50% point of a market move, in any case.) The decline then continued, at first sharply but then at a clearly more moderate angle. If you had measured segment A, when you saw segment B developing, you could have projected the length and time of segment B.

If you examine segment A more closely, you can see that that segment itself consists of two segments: a downward segment at one angle and a second segment at a steeper angle. The length of that first segment could have been projected along the second segment to secure the final time and price level of segment A.

Similarly, segment B consists of two segments. The first, in early March, is a vertical decline, lasting just two sessions—long enough, however, to be employed as a measure for the remainder of segment B after that segment changed its slope of decline.

eg Example 2

A second A, B sequence took place between April and May, immediately after the sequence just described. This time, the A wave started steeply. If you look carefully, you can see that this segment itself consisted of an A, B sequence. The A segment lasted for just two weeks or so. At that time, its path mediated into the angle of the B segment, which, in the end, fell just a touch short of matching the length of the A segment.

Notice that the B segment took approximately four weeks to complete, or twice the time of the A segment. It is not the time frame that is matched between the A and B segments of the full swing. It is the length of each of the two waves, created by a combination of angle and distance, which tends to be equal. It is not unusual for segments A and B to be unmatched in their time periods.

Example 3

Finally, Chart 4.1 shows an A, B segment sequence that ran between late May 2001 and mid-September 2001. The period began with a more moderate decline in the stock market that ran between late May and early August. The decline accelerated, with the more moderately sloped A segment transforming into the violent decline that took place in the B wave. The fit between the two segments was very close, indeed. You would have been able to make a fine call of the likely levels of the market lows after recognizing the transformation from the A segment to the B segment.

The Wedge Formation: Times to Accumulate and Times to Distribute Stocks

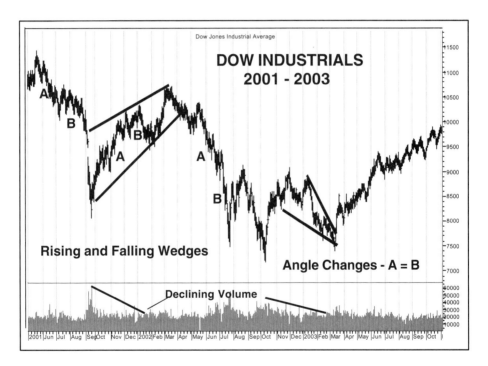

Chart 4.2   Recognizing Rising and Falling Wedge Formations

This chart illustrates both rising wedge formations, usually a precursor to imminent market decline, and declining wedge formations, usually a precursor to imminent market advance. Some examples of measuring angle changes are also shown. Many others have not been marked. For example, the advance from September 2001 into the end of the year took place in a two-segment, A, B pattern, as did the market decline from late winter to early spring during 2002.

The Wedge Formation

Rising wedge formations are created when the following conditions take place:

- The stock market (or other markets or individual investments) rises in price.
- Trendlines drawn that reflect support lines rise at a constant angle.
- Trendlines that reflect resistance, where prices turn down, can be drawn at a constant angle as well, but the angle of rise is less than the angle of the support trendline. The result is a converging channel.
- Trading volume decreases as the formation develops. This is an important condition because declining volume during uptrends suggests a reduction in buying pressures.

The pattern tells us that although buying pressures are remaining fairly constant, sellers are acting with increasing urgency.

What is actually taking place during the formation of the wedge? Buyers, perhaps to some extent influenced by the rising trendline itself, are buying with consistency and the angle of the supporting trendline remains constant. However, although buying pressures are holding firm, selling pressures are increasing; the descending resistance trendline indicates that selling is coming in earlier in comparison to new buying levels. Sellers are settling for diminishing amounts of profit relative to new buying levels; selling becoming more urgent with each minor market cycle. With net demand and supply relationships weakening, buying and selling pressures converge. The likely resolution is a downside break from the formation.

Please respect the phrase "likely resolution." Rising wedge formations, which carry bearish implications, usually provide accurate notice that rising price patterns soon will reverse to the downside. Sometimes, however, patterns resolve positively. Positive outcomes are most likely when wedges develop in an area of heavy resistance, a zone in which there has been heavy trading in the past. From time to time, the overhead supply of stocks that creates resistance simply slows but does not permanently impede gains in the market. When the resistance is overcome, stocks burst upward as investors become aware that a bullish breakout is taking place.

I have marked two wedges in Chart 4.2. Relatively brief retracements upward often take place following declines though the lower trendlines of rising wedges and downward following advances through the upper trendlines of falling wedges.

Declining Wedge Formations

Declining wedge formations have the following characteristics:

- The stock market is falling in price.
- Trendlines drawn across price highs decline at a constant angle, reflecting uniform selling.
- Support trendlines, drawn at price lows, also decline, but a lesser angle than selling trendlines, indicating increasing eagerness on the part of buyers, who are hoping to accumulate stock. Therefore, rising and declining trendlines converge.

- Trading volume decreases during the formation, indicating diminishing selling pressure. This is an important condition.

This pattern suggests that although selling pressures remain fairly constant, buying pressures are increasing; buyers are willing to step in at each minor cycle following less in the way of market decline. This pattern, which usually resolves to the upside, carries bullish implication.

Wedge formations tend to be very reliable for short-term and day-trading operations. This is one of my favorite personal charting patterns for day-trading purposes.

Appropriate Strategies

If you detect the development of a rising wedge, especially if the wedge is being confirmed by other indicators, you might take these actions:

- Sell at the upper boundaries of the wedge.
- Sell on a violation of the lower boundary of the wedge.
- Draw the trendlines forward to see the point at which the upper and lower boundaries would meet. If you are selling short because of a rising wedge formation, you might want to use that point as a stop. Cover if the market rises above the level of that point, which usually takes place with an upside run around and above the point of upper and lower trendline convergence.

If you detect the development of a declining wedge, especially if the formation is being confirmed by other indicators, you might take these actions:

- Buy at the lower boundaries of the wedge.
- Buy when the wedge's upper trendline is penetrated.
- Place protective stops at the convergence of the upper and lower trendlines.

Synergy in Chart Patterns

Chart 4.2 includes examples of synergistic chart patterns, which reinforce each other and thereby add weight to each separate bullish or bearish pattern.

For example, a very significant upside breakout from a declining wedge formation took place during the spring of 2003, shown in Chart 4.2. That breakout occurred simultaneously with the completion of the segment B decline within the wedge formation. The angle-measuring strategy suggested the completion of a decline right in the area of the breakout, so a recovery at that market juncture was not surprising.

The coincidence of the achievement of price objectives based upon A, B segment angle changes and the presence of rising and falling wedge formations adds to the significance of the wedge and the likely success of acting on wedge patterns. Synergistic thinking does produce its rewards.

Head and Shoulder Formations

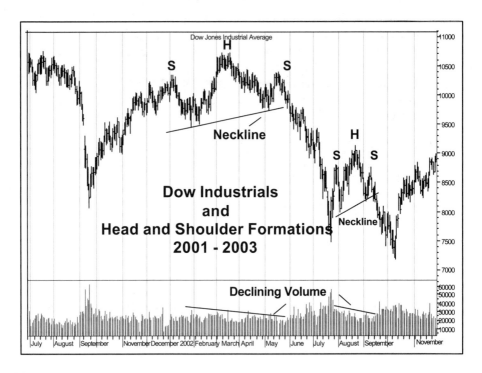

Chart 4.3   Head and Shoulder Formations for Buying and Selling

The head and shoulder formation is probably the best known of chart patterns, frequently significant in both its bullish and bearish configurations, although it is by no means 100% accurate in its predictions.

Chart 4.3 illustrates the head and shoulder formation, a formation that has a bearish and a bullish variant, for indicating significant market top and market bottom junctures, respectively. These are the conditions that define the head and shoulder formation.

At market tops, the following occurs:

1. The stock market rises to a high following a market advance. It then dips to an interim low before advancing to a new high. The original high point is referred to as the "left shoulder." The low of the subsequent dip ultimately develops in what will become the first point of the "neckline." The secondary new high that next develops will be the "head" when the formation is complete.

2. Following the advance to the secondary high, which is higher than the left shoulder, prices dip again. This dip might be to the level of the first dip to the neckline (flat head and shoulder formation), above the first dip to the neckline

(rising head and shoulder formation), or below that of a dip that followed upon the rise to the first shoulder (declining head and shoulder formation). The first two formations in Chart 4.3 are formations with rising necklines. The final formation on the right shows a flat neckline.

3. Following this dip, prices rise again, to a level that is not as high as the peak level of the head of the formation. This level is referred to as the "right shoulder."

4. The formation is considered to be complete when prices then turn down and decline to below the neckline, which is created by drawing a line across the two low points in the formation.

5. *Very important*: For the formation to have validity, trading volume must decline across the entire formation. Volume should be highest at the left shoulder, should diminish during the advance to the head, and should diminish still further on the advance to the right shoulder.

This reduction in volume indicates diminishing buying power during each leg of the topping formation. For example, even though the head lies above the left shoulder, the rally to the head fails to attract as much buying interest as the advance to the left shoulder. The advance to the right shoulder involves even less in the way of investor participation. Demand is clearly failing. Again, if these patterns of diminishing volume are not present, the formation loses validity.

Using the Head and Shoulder Formation to Establish Downside Price Objectives

This is probably a good time to review Chart 4.3.

To establish a minimum downside projection following the completion of a head and shoulder top formation, do the following:

1. Measure the distance from the peak of the head vertically down to the neckline drawn between the two dips in the head and shoulder formation.

2. When the penetration of the neckline takes place, measure from the point of downside penetration the distance secured from Step 1. This measurement is employed as a minimum downside objective for the formation.

Three head and shoulder tops are shown in Chart 4.3. The first developed at the start of 2002; its minimum downside objectives were achieved in May of that year. As matters turned out, additional declines carried the market down considerably further: The final decline did not end until July. (You might notice the angle change, A – B, in the decline from May to July, and the excellent projection that might have been made by using that angle change measurement.)

A second head and shoulder top, smaller in its magnitude, developed during the third quarter of 2002, between mid-July and September. This formation is marked in Chart 4.3. The distance from the peak of the head, h, projected down to the neckline of the formation provided a downside objective that turned out to be extremely accurate. The decline ended in October very much in the area of the projected downside target.

The chart shows another example of synergy in action. The decline from the right shoulder during September 2002 developed as an angle change. Prices first declined steeply and then at a more moderate pace. An almost perfectly executed downside objective was established by the angle change, which coincided almost exactly with the downside objective implied by the head and shoulder top formation. This provided considerable justification for "bottom fishing" in that area.

These are some general observations regarding head and shoulder top formations:

- Head and shoulder top formations that have rising necklines carry less bearish implications than head and shoulder formations with level necklines that are less bearish than head and shoulder formations with declining necklines. Downsloping necklines imply larger downside objectives than flat or rising necklines.

- Downside penetrations of necklines, which mark the completion of head and shoulder top formations, are frequently followed by rapid market recoveries back to the underside of the neckline just penetrated. This recovery, usually short-lived, is generally a good time for aggressive investors to sell short or for investors still holding positions in relevant issues to sell. Recoveries of this sort appear in the first head and shoulder pattern illustrated in Chart 4.3, frequently but not always taking place.

- Although head and shoulder tops are widely considered to be among the most reliable of chart formations, they are by no means infallible. Formations are rendered invalid if, following a break down through the neckline, there is a subsequent near-term recovery back over the peak level of the right shoulder. Failed head and shoulder tops are frequently followed by spirited market advances when the failure to follow through to the downside becomes widely recognized.

- Although it is often tempting to try to anticipate the completion of head and shoulder tops and to sell or sell short before the completion of the formation, it is probably a better policy to actually await the full completion of the head and shoulder pattern.

At Market Bottoms, the Inverse Head and Shoulder Formation

Head and shoulder bottom formations can appear as a formation that develops inversely to the head and shoulder top formation, in which case the pattern becomes a buying rather than a selling formation.

The same basic descriptive patterns occur, though reversed to the head and shoulder top.

1. A market decline takes place. At its conclusion, a high-volume spike often occurs. This ultimately becomes the left shoulder in the formation. Such a decline took place during June and July 2002.

2. A rally takes place, which is then followed by another leg down on lower volume than the first decline. This leg down generally carries to below the leg down that precedes it. When the decline ends, a rally carries to the area of the previous advance, with trading volume still decreasing.

3. The completion of this second market recovery provides the opportunity to define the neckline of the formation. A final decline from the new neckline on still-diminishing volume leads to the final and right shoulder of the formation. The formation is complete when the neckline is penetrated from below.

4. Minimum price objectives for the inverse head and shoulder formation, a bullish pattern, are secured by measuring the distance from the neckline to the head and projecting this measurement upward at the area where the neckline is penetrated. A very significant longer-term inverse head and shoulder formation developed in the Dow Industrials between the summer of 2002 and the spring of 2003. The price objectives of that formation were achieved during December of that year.

Head and shoulder bottom formations are among the more accurate of chart patterns, but there are occasional failures nonetheless. Sell stops should be placed below the lowest level of the right shoulder in the formation.

Confirmation by Measures of Market Momentum

Head and shoulder top and bottom formations are usually confirmed by measures of market momentum, such as the rate of change. Momentum generally declines as the formation develops along. Positive divergences (at market bottoms) and negative divergences (at market tops) provide additional evidence that significant changes in market climate might be developing.

Bearish head and shoulder formations often take place in Stage 3 (market topping), and bullish formations typically take place during Stage 1 (market base building). The time required to complete of such formations provides the opportunity for investors to carefully reduce or to accumulate positions.

Volume Spikes Are Very Bullish If the Stock Market Has Been in Decline

True or false: Conditions are bullish if market declines take place on low volume?

As a general rule, this is false—very false. This is a very common misconception.

Long-term and serious intermediate declines that take place on low volume tend to continue for some time. Low volume during market decline signifies two things. First, there is probably little panic on the part of investors; instead, there's complacency. Prices are likely to be declining not so much because of active selling, but because buying demand is drying up. When buying demand slows, prices frequently fall under their own weight. Second, prices have not yet fallen to levels that will attract aggressive buyers. Buyers are remaining on the sidelines while the typical, still complacent investor retains positions even through periods of slowly falling prices.

The Selling Climax

Sooner or later, even the most complacent holder becomes disturbed by the downward drift in prices. Selling pressures increase and become more widespread. Volume increases as shares of stock (or futures contracts, or option contracts, and so forth) pass from weaker, now nervous hands into the hands of aggressive buyers who are stepping in to take advantage of the developing selling panic.

This transition from slow, steady, complacent decline to aggressive, nervous selling and finally to nascent aggressive buying is referred to as a selling climax. It is largely driven by aggressive and fearful selling—the urge to sell at any price. Buying climaxes following extensive market advances sometimes take place as well. The demands of aggressive buyers are met by savvy traders who are perfectly willing to part with the stock that is being demanded. Buying climaxes are less usual than selling climaxes, but one did take develop in certain areas of the Nasdaq Composite Index in March 2000.

Again, market declines of any magnitude, even during intraday price swings (day traders, take note) frequently do not come to an end until trading volume increases, often dramatically.

Review Chart 4.3 one more time. Take note of the declines in the Dow Industrials that came to an end in September 2001, in July 2002, and in October 2002. Each one of those significant market low points developed on sharply rising volume compared to the days and weeks surrounding the actual market lows of those periods.

To sum up once more, although market declines sometimes end with a long, quiet, base-building process, low trading volume during market decline is, at best, a neutral indication. The most bullish development that can take place during a major or serious intermediate market decline is a dramatic build-up of stock market volume following a period of falling prices. This build-up often develops during the sort of terminal downside spikes that characterize stock market selling climaxes.

Support and Resistance Levels

Chart 4.4   Support and Resistance Levels for Nasdaq (1998–2004)

This chart shows the rising series of support lines that marked the market advance of 1998 to early 2000, and the declining series of resistance lines that marked the subsequent bear market. A significant angle change formation also did a fine job of defining the major phases of the 2000–2003 market period.

Support Zones

An awareness of patterns associated with support zones (areas usually associated with previous trading ranges, in which prices find support against further decline) and resistance areas (areas that resist further price advance) enables investors to more accurately define the direction of significant market trends. Such patterns also suggest areas in which price reversals are likely to take place.

Stock market advances do not take place in a straight line. They generally take place in a steplike series of advance, flat or retracement period, further advance, another flat or retracement period, and so forth.

During bull markets, retracements tend to take place at increasingly higher levels. The series of rising low areas between rising peak readings defines market trend. Suppose, for example, that a stock is trading at a high of $50 per share, having recently risen in price from $45. A certain number of traders who purchased at $45 will take profits at $50, creating, in the process, some temporary weakness in the stock. The stock might then back down to a price level of perhaps $47 to $48.

If the general trend for that issue is bullish, which is the case in an uptrend, there will be buyers at hand waiting for a some reaction from the $50 level to take positions. If the buyers are aggressive, they likely will step into the market quickly, taking positions in the $47 to $48 area. This $47 to $48 area might be taken as an area of "support," a zone in which buyers will take positions in that issue.

Prices then rise, crossing the previous high at $50 (a temporary resistance area because there was previous selling in that zone) and rising to perhaps $53 or so when a new round of profit taking takes place. If prices back down, they are likely to find support in the area of the old previous high—in this case, in the area around $50.

Chart 4.4 illustrates the rising series of support zones that developed in the Nasdaq Composite Index during 1999 and then the declining series of resistance zones that developed during the subsequent bear market.

Each rise, retracement, and new rise during 1999 left behind a sort of indentation in the chart pattern—a scoop of sorts, which represented a potential support zone for the next market decline. During uptrends, ideal buying zones often develop within those scoops or pockets between earlier market declines and the most recent market peaks.

Support Zones

Support levels, again, are zones in which investors show willingness to step in to purchase stocks (or other investment vehicles) that have backed off in price. There may be broad, long-term areas of support (zones from which market recoveries have taken place over considerable periods of time) or shorter-term areas of support (zones in which trading has taken place for only limited periods of time). The broader the support zone is, the more significant it is likely to be.

- Market uptrends are characterized by patterns of rising support levels and rising peaks achieved in rallies from those support levels.

- When a new peak is achieved, the area between that peak and a previous consolidation becomes a support level.

- Uptrends are considered intact for as long as support levels take place at progressively higher zones.

- During market uptrends, resistance zones tend to develop not at or below previous market peaks, but a bit above previous market peaks.

- The test of a bull market is the capability of the market to produce progressively higher support and resistance zones.

Resistance Zones

During declining and neutral market trends, resistance zones are likely to develop in areas in which there have been previous market trading, areas that have halted price advance in the past. How might a resistance zone develop? Well, suppose that a market advance has just come to an end, taking a particular issue down from a new high in price of $50 to a price of $44. There are likely to be many investors who regret not selling in the $49 to $50 zone, waiting and hoping for a second opportunity. If the issue recovers back to the $49 to $50 area, many of these investors, recalling that $50 was the last high, will offer shares for sale, perhaps driving the issue back down in price.

In this sequence, a "trading range" might develop between $44 (the most recent low for the stock, perhaps perceived as a buy zone) and $50 (the most recent high), perhaps perceived as an expensive area for that issue. The price of $44 to $45 will represent a support zone. The $49 to $50 area will represent a resistance zone.

If prices break down below $44 to $45—say, to $37 to $38—the former support zone of $44 to $45 is likely to become a new resistance zone. There will have been many buyers at $44 to $45 hoping and looking for a return to their buying level for an opportunity to achieve a breakeven on their investment. These investors, among others, represent a source of ready supply in that resistance zone of $44 to $45.

Conversely, if the stock penetrates the $50 level, moving perhaps to $55 to $56, that old resistance zone at $49 to $50 could become redefined as a favorable buying zone rather than a likely selling zone. The former resistance area will become a support zone.

These are significant concepts. When a support area is violated to the downside, the former area of support frequently becomes an area of resistance. When a resistance area is penetrated to the upside, this former area of resistance is likely to become an area of support.

Example: The 1999–2003 Stock Market Climate (Chart 4.4)

The basic trend for the Nasdaq Composite changed from bullish to bearish during the spring and summer of 2000. The parabolic, accelerating advance in that index ended in a spike formation during March 2000. Even within that terminal spike, an initial decline found rapid, though very temporary, support. A quick and sharp recovery to previous highs took place following the first downthrust, although a rapid and subsequent decline resulted in the end in a sharp and lasting break through the mid-March support zone.

This violation of support defined the major trend reversal that took place in the Nasdaq Composite in the year 2000. The stock market attempted another recovery during the early summer, although the attempt failed to penetrate the March support level, which had become resistance. Another support level was created in August; that support zone also failed to sustain prices, ultimately becoming a resistance area.

Bear markets are defined by a series of declining resistance levels, with market swings carrying to successively lower areas. The bear market that was so defined during the spring and summer of 2000 did not see even one penetration of a resistance area until the end of 2002. At that time, for the first time since the bear market began, a market rally carried above the peak of a previous recovery. Finally, in early 2003, a bullish pattern of progressively higher lows and progressively higher peaks was generated.

Market Downtrends

Market downtrends, which characterize major bear markets, represent periods of high risk for investors who are generally well advised to avoid assuming new positions and/or to reduce currently invested stock positions for as long as such downtrends are in effect. Just to review the tell-tale signs and patterns of behavior associated with bearish market climates....

- Market downtrends are characterized by a series of lower peaks (resistance zones) and lower areas (support zones) from which rallies emanate.

- For as long as a pattern of lower lows and lower highs remains in effect, a bear market is in effect.

- Resistance zones during bear markets generally develop at or slightly below peaks of previous market recoveries. Previous areas of support often become areas of current resistance.

- The capability of the stock market to penetrate a previous resistance zone could be an early indication of a significant trend reversal.

Chart 4.4 illustrates these concepts. As you can see, there were transitions from areas in which support factors dominated (1998 to early 2000) to areas in which resistance factors dominated (2000 to 2002), a transitional period (late 2002), and then a return to an area in which support factors were dominant (2003 to 2004).

Major Trend Synergy in Action

You can see in Chart 4.4 a major-term angle change that developed in the Nasdaq Composite between 2000 and 2003. The index declined first at a very steep rate and then, starting in early 2001, at a more moderate slope. The two stages of the decline were equal in the lengths of their slopes.

The second segment became equal to the first segment at the start of 2003. This measurement confirmed the capability of the Nasdaq Composite to first penetrate a resistance zone and then to establish a series of progressively higher lows and highs. The angle change pattern predicted the likely time and area of the market recovery. The coincidence of the downside projection implied by the angle change and the development of a bullish downside wedge in that area proved to be a fortuitous chart synergy.

Tricks with Trendlines

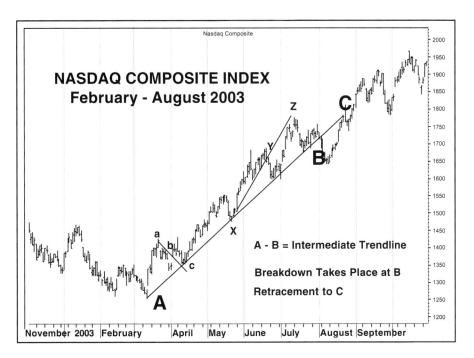

Chart 4.5   Resistance and Support Provided by Trendlines

This chart shows the intermediate trendline that defined the initial months of the 2003 bull market. The chart also provides examples of the tendency of trendlines to act as resistance when they are penetrated to the downside and to act as support when they are penetrated to the upside.

Trendlines are lines that can be drawn to connect the lows of market reaction moves during market advances or to connect the highs of market reaction moves during market declines. As Chart 4.5 shows, such trendlines often define the direction and slope of longer-term and shorter-term movement trends.

The more points are associated with any trendline, the greater the significance of that trendline is. For example, Trendline A–B on Chart 4.5 connects five points: the start at A in March; low points in April, May, and June; and a support area in July that finally gave way after two weeks of being challenged. This was a significant trendline that was actually established between its start in March and the first market reaction during April.

As you can see, less significant, more minor trendlines can be drawn within the context of significant market trends. For example, the X–Y trendline between May and June 2003 reflected a short-term uptrend that developed at a greater slope than the longer-term market advance between March and August. The short-term decline that took place when the X–Y line was violated ended at the support provided by the longer-term A–B intermediate trendline.

Significant market trends are frequently interrupted by shorter-term contratrend market movements, the brief A – B - C market decline that took place between March and the first days of April 2003.

Trendlines can be drawn for time periods that range from just a few minutes to many years, depending on the significance and length of market trend that is being defined. The trendline is a useful technical tool, but it should probably not be employed as a standalone indicator because of false trendline penetrations that occur and because trendlines tend to appear more accurate when they are drawn in after the fact than an actual real time. In any event, because definitions of trendline slopes are often somewhat subjective, it is advisable to employ trendlines in conjunction with confirming indicators.

Inverse Trendline Support and Resistance Zones

The inclinations of support areas, once penetrated, to act as resistance zones and of resistance areas, once penetrated, to act as support zones have already been mentioned. Trendlines, which represent support lines, have the same characteristics as other support areas.

A rising trendline, once penetrated to the downside, usually acts as resistance against repenetration to the upside. Advances following a downside trendline break likely will have difficulty passing through and above the trendline just violated, although such advances could well track along the bottom of that trendline.

For example, in Chart 4.5, you can see the longer-term A–B trendline that connected the March to July lows. That trendline was penetrated in early August; the Nasdaq Composite incurred a sharp, though not lasting decline. A retracement started quickly enough, but where did it meet initial resistance? Right at the under side of the A–B trendline, at C. The A–B trendline, no longer a support line, had become a resistance line.

A similar pattern developed following a break down through the X–Y trendline that developed between May and June 2003, with a downside break taking place in mid-June. The short-term decline that followed upon the X–Y trendline violation carried down to the A–B, longer-term, rising trendline, from which area prices recovered. But where did the recovery come to an end? Again, at Z, right at the underside of the X–Y trendline that had just been violated. X–Y, once a support line, became a resistance line.

A declining trendline, once penetrated, usually acts as support against repenetration to the downside. For example, a very short-term downtrend (A–B on the left of Chart 4.5) took place in March 2003. This downtrend lasted only for six trading sessions, with its downtrend line quickly penetrated. The stock market advanced for four sessions and then backed off. Where did this retracement come to an end? Right at the top of the A–B downtrend line. This time, a resistance trendline, once penetrated, acted as support.

Channel Support and Resistance

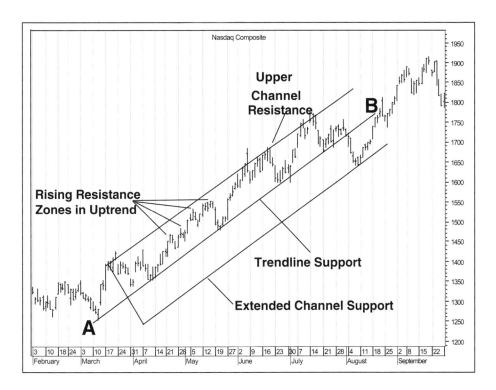

Chart 4.6   Resistance and Support Within Trading Channels

This chart shows the Nasdaq Composite and its movement within the bullish channel that developed between March and August 2003. Line A–B represents the supporting trendline of the advance. The upper boundary of the channel is created to best encompass the majority of peaks of minor moves within the channel. The lower extension is created to match the major channel in depth.

Continuing on the theme of support and resistance, Chart 4.6 illustrates the manner in which channels can be created based upon well-established trendlines. The upper boundaries of such channels frequently serve as ongoing resistance lines.

These channels can be drawn empirically by eye, with the upper boundary parallel to the primary supporting trendline. The upper boundary can be set to encompass all movement within the channel, but I recommend allowing for some overshoots here and there, to secure the best fit. A certain amount of subjectivity is involved.

Early Warnings Provided by Channel Patterns

The manner in which such channels operate is, I think, pretty apparent from the chart. Channels of this nature often provide advance notice of a change in the character of the stock market. For example, notice the nature of the series of recoveries that took place between April and early July whenever the midline of the channel, the primary trendline, was approached. Rallies during April and May were almost instantaneous. The rally in early July required a little more than a week of base building before the Composite could reach the top of channel; when prices did reach the top of the channel, they backed off quickly rather than running upward along the channel as they had done in June.

The recovery that started in mid-July never made a serious attempt to reach the upper boundary of the channel. Prices moved upward at a very moderate slope before they declined, for the first time since March, through the supporting, mid-channel trendline. In this case, the diminishing slope of the recovery, coupled with the failure over two weeks to reach the upper boundary, warned of the incipient breakdown.

The capability of stock prices to rise rapidly to and to even overshoot the upper boundary of a trading channel suggests a favorable market climate and higher prices to come. Diminished slopes of advance and failure to reach the upper boundary suggest incipient market weakness.

Extended Channel Support

The penetration of the supporting lower boundary of a trading channel carries an implication of further market decline. A likely objective for such a decline can be established by drawing a line parallel to the support trendline as far a distance below that trendline as the upper boundary of the channel is above that line. Simply double the width of the channel, placing the support trendline in the middle. That extended channel support line becomes the next support zone. The supporting trendline, which has acted as support, is likely to become a resistance area.

Sometimes the upper channel boundary is clearly penetrated by an amount sufficient to invite the creation of a new upper channel resistance line, as far from the original upper channel line as that line has been from the support trendline. In that case, the upper channel line serves as support.

Rising Resistance Zones

You can see how each wave of advance within the channel carried to the upper boundary of the trading channel. The upper boundary itself provides rising levels of resistance to penetration.

You might also notice in Chart 4.6 that, within the period of April to May, a series of minor peaks and troughs defined advancing resistance and support levels as the market moved from the April lows to the May peak.

To sum up, support and resistance zones are created and heavily influenced by areas in which previous trading has taken place. Resistance zones, once penetrated, transform into support zones. Support zones, once violated, tend to transform into resistance areas.

Support and resistance zones are also heavily influenced by current trends of investment markets, apart from influences created by previous trading activity. Look for rising areas of resistance and support during bull markets, and for declining areas of resistance and support during bear markets.

False Breakouts and Breakdowns: Key Market Patterns

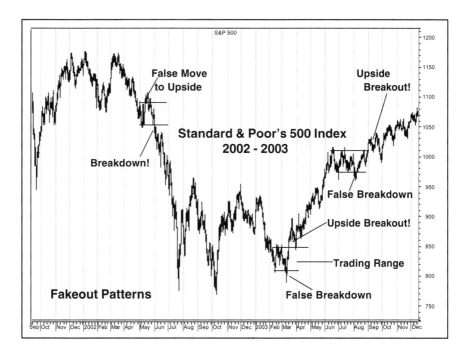

Chart 4.7   False Moves and Their Aftermath

This chart of the Standard & Poor's 500 Index shows one false move to the upside and two false moves to the downside. The rapid reversal of these false moves indicates the onset of sharp market moves in a direction contrary to the original false start.

False breakouts and breakdowns often precede dynamic market declines and advances. Here are two more very powerful chart patterns that frequently indicate the likelihood of a dynamic stock market advance or decline (the direction depends on the sequence of events).

The patterns are simple. In the first case, the following sequence develops:

A Significant Sell Signal

The most significant sell signals often take place following market advances that appear significant and favorable at first, but that rapidly fail. In this regard, you may want to recall that every major market decline originates from a market peak and that every bull market originates from a significant market low point. Here is a sequence of events that frequently takes place as the stock market reverses from a bullish to a bearish trend:

1. The stock market enters into a trading range.

2. A breakout takes place from within the boundaries of the trading range to a level above the trading range. It appears that a market advance is getting underway.

3. The advance ends almost immediately, indicating that the upside breakout was falsely deceptive. Prices fall to back within and then to below the lower boundary of the trading range in question.

4. The penetration of the lower boundary of the trading range when such a sequence takes place is generally followed by a sharp and extended market decline.

An example of this sequence of events appears in Chart 4.7 during May and June 2002. The trading range was narrow in this formation, but the concepts held true nonetheless.

This type of pattern exists on intraday charts as well; day traders are advised to look for it.

A Significant Buy Signal

A reverse sequence produces very significant buy signals:

1. The stock market enters into a trading range.

2. A breakdown takes place through the lower boundary of the trading range. This, perhaps, trips a few stop-loss orders in the process, extending the decline a touch, but there is basically little in the way of follow-through to the decline.

3. Prices quickly reverse upward back into and then through and above the trading range. The penetration of the upper boundary of the trading range is frequently followed by an extensive and dynamic market advance.

Sequences of this nature developed between February and March 2003 and again during July and September of that year. You might notice that the bullish implications of the early March pattern were reinforced by an angle change measurement just before the false shakeout that suggested the completion of the market's current downside objective.

The Key

The key in both cases lies with the false signal that is generated before the stock market embarks on a move in its final, significant direction. In both cases, the false moves attract very little in the way of investor follow-through. Breaks upward from trading ranges that represent false breakouts attract little in the way of investor interest, with advances faltering rapidly. The failure of subsequent trading range boundaries to hold as support confirms the bearish action reflected in the false move to the upside.

False breakdowns carry similar implications, in reverse. Violations of the lower boundary of the trading range draw very little in the way of further downside activity. Savvy investors realize that the breakdown is false, and large buying enters into the market as soon as the trading range is repenetrated, this time to the upside.

These are very powerful reversal patterns and, again, are among my personal favorites.

One last word on the subject of stock market reversals: Every stock market decline begins after the stock market has just reached a new high in price. New highs are not, in and of themselves, reason to remain bullish.

Every stock market advance begins after the stock market has just reached a new low in price. New lows are not, in and of themselves, reason to remain bearish.

You have been acquiring a number of tools that can provide warning of impending reversals in stock market trend. These tools can help you set price objectives, reveal diminishing market momentum, and provide notice of changing investor psychology. Hopefully you have been experimenting already with the material discussed so far.

5

Political, Seasonal, and Time Cycles: Riding the Tides of Market Wave Movements

It pretty much goes without saying that seasonal and other cycles that exist in nature are widely known and acknowledged. The seasons come and go pretty much on schedule year after year, bringing with them cycles of growth in vegetation; changes in the behavior of animals (migrations, nesting, births, deaths, hibernation); massive cyclical changes in the Earth's atmosphere, climate, and glacial movements; and changes in land mass.

Cyclical forces work their magic minute by minute and hour by hour as well. Tides roll in and tides roll out, their larger ebbs and flows interrupted by minor, contrawave movements at the shoreline and elsewhere. This action is similar to minor stock market retracements that take place even within strongly trended intermediate and long-term bull and bear market periods.

Political events appear to have their own particular cycles. For example, within the past century or so, wars seem to have taken place at fairly regular intervals of approximately 20 years. The cycle includes the Spanish-American War, World War I, World War II, the Vietnamese conflict, and the first Iraq War, the more recent conflict with Iraq, perhaps nearly a decade ahead of schedule. As we shall see, cyclical patterns carry significance but are not necessarily perfectly timed.

It is not known (to me, at least) why stock market behavior and the behavior of other investment markets appear to often develop along cyclical paths. Some analysts attribute patterns of investor behavior to influences exerted by interplanetary juxtaposition and the influence of phases of the moon. I, myself, can make no claim whatsoever to knowing why the cyclical patterns we observe take place. Instead, I can merely make some observations of what is and suggest how investors might identify and make use of time and seasonally oriented stock market behavior.

Calendar-Based Cycles in the Stock Market

Related to time cycles, if not technically a cyclical phenomenon, certain days of the month, months of the year, and holiday-related seasonal patterns seem to be particularly related to the performance of the stock market. These relationships are neither precise nor perfect in their correlation with the movement of the stock market, so trading on the basis of cyclical patterns alone is not necessarily the best of strategies. However, using seasonal and time-cycle patterns to confirm trading decisions based on other indicators or to determine the likely general mood and risk levels of the stock market could be a fine application of the principle of synergy.

Days of the Month

The stock market has had a definite tendency to achieve its greatest gains during the last and next-to-last trading days of each month and the first two to four trading days of subsequent months (the exact combinations have varied somewhat over the years). In fact, gains in stocks during the favorable four- to five-day turn-of-the-month trading period have typically equaled gains in stocks during all the rest of monthly trading days combined.

Pre-Holiday Pattern

Stocks have tended to show above-average strength within the days immediately preceding stock holidays and for three days following such holidays. There are definite bullish biases to periods of favorable monthly seasonality, which include the days at the turn of months and pre-holiday trading sessions. Lately, however, upside biases to holidays have generally excluded the days surrounding Good Friday, Independence Day, and President's Day. Pre- and post-holiday positive influences are most consistent during holidays that fall within the strongest months of the year, November to January.

The Best and Worst Months of the Year

There does not seem to be much of a contest in this regard. The three-month period of November through January has definitely been the strongest three-month period of the year for the stock market—not necessarily every year, but certainly overall. For example, this period produced nicely rising prices during 1995–1996, 1996–1997, 1997–1998, 1998–1999, and 1999–2000. Its performance dropped off, along with stock prices in general, during the nasty bear market period thereafter before returning to winning ways between November 2003 and February 2004.

July, September, and October have tended to be the weakest months for stocks. October has had a history of being the month most likely to see market turnarounds, which makes it a good month in which to plan or to execute the accumulation of shares in preparation for the more favorable year-end period that includes the months of November, December, and January.

October has marked turnarounds in major bear markets or significant intermediate market declines during years such as 1946, 1957, 1962, 1966, 1974, 1978, 1979, 1987, 1989, 1990, 1998, and 2002, the last of which finally reversed the most severe bear market in decades. It goes without saying, of course, that October was also the month of the fabled stock market crash of 1929.

Table 5.1 shows the month-by-month average performance of the Nasdaq Composite Index from 1971 to mid-2004 and the Standard and Poor's 500 Index from 1970-2004.

Table 5.1 *Performance by Month, Nasdaq Composite 1971 to August 2004*

Month	# Up	# Down	Winning Months Percent Up	Losing Months Percent Down	All Months Avg. Percent Change
January	23	10	69.7%	30.3%	+3.8%
February	18	15	54.6	45.5	+0.6
March	21	14	60.0	40.0	+0.3
April	22	13	62.9	37.1	+0.6
May	20	15	57.1	42.9	+0.6
June	23	12	65.7	34.3	+1.3
July	17	18	48.6	51.4	−0.3
August	19	16	54.3	45.7	+0.2
September	18	16	52.9	47.1	−0.9
October	17	17	50.0	50.0	+0.4
November	23	11	67.7	32.4	+2.0
December	21	13	61.8	38.2	+2.2

The Standard & Poor's 500 Index January 1970 to August 2004

Month	# Up	# Down	Percent Up	Percent Down	Avg. Percent Change
January	22	13	62.9%	37.1%	+1.7%
February	19	16	54.3	45.7	+0.2
March	23	12	65.7	34.3	+0.9
April	22	13	62.9	37.1	+1.0
May	20	15	57.1	42.9	+0.6
June	21	14	60.0	40.0	+0.7
July	14	21	40.0	60.0	+0.1
August	20	15	57.1	42.9	+0.2
September	12	21 (1 even)	36.4	63.6	−1.1
October	19	15	55.9	44.1	+1.0
December	26	8	76.5	23.5	+1.8

The Best Six-Month Period, the Worst Six-Month Period

Virtually all net gains in the stock market that have taken place within the last half-century or so have taken place between November 1 and April 30 of each year. May to October periods have essentially broken even, with stocks often returning slightly less to investors than risk-free income producing investments during these months.

Table 5.2 shows a quick-and-dirty seasonal trading system that has produced some surprisingly fine results on just two transactions each year.

Table 5.2 *Seasonality Trading System: Enter Market the Last Trading Day of October and Exit Closest Trading Day Before or on May 4 (Index Employed: Standard & Poor's 500 Index, Excluding Dividends, 1969 to May 2004)*

Total trades	35
Winning trades	28
Losing trades	7
Winning percentage	80.0%
Average gain	7.48%
Compounded gain per year	6.91%

Let's compare this to being invested during the most unfavorable six months of the year, buying on the closing date closest to May 4 and selling on the next-to-last trading day of October.

Table 5.3 *The Standard & Poor's 500 Index Being Invested During the Most Unfavorable Six-Month Period from 1970 to September 2004*

Total trades	35
Winning trades	22
Losing trades	13
Winning percentage	62.9%
Average gain (loss)	+0.7%
Compounded gain per year	+0.3%

Evaluating the Tabulations

Although gains were recorded in most months during both the favorable and unfavorable six-month periods, there has been a considerable difference in the magnitude of the average gain achieved during favorable seasonal periods and unfavorable periods. (Stocks advance approximately 75% of the time but, apparently, there are advances and, then again, there are advances.)

Returns during unfavorable six-month periods have averaged just a bit less than 1% per period, with the rate of return while invested approximately 2% per annum, less than risk-free interest rates in most years. As a rule, investors would have been better off in the stock market for just six months each year and out for six months than being fully invested at all times (although this is not true for every year, of course).

The performance of this seasonal six-month period timing model has been essentially similar to the Nasdaq/NYSE Index Relative Strength Indicator and the 3- to 5-Year Monetary Indicator, which also produce virtually all net market gain within defined and limited holding periods. These "mood indicators" are not precise on their own in terms of market timing, however, so they are probably best employed as an influential backdrop to investment decisions based upon more specific timing tools or as a consideration for decisions regarding the extent to which you want to be invested at any time.

There certainly do appear to be significant differences in performance between the favorable and unfavorable six-month periods. Table 5.4 divides performance into four periods and shows the breakdown of performance for the Nasdaq Composite Index and the Standard & Poor's 500 Index by seasons from 1970-2000. (Yale Hirsch, longtime publisher of the *Stock Trader's Almanac*, has been a major pioneer in areas regarding the relationships between seasonality and stock price movement. The six-month seasonal timing model described previously, as well as other concepts in this section, draw upon Yale's work and the timing model, Seasonal Timing Strategy, developed by Sy Harding, publisher of *Street Smart Report Online*.)

Table 5.4 *Seasonal Performance of the Nasdaq Composite February 5, 1971–September 2004*

Season	# Gain	#Lost	Average Change	% Profitable
Spring	25	9	+2.68%	73.5%
Summer	20	13	+0.42	60.6
Autumn	18	15	+2.18	54.6
Winter	24	9	+6.91	72.7

Seasonal Performance of the Standard & Poor's 500 Index 1970–September 2, 2004

Season	# Gain	#Lost	Average Change	% Profitable
Spring	22	13	+2.09%	62.9%
Summer	19	15	– 0.29	55.9
Fall	21	13	+2.53	61.8
Winter	24	10	+4.54	70.6

The Presidential Stock Market Cycle

This is a well-known, though hardly flawless, stock market political cycle. Basically, the stock market's best performances take place during the years that immediately precede the years of presidential elections. Its second-best annual gains tend to take place during the years of presidential elections, with the stock market often peaking shortly after the elections held during those years. The worst years for the stock market have been the years following presidential elections.

For example, positive stock market returns were achieved during every pre-election year but one since 1948. The same ratio of success has almost existed for election years (although the year 2000 was a notable failure), but gains during election years have not generally been as great as gains achieved during pre-election years. Post-election years and midterm years have produced only modest net returns to stockholders throughout the years. In fact, some portfolio managers maintain portfolios in equities only during years that are normally favorable for the presidential market cycle; they turn to interest-producing instruments during the remainder of the time.

This is, again, an indicator that has been highly reliable over the long run but one that has been prone to error in certain years. For example, the stock market advanced during the first year of President Reagan's second term in office (1985), during the first year of President Bush's term in office (1989), and again during the first years of President Clinton's two terms of office (1993 and 1997), but the year-after election hangover returned with the election of George W. Bush, whose first full year in office (2001) was marked by a serious extension of the 2000–2002 bear market.

Table 5.5 *The Election-Year Cycle: 1971–2003 Average Gain/Loss Per Year*

Year of Cycle	Nasdaq	NYSE Index	S&P 500 Index
Election year	+9.43%	+12.38%	+10.86%
Year after election	+5.07	+4.47	+4.19
2 years after election	–1.41	–1.50	–0.47
Pre-election year	+32.27	+18.65	+19.53
Percentage of Profitable Months			
Election year	50%	83%	83%
Year after election	67%	67%	67%
2 years after election	42%	58%	58%
Pre-election year	83%	75%	75%

Comments

The first section of Table 5.5 shows the average gain per year based upon its position in the election year cycle. The second section shows the percentage of profitable months within years according to their place in the cycle. The Nasdaq Composite tends to lead New York Stock Exchange–oriented market indices during the years before presidential elections but is not as consistent a performer during other years. The relative (not absolute) weakness of the Nasdaq Composite during election years, the years in which bull markets tend to peak, suggests that the Nasdaq tends to reach its bull market maximum strength before the primary market areas and falls in advance of stocks associated with primary market indices. (For example, the bear market in the Nasdaq Composite was actually underway by April 1972, whereas the Standard & Poor's 500 Index did not peak until January 1973.)

Time Cycles: Four Days to Four Years

Although they are not always apparent, there are a number of fairly regular wave patterns in the movements of stock prices that appear to be based upon time. There seem to be regular and repetitive cyclically determined time periods between low points, which is how cycles are defined. Frequently there are equal lengths of time from highs to highs as well within full market cycles, generally during neutral market periods, but cycle lengths are normally measured from lows to lows of market cycles.

Example of Market Cycles: The 53-Day Market Cycle

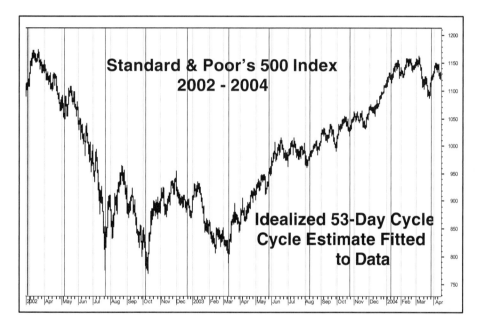

Chart 5.1 The 53-Day Cycle of the Standard & Poor's 500 Index During 2002–2004

This chart shows the 53-day idealized time cycle of the Standard & Poor's 500 Index, illustrating lows in the stock market that appear to develop at intervals of 53 trading sessions or between 11 and 12 weeks. This is an idealized cycle, whose parameters best fit the data stream for this period. In actuality, cyclical lows do not generally take place at such precise and regular intervals.

Chart 5.1 illustrates the concept of the stock market cycle. The vertical lines, placed at intervals of 53 trading sessions, appear to produce a fine fit with significant intermediate low areas for the Standard & Poor's 500 Index between 2002 and early 2004.

As you can see, the following holds true for the chart:

- The cycle, a full wave of rising and then declining price movement, is measured from low point to low point.

- Shorter-term cycles take place within the 53-day period. The full 53-day cycle is more dominant and produces significant market swings of a larger amplitude than market fluctuations based upon its shorter cyclical components. The amplitude of a cycle is the amount of average price movement that takes place during the typical range from the lows of that cycle to its peak. It goes without saying that cycles of longer length typically carry more amplitude and significance than cycles based on shorter time frames.

- It is not apparent on this chart, but the 53-day cycle itself is part of a longer sequence of cycles that have larger amplitudes than the 53-day cycle.

- The time fit between actual market lows and the idealized cyclical length is not exact but is often surprisingly accurate and predictable.

- The stock market cycle defines when market upturns are likely to take place but does not predict the length and extent of market advance that will follow. (However, clues are presented by patterns of cyclical market action that do present themselves, as discussed later in this chapter.)

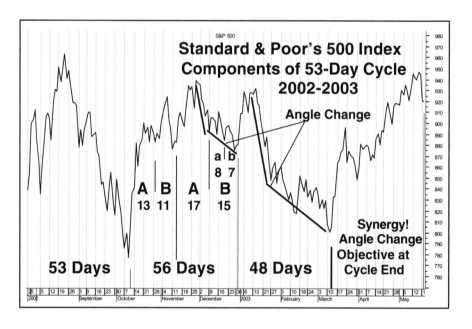

Chart 5.2 Actual Cyclical Behavior of the Standard & Poor's 500 Index Based Upon the 53-Day Time Cycle

The 53-day time cycle should actually be thought of as the "nominal" or "idealized" 53-day cycle. This chart, which covers a smaller time frame than Chart 5.1, more clearly defines the cyclical patterns reflected by the nominal 53-day cycle. The actual cyclical low-to-low measurements that developed within this period spanned a range of 48 to 56 days.

Cyclical measurements can provide fine projections for when market turns are likely to take place, but they are not absolutely precise in their outcomes:

It would be very nice if cyclical measurements were totally precise in their ability to project calendar turning points, but this is not actually the case. As you can see in Chart 5.2, there are certain discrepancies between the nominal lengths of market cycles and the actual time periods between cyclical lows. For example, actual time spans between lows based upon the 53-day cycle ranged between 48 and 56 days from July 2002 through May 2003.

Shorter time cycles—for example, the four- to five-day market cycle—are not likely to miss their projection by more than a day or so. The longer the time cycle is, the larger the potential error. Interestingly, cyclical errors tend to be self-correcting. So, if one cyclical swing tends to be longer than its nominal length, the subsequent cyclical swing will tend to be shorter than its nominal length, and vice versa. You can see in Chart 5.2 that an extended 56-day cyclical swing was followed by a shorter than 48-day cyclical period between market lows.

It is probably helpful to define your cycles as representing a range of likely time frames. For example, you might think of the 53-day cycle as representing a cyclical length of between 10 and 12 weeks, 50–60 calendar trading days, rather than as a cycle of precisely 53 days.

Return to Chart 5.2, which shows segments of the nominal 53-day cycle that we have been examining, concentrating on the cyclical period of the nominal 53-day cycle that was actually 56 days in length. As you can see, each cycle consists of two waves, an A wave and a B wave, and is itself either an A or a B wave of a larger cycle. Therefore, there are myriads of cycles, with smaller cycles nested within larger cycles, which themselves are nested within still larger cycles.

Segments of Market Cycles

The movement of stock prices actually takes place within a series of cyclical segments, which comprise larger cycles, which, themselves, comprise still larger cycles.

Each cycle, again, consists of two segments, an A segment and a B segment. For example, the 56-day cycle shown in Chart 5.2 can be divided into two segments, the first lasting 24 days and the second lasting 32 days. Segments do not necessarily match precisely in time length, length of price movement, or even basic direction, but A and B segments tend to be relatively equal in length.

Each of these segments, A and B, can itself be divided into two segments. In Chart 5.2, the 24-day segment could be divided into a 13-day segment and an 11-day segment. The 32-day A–B segment can be divided into a 17-day segment and a 15-day segment, which, themselves, represent market cycles of a lesser magnitude.

Each of these segments, ranging from a low of 11 days to a high of 17 days in length, could be subdivided again, into smaller A–B segments. For example, the 32-day B segment of the 56-day cycle in Chart 5.2 could be divided into a 17-day segment and a 15-day segment. The 15-day segment could be divided into two segments, eight and seven days in length. As you can see, each cyclical segment tends to divide into two segments, each approximately half its length.

The segmentation can be continued further, of course, down to cycles that last for less than an hour, if you like, or possibly even shorter than that. Conversely, if we were working in the other direction, the 56-day cycle could be viewed, again, within the context of longer-term cycles.

The Significance of Segmentation

If this total 56-day cycle is viewed in the context of its different segments, it will be seen not just as one cycle, but as a composite result of a myriad number of smaller cycles, some rising, some falling, some confirming others, and some in contradiction. The final effect of the cycle is the sum of the influences of smaller cycles within and the larger cycle of which it is a part.

For example, consider the initial segment A in Chart 5.2 and its components. The first portion of A lasts for 13 days. Its turndown does not create much of an effect on either the 56-day cycle or the 24-day segment, A, largely because that turndown in the 13-day segment is unsupported by any other meaningful cycle.

The subsequent turndown of the 11-day cycle, whose influence is augmented by the turndown in the longer-term 24-day segment, had a greater effect. Although the more significant 56-day cycle was still rising, which limited the negative cyclical influence, the cyclical turndown in early November 2002 resulted in a sharp short-term market decline.

The final quadrant of the 56-day cycle saw greater cyclical weakness as the 56-day cycle and its shorter-term segments simultaneously declined into a nest of lows. At this time, the 56-day cycle, the 32-day segment, the shorter-term 15-day segment, and the final seven-day segment all coalesced to the downside: a period of uniform cyclical weakness.

The areas in which a number of shorter- and longer-term market cycles come together at a market low is called the nesting of cycles. The stock market is most likely to show serious cyclical weakness as larger numbers of cycles simultaneously move down into these nests. Upward turns from these nests as multiple cycles simultaneously reverse back to the upside provide very bullish cyclical influences on the stock market.

Areas in which numerous cycles and segments lie in contradictory directions represent areas in which cyclical influences tend to be moderate.

Distinguishing Bullish Cyclical Patterns from Bearish Patterns

The 56-day cycle represented in Chart 5.2 was actually a bullish market cycle. For one thing, its second segment, or leg, B, carried above the level of the first leg, A. For another, the total length of the rising phase of the swing, seven weeks from mid-October to early December, occupied seven weeks of the 11-week cycle, clearly more than 50% of the total cyclical period. Neutral cycles generally involve rising and falling periods of equal length. Bearish cycles usually involve more of the cycle being down than up in price movement.

However, by December 2, cyclical forces were beginning to line up on the bearish side. For one thing, the 56-day cycle had already been rising for seven weeks, for nearly two-thirds of its nominal cycle length. By December 9, Segment B was running out of time and moving into its second half, confirming in its own increasing weakness the building weakness of the entire 56-day cycle. The final 15-day period of Segment B could be divided into two smaller segments yet: eight days and seven days. Declines at the very end of December were supported by a confluence of declining short- and medium-term cycles. This confluence resulted in a fairly serious market correction during the final four weeks of the larger 56-day cycle.

Lest We Forget the Concept of Synergy...

In Chart 5.2 is an angle change movement that took place during December 2002 that provided an excellent price/time objective for the market decline that continued from December 9, when the angle change took place.

The ultimate workout of that angle change coincided with the projection that could have been made on December 9 just about as perfectly as one might hope. Again, you might notice how Segment A divided into two very nearly equal sub-segments of 13 days and 11 days; how its counterpart, Segment B, divided into two very nearly equal halves of 17 and 15 days; and how that 15-day segment divided into two halves of eight days and seven days.

A sharp downward thrust in the stock market in January 2003 changed its angle of fall. The second- more-moderate angle produced a price/time projection that fit almost perfectly the completion of the bottom in March 2003, which itself took place 49 days from the previous cyclical low. This is a fine confluence of angle change measurement and cyclical time projection.

Lengths of Market Cycles

Again, numerous market cycles exist, each simultaneously exerting its influence at any given time. Some cycles are more significant than others, with their amplitudes (the amount of movement that takes place as a result of that cycle) greater than those of other cycles. The reliability of some cycles appears to be greater than the reliability of others. The major concept to be recalled is that cyclical influences on the stock market are greatest when a number of significant cycles coalesce in their direction, nesting, falling, or rising together. Cyclical influences are likely to be weakest when a number of significant cycles lie in opposition or are in neutral territory.

Here are some of the cycles that I have found to be most significant throughout the years. These are presented with the caveat that shifts in strength and length do take place from time to time, as with shifts in seasonal patterns.

- The four-year market cycle
- The one-year market cycle
- The 22- to 24-week market cycle
- The 11- to 12-week market cycle
- The five- to six-week market cycle
- The 15- to 17-day market cycle
- The 7- to 10-day market cycle

- The four- to five-day market cycle
- The 17- to 20-hour market cycle

Each cycle tends to be roughly half the length of the cycle just above it and roughly twice the length of the cycle below it. This pattern coincides with the A–B sequence that we have been observing.

We return now to examining cyclical patterns that have taken place throughout the years.

The Very Significant and Regular Four-Year Market Cycle

Chart 5.3 The 48-Month or 4-Year Market Cycle: The Standard & Poor's 500 Index, 1970–2004

This chart shows the very significant 48-month or 4-year market cycle of the stock market, with prices posted on a monthly basis.

The four-year market cycle, probably the most significant operative cycle in the stock market, actually comes and goes with surprising regularity and relatively little variability, particularly considering its length. It appears to be operative in many foreign stock markets as well as our own.

This cycle, of course, is tied to the presidential election cycle, which has been discussed. It is difficult to say whether the presidential cycle is the cause of the four-year market cycle, whether it is the effect of the cycle, or whether, in this case, political and cyclical influences actually reinforce each other. Whatever the cause, the effect is a cycle that exerts powerful influences upon the stock market.

Chart 5.3 begins with the conclusion of the 1969–1970 bear market. In fact, before the market lows of 1970, bear markets came to conclusions in 1962 and 1966, so the cycle could easily have been extended back to 1962, at a minimum. As you can see from the chart, bear market bottoms took place in 1970, 1974, 1978, and 1982.

Bear markets following 1982 were generally brief, measurable in months rather than years, until the bear market of 2000 took place. Nonetheless, significant market low points took place right on cyclical schedule in 1986, 1990 (after a significant decline), 1994 (a year of no progress to speak of in the stock market), 1998 (significant third-quarter decline), and, finally, in 2002 when the most serious bear market in decades ended just in time for the nominal conclusion of the four-year cycle and for the start of the strongest year of the presidential cycle.

The period from 1966 to 1982 was actually fairly neutral in terms of the longer-term secular trends in the stock market. The cyclical patterns of four-year cycles during these years were neutral as well, with roughly half the four-year cycles up and half down. With the secular trend strengthening into the bubble of 1999–2000, the stock market spent more of its cyclical wave periods rising; prices held well until the very end of each cycle, when the most downside pressure is normally felt. The downturn in 2000 was the first market downturn in 30 years marked by a downturn in the major four-year cycle before its midpoint. Downturns in market action early in market cycles imply more than average weakness to come.

An Intermediate Market Cycle with a Confirming Indicator

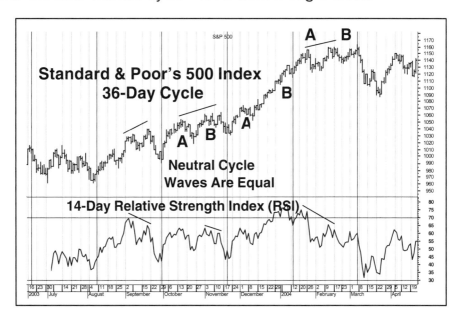

Chart 5.4 The 36-Day Cycle of the Standard & Poor's 500 Index Confirmations by Indicator of Stock Market Momentum, RSI

Chart 5.4 shows a fairly significant 36-day or 7-week market cycle and its A–B components. The 14-day Relative Strength Index, a measure of market momentum, provides fine confirmation of the position of the cycle's intrawave segments, along with implications regarding the strength of market momentum.

The interplay between cyclical waves and a popular measure of stock market momentum, Welles Wilder's Relative Strength Index (RSI), is demonstrated in Chart 5.4.

This chart illustrates a basis concept in the application of time cycles. Buy and sell signals produced by timing indicators are more likely to prove timely when they are supported by cyclical patterns. Conversely, cyclical patters are more likely to prove useful when they are supported by key technical indicators. The best signals are produced when momentum and other technical indicators approach buying or selling areas simultaneously with key cyclical elements.

Chart 5.4 is configured for the 36-day or roughly 7.5-week cycle in the stock market. Price movement within the 36-day cycle segments takes place along what by now should be familiar patterns. A–B segments are marked in three of the four cyclical periods shown on the chart, with three of those segments readily divisible into equal subsegments that are apparent in both the price and the RSI areas.

It might be slightly more difficult to recognize and identify the A–B sequence by price during late November to early January, but these A–B sequences are more readily apparent in readings of RSI.

The length and the amplitude of the A segment and the B segment are more likely to be relatively equal during neutral market periods, such as between early October and mid-November, and again at the start of 2004. The cycle that started in mid-November was very bullishly skewed: Segment B was well above segment A, with no decline to speak of in price (although one in momentum did emerge) as the cycle drew to a close.

Cycles that end up with prices at their maximum levels usually follow through during the onset of the next cyclical period with early market strength. In such situations, cyclical patterns could become more apparent in charts that include measures of market momentum, as compared to charts that measure market price movement alone.

How the Confirming Indicator Helps the Cause

If you choose to maintain one or more, which is a recommended practice, you might have made the following observations as the 2003–2004 period moved along.

The August–September Cycle

First, you can observe the level of RSI at the market low in early August, where this study begins. As you can see, RSI resided at the time in the 40 area, an oversold region for the 14-day RSI during neutral to bullish market periods. RSI advanced during the new cycle, ultimately peaking right at the cycle midway point. Prices continued to advance into the cycle, but the RSI failed to achieve new peaks along with price. This represented a negative divergence that, as we have seen, carries bearish implications.

Two developments took place as this 36-day cycle drew to its nominal close. First, the RSI, failing to reach a new high along with price (a sign of failing momentum) suggested near-term problems ahead. Second, both price and RSI turned down, price from a maximum peak and RSI from a secondary peak. Key elements were in negative harmony. The cycle was due to move into a low. The RSI had failed to achieve a new high along with price. The price level of the Standard & Poor's 500 Index turned down as well.

Now, what took place as the cycle reached its nominal low at the end of September? A number of bullish elements supported that low area, indicating the likelihood of a tradeable market advance. For one thing, the cycle was due to reach its cyclical bottom. For another, the RSI had by then descended to the area that had been the launching pad for the September advance. For still another, as the bottoming process moved along, the RSI traced out a rising double-bottom pattern, a type of pattern that tends to be quite significant when it develops within areas that mark oversold levels during bullish market periods.

The October–November Cycle

This was a slightly bullish cycle, with prices moving up gradually and more market time taking place in advance than in decline. The division into virtually equal A and B segments is very clear, as was the negative divergence between price movement and the patterns of RSI that closed the cycle with a classic negative divergence.

The RSI indicator closed the cycle at its oversold zone, again with a double-bottom formation, confirming the start of the next cycle.

The November to Early January Market Cycle

The cycle was very bullish in its development, with a small dip at the end of an early A segment followed by rising prices right into the end of the period. Sometimes cycles during very bullish market periods show patterns of price movement that make it very difficult to determine the completions of cycles that become more readily discernible in indicators that track the momentum of the price advance.

For example, the RSI dipped a few days before the end of the cycle, failing to confirm new highs made in the Standard & Poor's 500 Index at the start of 2004.

Cycles that end as strongly as the cycle from November to early January are usually followed by very strong market action at the start of the following cycle, which is what took place in this instance. The RSI indicator, incidentally, clearly indicated the A, B sequence of the November–January cycle, which was not as apparent in the price pattern.

The January–March Cycle

Following the late 2003 market advance, the stock market resumed a more neutral track at the start of the following year. The stock market started 2004 well, but the price thrust weakened rapidly.

As matters turned out, the relative weakness of the RSI indicator during the cycle presaged the more severe market decline that took place in March 2004.

The 18-Month Market Cycle with a Rate of Change Confirming Indicator

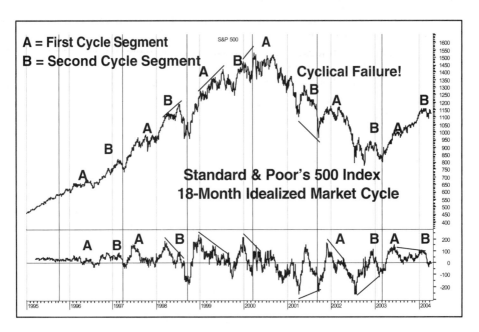

Chart 5.5 The Standard & Poor's 500 Index and the 18-Month Cycle (March 1995–March 2004)

Longer-term market cycles often break up into 18-month cycles, which are reflected on this chart. A and B waves are quite distinct, rising during the bull market periods and falling during bear market periods, clearly expressed in price movement as well as in the patterns of a 50-day rate of change indicator.

Synergy Between Rates of Change and Cyclical Patterns

Chart 5.5 further demonstrates the regularity and power of significant market cycles—in this case, the powerful 18-month market cycle that produced very regular and powerful market fluctuations for the full nine-year period between March 1995 and March 2004. The idealized cycle lines shown on the chart are evenly spaced. Virtually no adjustment appears required to allow for the usual variances in the actual lengths of time between cycles, particularly cycles of this length.

Slopes of the A and B sequence often reflect the direction of the major trends of the stock market. For example, each 18-month cycle between 1995 and early 2000 was marked by a pattern in which the B wave completed its cycle at or above the highs of the A wave that preceded it. Trends were obviously favorable.

This pattern of rising waves came to an end during the second half of 2000, when the first A wave of the new cycle failed to surpass a previous B wave in height and then turned down to below the level at which that A wave started.

A pattern in which a rising wave starts upward and then turns down to below its starting point is referred to as a cyclical failure, particularly if the turndown carries to below a previous support level. This sort of pattern is usually quite bearish, reflecting a change in basic market trend. From the point at which this failure (marked on the chart) occurred, the stock market witnessed a reversal of the 1995–1999 pattern, with B segments developing below rather than above A segments. This bearish sequence continued until the first quarter of 2003, when a reversal in the wave structure (the A segment surpassed a previous B segment) indicated the start of a new bull market. In short, during bull markets, B segments generally end above A segments. During bear markets, B segments generally end below A segments.

Enter the Rate of Change Indicator

The rate of change indicator certainly proved its worth between 1995 and 2004.

For starters, in its patterns of movement, the indicator clearly reflected the A–B wave sequences that took place during this period. Rate of change measurements frequently provide advance notice of market reversals, reversing direction before rather than after or even simultaneously with the trend of stock prices. As a general rule, rate of change indicators peak approximately 50-65% into a market upswing. The area at which these indicators turn down is an area in which it is probably too late for buying, possibly a touch early for selling; this is an area during which it might be appropriate to prepare for the next downside move.

As you can see, every cyclical peak that took place between 1995-2000 was presaged by a negative divergence, with prices rising to new highs, the rate of change indicator turning down to reflect diminishing upside price momentum. This characteristic, in reverse, was also present during the market declines of 2000–2002, with cyclical market lows characterized by advance positive divergences and the rate of change indicator reversing to the upside as prices moved toward their final lows.

The 50-day rate of change indicator provided a fine notice of market rallies that developed in late 2001 and 2002.

Investors received clear notice of market recoveries that took place based upon the 18-month cycle, notice provided by the cyclical lengths and by the action of the 50-day rate of change indicator.

For Future Readers of This Work

This section is being written during March 2004. At this time, price levels of the Standard and Poor's 500 Index have remained relatively firm, but there have been clear negative divergences developing in the 50-day rate of change indicator because the 18-month cycle is now 13 months along. The general pattern appears to suggest some further strength—not a dynamic continuation of the bull market—with mounting market danger developing until the late summer of the year, 2004, when a new 18-month cycle is scheduled to begin. Future generations of investors will be able to determine how prescient (I hope) the 50-day rate of change indicator turned out to be....

(Year-end update! As a matter of fact, the stock market remained firm through April, when seasonal weakness did set in that brought prices sharply down into mid-August, at which time a market recovery began that carried into the end of the year.)

Day Trading with Short-Term Cycles

Our discussion has focused upon longer-term market cycles, which are of more significance to the typical investor than very short-term market cycles. However, online trading, including active day trading and other forms of short-term trading carried out by computer, has been gaining a following. Investors now can employ computer screens and trading programs to track the hour-by-hour and day-by-day perambulations of the stock market. In this regard, I have found the 24- to 30-hour or four- to five-day stock market cycle to be very helpful.

This cycle can be tracked with price, rate of change indicators, RSI and, as you shall see later, MACD patterns, which are of special use for this purpose. I refer to this cycle in terms of days rather than hours, but turns in the cycle tend to occur within rather than at the ends of days, so hourly tracking can be very useful.

The four- to five-day cycle can often be broken down into the following sequence, with market turns developing rapidly because day traders tend to demonstrate rapid reflexes and often act in concert.

Day 1: It becomes apparent to traders at some point in the day that the previous cycle has been complete, that declines are ending, and that the next market swing will be upward. Clues develop from positive divergences in MACD, RSI, and rate of change measurements, often accompanied by the development of falling wedge formations and positive T-formations (to be discussed shortly). Prices usually have their longest and strongest moves on that first day. It is important to be ready for the turn and to act either just before or right at the start of market-reversal junctures.

Day 2: In the past, strong market closes tended to be followed by strong market openings. This has become less true in recent years: Each day now seems to have a separate character. Still, cyclical odds favor an extension of the gains of Day 1 into at least a portion of Day 2; unless market trends are very strong, though, the advance is likely to end at some time during the second day, and certainly by the third.

Day 3: During most market periods, this is a day of relatively little price change as the stock market prepares for Day 4, when most of the short-term cyclical damage takes place. Occasionally, the entire cycle spreads out into another day.

The primary tasks lie with recognizing the phases of the four- to five-day cycle and the patterns associated with your confirming indicators (remember synergy?) that will support your new long (or short) positions. To profit, day traders have to be successful in a very high percentage of their trades because the profit potential of each short term, or day trade, is relatively limited as a percentage of investment expenses compared to longer-term position trading, which also benefits from the secular upside bias of the stock market.

T-Formation: The Ultimate Cyclical Power Tool?

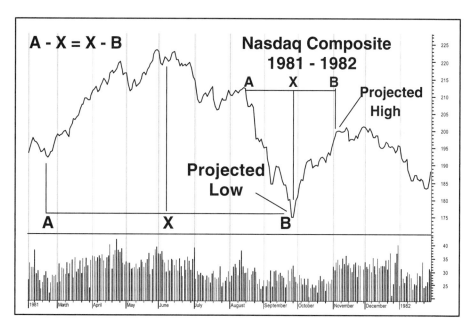

Chart 5.6 The Nasdaq Composite Index and T-Formations (November 1981–May 1982)

Chart 5.6 provides examples of T-formation measurements that might have been made between 1981 and 1982. As you can see, these formations provided some excellent projections of market tops and lows prior to their completion.

The T-formation is one of my favorite technical power tools. This tool is applicable to both long- and short-term trading operations, although it usually requires minimum time for construction and calculation. T-formations appear applicable to a wide variety of investment markets.

The viability of the formation is based upon the concept that time cycles often are relatively neutral, in the sense that wave lengths or segments are likely to be quite equal in time. Given this assumption of relative neutrality and time constancy between cyclical waves, it becomes logical to assume that if you know the time that the stock market has spent in a cycle or segment of a cycle, and recognize when a new cycle or cycle segment has gotten underway, you should be able to project when the new cycle or segment cycle is likely to come to an end. The process is less complicated than the verbiage here and should be clear enough after you examine Chart 5.7.

The Construction of T-Formations

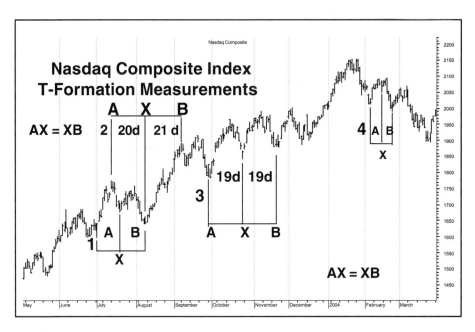

Chart 5.7 Nasdaq and T-Formations 2003–2004

Chart 5.7 illustrates the construction of T-formations. The major concept involved is that the left side of T-formations is equal in terms of time to the right side of the formation. Time projections of market reversals can be made as soon as you know the length of the left side of the T-formation.

Area 1

We start in Area 1, on the left of Chart 5.7. The Nasdaq Composite rises from a low at the beginning of July, reaches a high point in mid-July, dips down, starts upward once again, and thereafter dips once more as a double-top formation is completed. The goal is to project the time frame in which the next market low area will take place.

Step 1: Measure the distance from the low at the start of the formation (A) to the center of the formation (X), to secure the measurement A–X. X is a vertical line drawn from the starting low to the peak price area of the cycle. Important variable: If the peak area of the cycle develops as a double top rather than as a single peak, employ the valley between the two spikes as the center of the cycle, and take the X measurement from that area. The top area in July took the form of a double-top M formation, so the X measurement is taken from the center line of the M.

Step 2: After you have secured the horizontal distance between the start of the formation and X, the vertical line drawn from the cycle high, draw a horizontal line of that horizontal distance to create the left T-bar; the length of this is referred to as A - X. The vertical line, X, can be drawn as soon as the cycle starts to turn down.

Step 3: Project the distance A – X to secure the length of the right side of the T-bar, X - B. This provides a projection of where the next down cycle will come to an end, at the right side of the line X – B.

The basic T-formation construction is really quite straightforward. The first concept to keep in mind is that, in a double-top formation, you draw the line X from the center of the M formation rather than from one of the two peaks in the double-top formation. The second concept is that the distance A – X is equal to the distance X – B. The third concept is that the T-formation indicates when B waves are likely to come to an end. These formations do not project the price level at the conclusion of the cycle; they project just the time duration of the cycle. Actually, your projections often will include accurate price as well as time projections. Price projections can often be estimated from the slopes of price movement.

Area 2

Prices declined from a peak in mid-July to a low area early in August, when a single-spike bottom formation developed and prices moved straight upward. How long is the advance likely to continue?

When the move upward gets underway, we can recognize the low of the formation and draw the vertical line X from that area. We then carry the time distance from the most recent peak, A, across the chart horizontally to create the left bar, A – X, of the T-formation. In this case, the time period involved is 20 days. This time distance is projected forward to secure the projected length of the right bar of the T; this distance, X – B, will theoretically be 20 days. In actuality, in this particular case, it worked out to 21 days; the projection missed the actual peak by just 1 day.

The basic rule, as you can see, is that Distance A – X equals distance X – B.

To restate, in Area 2, the center of the formation took the form of one clear spike that reflected the low of the formation and the center of the cycle. In Area 1, the center of the formation was reflected in the midpoint of the double-top formation. It is sometimes something of a judgment call regarding whether the formation is showing a one-point spike reversal or a double-top or bottom reversal.

Area 3

The construction and interpretation of T-formations should be a rather familiar process by now. Area 3 illustrates a projection of low formation created around the midpoint of a double-top, M, formation. An accurate projection of the low at B was achieved by using the T-formation.

Area 4

This area illustrates the application of T-formations to minor stock market cycles. In this case, two tops of a double-top formation are separated by a decline lasting just one day.

Several other potential T-formations might be constructed on this chart. Readers might want to copy this page and practice on the chart.

Further Examples of T-Formations, Including the Application of Synergy

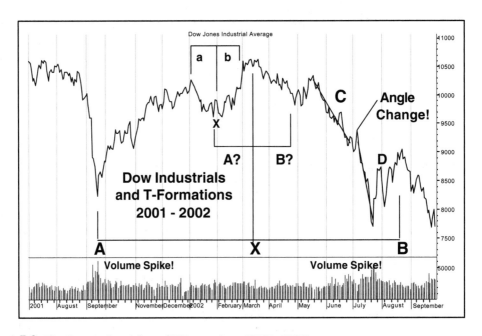

Chart 5.8 The Dow Industrials and T-Formations (2001–2002)

Chart 5.8 shows T-formations associated with the Dow Industrials from 2001 to 2002, along with other indicators that might well have been employed with the T-formations.

Three T-formations are shown on Chart 5.8: a relatively short-term top-to-top formation that developed between December 2001 and the end of February 2002, a low-to-low formation that ran between late January and late April, and a broader bottom formation that ran between September 2001 and August 2002.

The first two formations provided projections of market turns that missed the mark by only a few days—not a bad miss, considering the fact that projections were being made for market turns scheduled between 1 and 1.5 months from the point of projection.

The longer-term September–August projection missed by approximately one month. The market reached its actual bottom during the latter half of July 2002, coming in a little less than a month before the low in August that had been projected by this larger T-formation. The time discrepancy between the projected low and the time of the actual low was not all that great, considering the time span of the projection, but if the miss was not great in terms of time, it was more significant in terms of the price movement that took place between the actual low and the low that had been projected to take place three weeks thereafter.

Were there indications that might have led traders to recognize the validity of the developing July 2002 lows instead of awaiting a final bottom in August? As a matter of fact, yes. It might have been very helpful to use certain tools. For example, a volume spike developed at the lows of July, suggesting the presence of a selling climax. Compare the trading volume at the lows of July with the lows of the previous September, in 2001. Volume patterns were similar: An amount of volume developed in July 2002 that had turned the stock market upward ten months before. In addition, an angle change formation (C–D in the chart) had developed that produced a price projection that was met simultaneously with the volume spike; this was a further indication that even though the lows were taking place earlier than anticipated, they were probably valid.

This sequence of events is one further example of the benefit of employing multiple indicators for market forecasting rather than reliance upon one indicator alone.

T-Formations and Mirror Patterns of Stock Movement

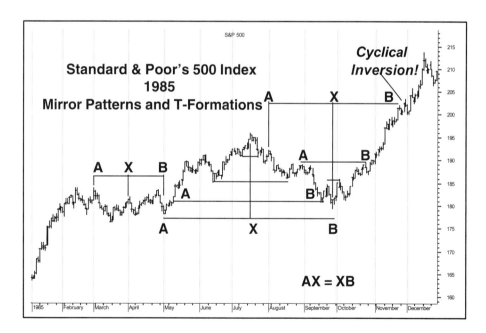

Chart 5.9 T-Formations and Mirror Patterns: The Standard & Poor's 500 Index (1985)

Chart 5.9 illustrates mirroring patterns of market movement, in which the right side of an advance or decline mirrors a pattern that appears on the left side of the chart. T-formations tend to be particularly useful when such formations develop.

From time to time (actually, for short-term swings, more often than that), the stock market traces out advancing and declining waves of rise and fall, with one side almost exactly mirroring the other. The development of such patterns is not all that surprising. For one thing, support and resistance levels that develop on the initial side of the mirror are likely to become reflected as pauses in price movement on the other side in a neutral cycle, as support and resistance levels created on the one side affect price movement on the other. For another, time cycles in neutral market climates, when mirroring most frequently takes place, naturally lead to market reversals that will occur following neutral cyclical patterns.

In any event, Chart 5.9 illustrates a market period in 1985 that was marked by repetitive mirror imaging. As you can see in the chart, T-formations measured from centers of formations frequently indicate not only the final resolution of significant market cycles, but many steps along the way as well.

The first T-formation in the chart, March to May 1985, was a top-to-top formation, with its center being the center of a W formation. The actual market top that might have been scheduled on the basis of the formation was early by just a few days.

If you examine Chart 5.9 carefully, you might notice a number of minor-term T-formation projections along the way that I have not marked. For example, between mid-March and the end of April, at the left of the chart, two consecutive short-term T-projections appear that were very accurate in defining short-term market cycles.

The most significant T-formation during this period took place between May and late September. When the stock market began its decline in mid-July, you could have secured the measurement $A - X$, which, projected forward from the center line at X, produced a virtually perfect time projection (B) of the final downside target of that cycle.

Along the way to that final low, moreover, were a number of interim market reversal areas that could have been very well defined by using T-formation measurements.

A significant inversion in November illustrates the development of a cyclical failure: Cyclical projections do not always work out—not even those made by T-formations.

A cyclical T-formation suggested the likelihood of a stock market downturn in November 1985. For a day or two, the turn downward appeared to be taking place, but it was immediately reversed and prices soared once it became apparent that there would be no follow-through to the cyclically projected market decline. This reversal of cyclical direction is referred to as a cyclical inversion and is generally followed by a strong move in the direction of the inversion. In this case, instead of following through with a cyclically indicated reversal to the downside, the market moved upward—and did so very strongly. Inversions can be troublesome, but if you recognize them and respond quickly, they often provide special opportunities for rapid trading profit.

T-Formations and Longer-Term Time Periods

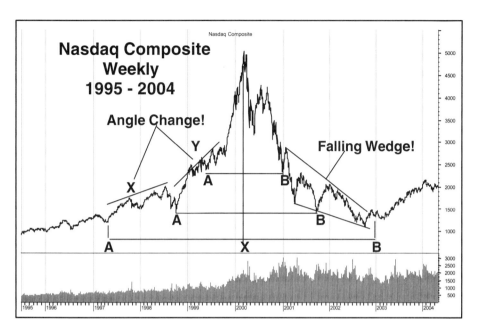

Chart 5.10 A Long-Term Market Cycle and T-Formations: The Nasdaq Composite (1995–2004)

The Nasdaq Composite traced out a massive T-formation between 1997 and 2003, a formation that also had many of the characteristics of mirroring.

Technical patterns in the stock market, as we know, tend to persist regardless of the time frame that is being studied. The forces that create patterns relating to time, momentum, supply and demand, and emotional buying and selling tend to exist for short-term market movements as well as long-term market trends. We will return to this concept when we review timing tools such as MACD and moving average trading channels.

Chart 5.10 illustrates the application of T-formations to very long-term market trends and to charts that reflect such trends. Vertical line X remains, of course, the center line of the T-formation, drawn from the peak of the Nasdaq Composite during March 2000. When the Nasdaq started down in price, you could have employed the distances between areas of pause and the center line (X) that took place during the major term advance in that index to project likely stopping areas that develop as the decline moves along.

The price movement of the Nasdaq Composite from 1995 to 2004 shows many of the mirroring characteristics that we saw in Chart 5.9, the Standard & Poor's 500 Index in 1985. In the one case, the mirroring period lasted for six years. In the other case, the mirroring period lasted for five months. Yet, these two disparate charts have much in common.

Supplemental Indicators

Angle changes also can take place over long periods of time. An excellent long-term angle change projection (A, B) took place in the Nasdaq Composite between early 1998 and late 1999. The bear market ended for the Nasdaq Composite in a falling wedge: Notice the reduction in trading volume during the 2001–2002 period that confirmed the wedge formation. Also worth noting is how the upper boundary line of the wedge, once penetrated, acted as support against prices returning within the wedge formation. The completion of the wedge formation and the upside breakout that followed took place right where the T-formation called for a significant market low point, a positive synergistic development.

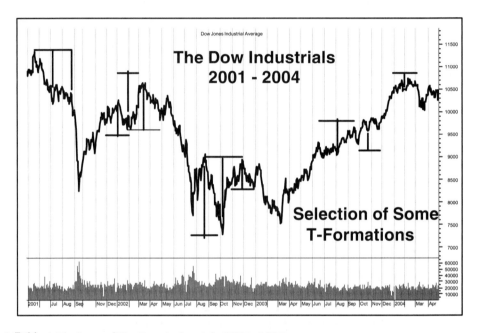

Chart 5.11 A Plethora of T's: Dow Industrials (2001–2004)

This chart shows ten of the many T-formation patterns that developed during the 2001–2004 period. Many more formations have not been marked.

One Final Set of T-Formations

Here is a final chart relating to the subject of T-formations.

T-formations actually occur with considerable frequency, on daily and weekly charts, and also on hourly and even more short-term charts employed by day traders for intraday scalping activities.

Marked on the chart are ten of the more significant T-formations that presented themselves in the price patterns of the Dow Industrials from 2001 to 2004. Numerous other instances and examples of T-formations during this period have not been marked. The point, of course, is that T-formations develop very frequently, that they are very useful in their own right and as confirmations of other signals, and that they are applicable to a broad range of investment markets and to a broad range of time frames.

In other words, if you look, you will find....

In Summary

Seasonal and Calendar Influences on the Stock Market

The best days to purchase stocks have generally been the first two to three days and the last one or two days of each month. Stocks also have tended to perform well on the days before most holidays.

The period of November to April has been the best period in which to own stocks. The period of May to October has historically produced stock market returns that have been below rates of return of short-term income investments.

The best years to own stocks have been the years before and the years of presidential elections. The two years following presidential elections have shown lesser rates of return.

Time Cycles

Time cycles can help you anticipate when stock market turning points are scheduled to take place. In addition, the behavior of the stock market as cycles work their way along provides clues to the strength of the stock market.

Most market cycles can be subdivided into two segments, A and B. A market cycle itself is either an A or a B segment of a longer market cycle. It is a sign of market strength if the B segments take place at higher levels than the A segments, and it is a sign of market weakness if the reverse is the case.

Cyclical influences are most significant when high percentages of cycles of various lengths are pointing in the same direction, or when a number of significant cycles are reaching bottoms ("nesting") simultaneously.

The four-year market cycle has been a very dominant cycle for decades.

T-Formations

T-formations are cyclically related formations that can be drawn to project the time frame of likely turning points in the stock market and other investment markets.

Basically, T-formations are based on the concept that the time distance between the starting low of a cyclical wave and its peak is likely to be subsequently repeated between that peak and the final low of that cycle. Similarly, the time span between the peak of a cycle and its final low is likely to be at least approximately repeated in the time span between that low and the peak of the subsequent cycle.

Time cycles can provide fine indications of the likely periods in which significant stock market buy and sell junctures are likely to take place. However, time cycles and T-formations should be employed in conjunction with other stock market indicators and not employed as standalone buy or sell signals.

6

Bottom Fishing, Top Spotting, Staying the Course: Power Tools That Combine Momentum Oscillators with Market Breadth Measurements for Improved Market Timing

A Quick Review of Where We Have Been

In Chapter 1, "The No-Frills Investment Strategy," we reviewed concepts regarding and methods of creating investment portfolios that are likely to produce above-average rates of return at below-average risk. Chapter 2, "Two Quick-and-Dirty Stock Market Mood Indicators," featured two easily maintained market mood indicators that have had excellent long-term histories of separating higher-risk from lower-risk investment climates. Chapter 3, "Moving Averages and Rates of Change: Tracking Trend and Momentum," discussed how to use moving averages to define the direction and strength of market trend, along with rate of change indicators to further clarify the momentum of such trends.

Chapter 4, "More Than Just Pretty Pictures: Power Tool Chart Patterns," featured special chart patterns—angle changes that project, sometimes months in advance, likely price and time objectives for market cycles; wedge formations, which provide indications of coming direction changes in stock prices; and other charting techniques that can help you determine likely stopping places of price movement in the stock market. Finally, Chapter 5, "Political, Seasonal, and Time Cycles: Riding the Tides of Market Wave Movements," investigated the significance of political and calendar time cycles, and how these can be used to predict when and where significant stock market junctures might occur.

Our goal, again, is to develop a battery of diverse and useful timing tools so that investment decisions can be based upon a consensus of stock market indicators rather than on just one or two investment techniques. At times, of course, various different indicators will produce contradictory signals. In fact, this is probably more the norm than the exception. At other times, messages received from chart formations, cyclical analysis, measures of momentum, the interest rate structure, and relative strength of the various market sectors are consistent, producing buy or sell signals that, in synergy, are more significant than any single timing indicator.

This chapter explores concepts that relate to patterns of market movement as they apply to measures of internal market breadth and strength (as opposed to more obvious price measures), ways to test for indicator confirmation, and other areas that thus far have been only partially touched on or that are new.

We start with one of the most significant areas of technical analysis: areas related to market breadth.

The "Internal" as Opposed to the "External" Stock Market

Financial news reports tend to focus on gains and losses recorded by a selective group of popularly followed stock market indices. These include the Dow Industrials, with 30 issues, unequally weighted (higher-priced issues have a larger influence, on the index); the Standard & Poor's 500 Index, with 500 stocks (weighted by capitalization so that the index is unequally weighted, with larger companies more influential than smaller companies); the Nasdaq Composite Index, with approximately 3,500 separate issues (heavily weighted by capitalization so that at times perhaps only a dozen or so issues carry a very disproportionate effect); and the New York Stock Exchange Index, which includes all issues on the New York Stock Exchange (also weighted so that larger companies most heavily influence the average).

Another index, the Value Line Arithmetic Average, includes approximately 2,000 issues traded on various exchanges and is not weighted by capitalization: All companies in that average are afforded equal weight.

Arguments can be made for or against the weighting inherent in most of these market indices, but the simple fact is that there are often serious discrepancies between the movements of one or more of the weighted indices and the movement of the typical listed stock. It is very possible for a weighted market index to advance in price as a result of strength in a handful of larger companies while the majority of stocks is actually declining. Popular market indices represent the "external stock market," a view of the market most frequently observed. Indicators that measure the numbers or proportions of issues that actually participate in market advances and declines are measures of the internal strength or breadth of the stock market, a generally truer reflection of the strength of the typical stock and mutual fund.

As a general rule, the stock market is on firmer ground when market advances are broad and include large percentages of listed issues than when they are selective, with advances in market indices created by strength in a relatively narrow group of highly capitalized issues. This is actually quite logical. If larger percentages of stocks are participating in market advances, the odds of selecting and holding profitable positions increase. If only a relatively small number of stocks are carrying market indices upward, the odds of successful stock selection narrow. Investors are more likely to find themselves taking losses in a stock market that seems to be rising if judgments are based on weighted indices, but that, in fact, is rising only selectively. External readings are strong. Internal breadth measurements indicate otherwise.

Measures of Market Breadth

One useful measure of market breadth lies with the advance-decline line, a cumulative total of advancing minus declining issues on each of the various exchanges. You can start these cumulative lines from any level, using daily readings for daily-based advance-decline line readings, or weekly readings for weekly advance-decline line measurements.

For example, if you started an advance-decline line of the New York Stock Exchange at an arbitrary level of 10,000, and on the first day there were 1,500 issues advancing in price on that exchange and 1,000 declining (unchanged issues are not included), there would be 500 more issues advancing than declining that day. The advance-decline (A-D) line would advance by +500 units, from 10,000 to 10,500. If there are 200 more declines than advances on the subsequent day, the A-D line would decline from 10,500 to 10,300.

We will return to applications of the advance-decline lines of various market indices, but first we take a more detailed look at the relationships of the number of issues rising to new highs and falling to new lows. This is another area that reflects the internal breadth and strength of the stock market.

New Highs and New Lows

Another indicator reflects market breadth, a measure of the true internal strength (or weakness) of the stock market. This is the new high/new low indicator, including various derivatives of the related data. The number of issues making new highs, measured on either a daily or a weekly basis, is the number that reach new 52-week highs in price at any time on a given day or, for weekly-based readings, at some point during the week. This would be a price level higher than any level recorded in the previous 52 weeks. The number of issues falling to new lows refers to the number of issues whose prices have declined to their lowest level in the most recent 52 weeks.

It goes without saying that it is more positive when large numbers of issues advance to new highs than when the numbers of stocks in rising trends diminish. It is more negative when large numbers of issues keep falling to new lows than when increasing numbers of stocks find support, perhaps beginning new uptrends.

New High/New Low Confirmations of Price Trends in the Stock Market

We have already reviewed concepts relating to confirmation and non-confirmation of price advance and decline by indicators that measure market momentum, such as rate of change measurements. Among these are concepts related to positive divergence and negative divergence, based on the relationships between momentum and price movement.

Concepts related to confirmation, non-confirmation, positive divergence, and negative divergence can be related as well to the relationship between external price strength and measures of the internal strength of the stock market. For example, if the number of stocks that reach new highs expands with gains in market indices, we can think of this as a positive confirmation of market advance: Internal strength measurements are confirming external strength measurements. However, if the number of issues making new highs does not keep pace with gains in the market averages, internal strength can be thought of as underperforming the external stock market. Negative breadth divergences are taking place, a warning of probable trouble down the road.

Conversely, if price levels remain down trended but fewer issues fall to new lows along with weighted price indices, this divergence could be evidence of internal strength building in the stock market as external indicators continue to weaken. Such conditions reflect positive breadth divergences, situations in which more stocks are finding support even within the context of declining price averages, usually a bullish portent.

Positive and Negative Confirmations, 1995–2004

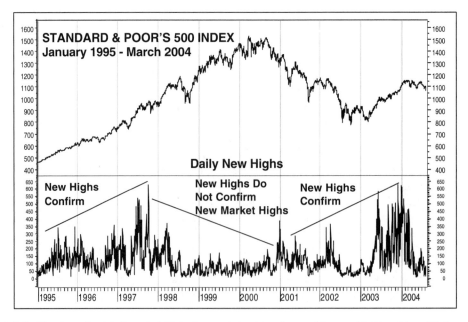

Chart 6.1 The Standard & Poor's 500 Index and the Numbers of Issues Making New Highs, 1995–2004

Chart 6.1 shows the relationship of the price movement of the Standard & Poor's 500 Index and the number of issues making new highs. New highs confirmed the advance of the stock market between 1995 and 1997 but fell off badly as 1998 moved along, belying gains in market indices that took place into early 2000.

These points are illustrated in Chart 6.1, which shows the number of issues reaching new highs in price between 1995 and early 2004, along with the price movement of the Standard & Poor's 500 Index. The stock market had started in 1994 with relatively little strength but seemed to firm later in the year, with better strength developing early in 1995. Between 1995 and 1997, the number of issues on the New York Stock Exchange that rose to and achieved new highs in price expanded, with gains in the Standard & Poor's 500 Index. The number of new highs that contracted during periods of price consolidation was normal even during a bull market, in as much as the amount of issues reaching new highs renewed its rise as prices renewed their advance. Breadth, as measured by new highs and new lows, confirmed the advance in the Standard & Poor's 500 Index, with new highs peaking into the final quarter of 1997.

Negative breadth divergences began to appear at the beginning of 1998, with new highs rapidly diminishing as the year developed. By midyear, the numbers of issues making new highs had contracted dramatically, although the levels of weighted market indices continued upward. The negative implications of these price/breadth divergences were realized in the very serious intermediate decline that took place in the stock market during the late summer and early autumn of 1998.

Prices ultimately rebounded, and the stock market produced a choppy advance into early 2000 that lacked broad participation; new highs failed to expand at any point. (As a matter of fact, the number of issues making new lows showed a definite increase even as prices moved upward to their final peak.) The 1999–2000 period is an example of a market advance that appeared powerful but was actually rather narrow in scope.

New highs expanded at certain points of the 2000–2002 bear market, particularly after the start of 2001, but the bear market did end, as we might expect, with relatively few highs being achieved; price movement and breadth, reflected in the number of issues making new highs, were consistent. New highs again confirmed rising prices as the bull market accelerated during the spring of 2003, a very strong joint price-breadth acceleration that carried market indices as well as breadth readings upward pretty much throughout the final three quarters of the year.

Chart 6.2 Standard & Poor's 500 Index and Daily New Lows, 2002–2004

Diminishing numbers of issues falling to new lows at each market low indicated an improvement in internal market strength, suggesting the onset of the bull market that followed.

New Lows at a Developing Stock Market Bottom

In a similar but converse vein, reductions in the number of stocks falling to new lows as market declines proceed represent positive breadth divergences; internal market strength improves as price levels decline.

Chart 6.2 illustrates a fairly typical pattern that develops from time to time at significant intermediate and major market lows. A major stock market bottom formation developed between the summer of 2002 and March 2003, a bottom formation characterized by three downside spikes in the Standard & Poor's 500 Index—three spikes in the number of issues falling to new lows.

However, whereas the Standard & Poor's 500 Index traced out one lower low and another nearly lower low during this period, the number of issues declining to new 52-week lows in price contracted sharply between the lows of July 2002 and March 2003. Although the Standard & Poor's 500 Index stood at almost the exact level in March 2003 as it had been at the lows of July 2002, the number of issues falling to new lows had shown a decline from more than 900 to slightly more than 300. Clearly, the stock market was building internal strength, a precursor to the bull market that soon ensued.

A summary of the basics follows:

• Market advances accompanied by increases in the number of issues reaching new highs in price are advances that are well confirmed by market breadth. Such advances are likely to continue.

• Market advances that are not accompanied by increases in the number of issues reaching new highs in price are not as well grounded in internal strength as fully breadth-confirmed market advances. There are no precise and regular intervals in time between peaks in the number of new highs and ultimate peaks in the stock market averages. For example, in less than a year, the summer decline in 1998 followed peaks in new highs that had developed during 1997, whereas the full-scale bear market of 2000–2002 did not begin until more than two years after the 1997 peak in new highs. As a general rule, significant peaks in new highs tend to be seen perhaps one year or so before final bull market peaks.

- Market declines accompanied by increasing numbers of issues falling to new lows are likely to continue. If new lows reach bear market peaks during a downside selling climax, with prices spiking down at the time, there are likely to be further tests of those price and breadth lows before final bear market bottoms are achieved. Chart 6.2 illustrates this observation.

- Failures of new lows to expand with price declines represent positive breadth divergences and tend to be forerunners of stock market reversals to the upside.

Again, breadth divergences, positive and negative, do not signal immediate market reversals. This family of indicators usually requires time for its effects to be felt. However, triple-bottom formations, representing declining numbers of new lows during bottoming formations, often resolve in market advances fairly rapidly after the third spike reversal has taken place. The market bottom that developed during 2002 is an excellent example.

Creating a New High/New Low Indicator to Keep You in the Stock Market When the Odds Heavily Favor the Stock Market Investor

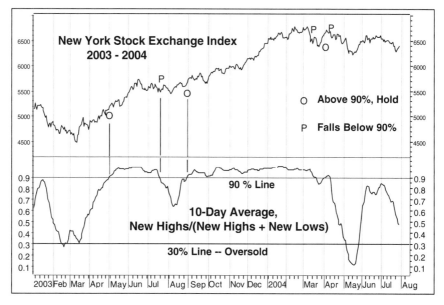

Chart 6.3 The New Highs/(New Highs + New Lows) Indicator, 2003–2004

Chart 6.3 shows the new highs/(new highs + new lows) indicator, which remained consistently strong from the onset of the 2003 market advance through the end of the year. New high/new low ratios fully confirmed the strength of the stock market during this period, in the process suggesting largely invested positions.

As a general rule, the stock market prefers positive breadth unanimity during market advances: high percentages of issues reaching new highs in price, and low percentages of issues falling to new lows. (At market tops there are often high levels of issues making both new highs and new lows, reflective of very split market breadth. When the number of new highs and the number of new lows on the New York Stock Exchange *both* amount to more than 5% of the total number of issues traded on that exchange, serious market declines frequently, though not always, follow shortly.)

A useful indicator that measures the level of positive breadth unanimity can be maintained by dividing the number of issues reaching new highs in price by the total of issues reaching new highs and falling to new lows. For example, if 100 issues reach new highs on a given day and 25 issues fall to new lows, you can divide 100 (new highs) by 125 (sum of 100 new highs plus 25 new lows) for a daily ratio of .80, or 80%. Single-day readings can be beneficially employed, but the maintenance of a ten-day simple moving average of daily readings smoothes the data.

Method of Interpretation

Buy signals can be said to take place when the ten-day moving average of the NH/(NH + NL) ratio first falls to below 25% (very oversold) and then rises by approximately ten units—say, from 13% to 23%—indicating that downside breadth momentum has begun to reverse.

Buy signals also can be said to take place when the ten-day moving average of the ratio falls to below 30% (oversold) and then rises upward through the 30% level.

Finally, buy signals can be said to take place if the ratio rises from below 70% to above 70%, if a buy signal is not currently in place.

Sell signals can be said to take place when the ratio falls from above 70% to below 70%, or, if you prefer, from above 80% to below 80%—a somewhat safer exit, though sometimes premature.

These parameters are not recommended as stand alone timing models, but more as a part of your general arsenal of indicators that can be used as a group for market analysis and forecasting.

The following, however, represents a fine set of buy or hold parameters related to new high/new low data that stands well on its own. The combinations of parameters that appear to have provided the best risk/reward ratios over the years are highlighted in the tables that follow.

These are the basic operating rules:

- Buy or commit to hold existing stock positions when the ten-day average of new highs on the NYSE divided by the total of new highs and new lows reaches 90%.

- Hold for as long as the ten-day average of the ratio NH/(NH + NL) remains above your choice of 90%, 85%, 80%, 75%, or 70%.

• Sell when the ten-day average of NH/(NH + NL) falls below the sell parameters you are employing.

Table 6.1 shows the historical results of the ratio, employed as a timing model in this manner.

Table 6.1 *Trading the Standard & Poor's 500 Index on NH/(NH + NL) Ratio Signals: Ten-Day Moving Average of Ratios Employed, 1970–2004. Buy When the Ten-Day Average of the Ratio Climbs Above 90%. Sell When the Ratio Falls to Below the Levels Shown.*

	90%	>85%	>80%	>75%	>70%
Round-trip trades	75	55	44	40	36
Percent profitable	54.7%	49.1%	52.3%	57.5%	58.3%
Average % gain, winners	3.4%	6.6%	8.1%	7.9%	8.9%
Average % loss, losers	–1.9%	–2.1%	–2.4%	–2.9%	–4.0%
Gain per annum	2.0%	3.2%	3.6%	3.6%	3.3%
Annualized rate of return	11.8%	16.1%	15.3%	13.9%	11.9%
% of time invested	17.6%	21.0%	25.0%	27.0%	29.2%
Maximum drawdown	19.7%	12.3%	15.7%	14.8%	24.8%
Buy and hold	7.6%	7.6%	7.6%	7.6%	7.6%

Results are hypothetically derived from back-testing. No guarantees are implied for the future.

Percentage of trades profitable: As a general rule, the majority of trades have been profitable. Parameter sets that generally involve longer-term holding periods tend to produce higher percentages of profitable trades but lower rates of return while invested.

Average % gain, winners: The average gain for trades that were profitable.

Average % loss, losers: The average loss for trades that were unprofitable.

Gain per annum: Average annual total gain achieved by trading via these signals. For example, if you had purchased the Standard & Poor's 500 Index whenever the ten-day ratio of new highs divided by the sum of new highs and new lows rose to above 90%, and held until the ratio fell to below 85%, your average total gain per year would have come to 3.6%. This is not a total timing model for investing in the stock market. It is a model that is invested only a relatively small percentage of time but that produces excellent results for the periods in which it is invested.

Annualized rate of return: The rate of return while invested—in this case, 15.3%—or approximately twice the annualized rate of return of buy-and-hold strategies, with dividend payouts and interest while in cash excluded.

Maximum closed drawdown: The maximum ongoing loss created by using this model before capital reaches a new peak in value. The lowest drawdown was achieved by using the 85% level as the sell trigger.

Using the 90% (buy) and 85% (sell) parameters produced 42.1% of annual gains achieved by buy-and-hold strategies, while being invested only 21% of the time. Using the 90% (buy) and 80% (sell) parameters produced 47.6% of annual gains achieved by buy-and-hold strategies while being invested only 25% of the time.

Periods marked by very favorable new high/new low relationships tended, on average, to show approximately twice the average rate of gain of the stock market.

The Application of the New High/(New Highs + New Lows) Indicator to the Nasdaq Composite

For whatever reason—and, no doubt, there might be many—timing models tend to produce better results when applied to the Nasdaq Composite than when applied to New York Stock Exchange–related market indices, such as the Dow Industrials and the Standard & Poor's 500 Index.

For one thing, over the years, the Nasdaq Composite has tended to be more trending (greater autocorrelation, the tendency of prices to move in the same direction as the price movement of the previous day) than indices such as the Standard & Poor's 500, whose movements generally appear more random day by day. Therefore, everything else being equal, there is likely to be better follow-through to buy and sell signals related to the Nasdaq Composite than to signals related to, for example, the Standard & Poor's 500 Index.

For another thing, the Nasdaq Composite is generally more volatile (average higher absolute price movement over various periods) than the majority of New York Stock Exchange–based indices. As a rule, timing models tend to be more efficient when applied to volatile, trending vehicles than when applied to quieter, more randomly moving investment vehicles. Keep these observations in mind as we evaluate the application of the new highs/(new highs + new lows) timing model to the Nasdaq Composite. Also keep in mind that although we are tracking the Nasdaq Composite, we are doing so via New York Stock Exchange–based new high/new low data.

Table 6.2 *Trading the Nasdaq Composite Index on New York Stock Exchange NH/(NH + NL) Ratio Signals: Ten-Day Moving Average of Ratios Employed, 1971–2004. Buy When the Ten-Day Average of the Ratio Climbs Above 90%. Sell When the Ratio Falls to Below the Levels Shown.*

	90%	>85%	>80%	>75%	>70%
Round-trip trades	73	70	51	44	35
Percent profitable	63%	57.1%	64.7%	65.9%	74.3%
Average % gain, winners	5.7%	7.6%	9.4%	10.4%	11.3%
Average % loss, losers	2.1%	2.6%	3.9%	5.0%	8.1%
Gain per annum	5.1%	5.9%	6.4%	6.0%	5.7%
Annualized rate of return	32.3%	28.9%	26.4%	22.7%	20.6%
% of time invested	17.8%	22.5%	26.4%	28.4%	29.5%
Maximum drawdown	18.4%	22.9%	32.3%	36.6%	42.5%
Buy and hold	9.4%	9.4%	9.4%	9.4%	9.4%

Results are based upon hypothetical back-testing. No guarantees are implied for the future.

Annualized rates of return are considerably higher when this model is applied to the Nasdaq Composite than when it is applied to the Standard & Poor's 500 Index. For example, long positions taken at 90% and sold at 85% levels of the NH/(NH + NL) ratio produced an annual gain of 5.9%, or 62.8% of the total buy-and-hold gain (9.4%) of the Nasdaq Composite Index, while being invested only 22.5% of the time. This represented a rate of return while invested of 28.9%.

Using the 90% (buy) and 80% (sell) parameters produced annual gains of 6.4% while being invested 26.4% of the time, which represented an annualized rate of return while invested of 26.4%. 68.1% of the total buy and hold gain (9.4%) of the Nasdaq Composite was achieved while being invested only 26.4% of the time.

Trading in the Nasdaq involves greater risk than trading in the Standard & Poor's 500 Index. Maximum drawdown for the 90% to 85% parameters was 22.9% when trading in the Nasdaq Composite, and only 12.3% when these parameters were applied to the Standard & Poor's 500 Index.

Pre–Bear Market Comparisons

It is interesting to compare the results of the 1971–2000 period to the 1971–2004 period, which includes the bear market of 2000–2002. Using the 90% (buy) and 80% (sell) parameters between 1971 and 2000 would have produced rates of return while invested of 34% and maximum drawdowns of only 8.6%, with 72% of trades profitable. Major drawdowns of the new high/new low timing models took place during 2001 and 2002.

The bear market certainly affected the historical performance of this and many other stock market timing indicators, which underlines the importance of employing long and diversified periods of stock market history in research and in any evaluation of stock market–timing techniques.

The New York Stock Exchange Advance-Decline Line

Relating to Advance-Decline Breadth Data

In a general sense—I know of no really firm parameters—certain observations can be made regarding the relationships between the movements of the daily and weekly advance-decline lines (internal market) and the various weighted market indices (external market). The Value Line Arithmetic Index, an unweighted index that includes all the issues in the Standard & Poor's 500 Index plus 1,200 additional stocks, appears more correlated with the New York Stock Exchange–based advance-decline line than other market indices, such as the Dow Industrials and the Standard & Poor's 500 Index.

The advance-decline line and the Value Line Arithmetic Index are both fine indicators of how the typical mutual fund is likely to perform, but the performance of neither is as closely correlated to the mutual fund universe as the performance of the broadly based New York Stock Exchange Index.

General Observations

The stock market is likely to be on firmer footing when strength in the daily- and weekly-based advance-decline lines confirm strength in the various indices that reflect different sectors of the stock market. In other words, new highs in indices such as the Standard & Poor's 500 Index should be confirmed by new highs in the weekly- and daily-based advance-decline lines, and vice versa.

Stock market technicians frequently take negative note of periods in which market breadth readings fail to confirm new highs in market indices such as the Standard & Poor's 500 Index and the Dow Industrials, but bear markets have started during periods that market breadth readings have remained stronger than readings of popularly followed market indices. For example, the 1981–1982 bear market started with more apparent weakness in major market indices than in the advance-decline lines, but eventually the decline spread across the entire stock market universe.

The stock market prefers strength in all of its areas. Although it is probably better if measures of breadth lead market indices than vice versa, universal strength is the best.

It is more bullish for stocks when peaks in major market indices are confirmed by new peaks in the advance-decline lines, or when new lows in market indices are unconfirmed by new lows in the advance-decline lines.

Again, unanimous strength is best. But if you have to choose, breadth strength is generally the most decisive, especially if your portfolio includes a fairly high percentage of broadly based, smaller company–oriented mutual funds that tend to track with market breadth measurements.

Market breadth data is available for Nasdaq-based as well as New York Stock Exchange–based markets. The advance-decline line of the Nasdaq Composite Index often provides clues and cues that are not apparent in the price action of the Nasdaq Composite Index alone.

The price level of the Nasdaq Composite Index is frequently more influenced by a relatively smaller group of companies than the price levels of either the New York Stock Exchange Index or the Standard & Poor's 500 Index. Certain mutual funds and ETFs reflect larger-capitalization companies such as Microsoft and Intel that trade on the Nasdaq, but mutual funds that invest in emerging companies usually more closely reflect the Nasdaq advance-decline line in their price movement.

The level of strength in the advance-decline lines of the various market sectors can be tracked with rate of change measurements that reflect changing patterns in the strength of market breadth. This will become clearer as we examine Chart 6.4 and other charts related to advance-decline data.

Chart 6.4: The Advance-Decline Line Between 2002 and 2004

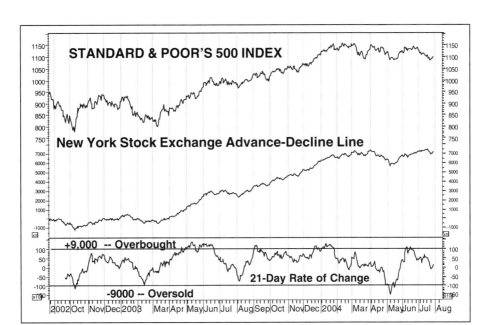

Chart 6.4 The New York Stock Exchange Daily-Based Advance-Decline Line and the Standard & Poor's 500 Index, 2002–2004

The daily advance-decline line reflects the cumulative differential between the number of issues that advance in price during each day and the number that decline. Below the advance-decline line is a scale that reflects a 21-day rate of change of that indicator, the level of the advance-decline line minus its level 22 days previous. The chart illustrates the gradual development of strength in market breadth as the bear market came to an end, continuing strength in breadth during 2003 and its sharp weakening at the onset of 2004.

Chart 6.4 illustrates many of the points that have just been discussed.

The chart encompasses the period during which the 2000–2002 bear market came to an essential end, during which the bull market year of 2003 took place and, finally, the start of 2004 and its attendant market correction.

The daily-based advance-decline line and the Standard & Poor's 500 Index were very highly correlated during this period, with the price levels of the Standard & Poor's 500 Index and the daily perambulations of the advance-decline line in almost perfect harmony between mid-2002 and early 2004. The Standard & Poor's 500 Index peaked earlier in 2004 than the advance-decline line, but by early April, both measures of market strength were in decline.

Basically, this was a period in which breadth and price movement were in harmony, with breadth confirming price strength and vice versa. This pattern is fairly typical of market action at the onset of bull markets.

The 21-Day Rate of Change of the Advance-Decline Line

Overbought Levels

The lowest scale on Chart 6.4 reflects the 21-day rate of change of the advance-decline line, again today's level of that indicator minus the level of the indicator 22 days before. In recent years, intermediate swings have tended to range from high levels of about +9,000 to +10,000 and –9000 to –10,000, which are highly overbought and oversold levels, respectively.

Highly overbought readings generally take place only during fairly strong periods within bull markets. They rarely first occur right at the peaks of market advances; they usually develop when intermediate market advances are roughly 50–65% complete. Actually, the +10,000 level was reached in late April 2003, well in advance of the next market peak, and again during December of that year, some months before the final advance-decline line peak at the start of the second quarter of 2004. Again, the ability of overbought-oversold oscillators to reach highly extended positive levels is generally a sign of strength, suggesting market conditions that could be a little late for buying but that are probably too early for aggressive selling.

Oversold Levels

At the present time (2004), oversold readings in the 21-day rate of change of the advance-decline line can be considered to be taking place when readings decline to the area of –9,000 to –10,000 or below. (In past years, fewer issues were traded on the New York Stock Exchange, so rate of change readings moved within narrower ranges. In addition, the decimalization of prices, the conversion of pricing variations to small increment decimals, has led to fewer issues being unchanged in price.)

The stock market tends to behave differently at market low points than at market tops, particularly during bull markets. Market bottoms tend to be sharper and more climactic than market peak areas, during which prices tend to more slowly roll over. Therefore, whereas overbought readings in timing oscillators such as the 21-day rate of change of the advance-decline line usually provide advance notice of at least a few weeks before market reversals to the downside, upside reversals in such indicators from deeply oversold levels, particularly during bull markets, often suggest immediate bullish action.

Review Chart 6.4 again. As you can see, the stock market embarked on at least intermediate market advances between 2002 and 2004 every time the 21-day rate of change of the advance-decline line approached or fell to below –10,000 and then turned up. Of course, the indicator does not always work quite that well, but, in general, it produces excellent buy signals during market climates characterized by favorable market breadth.

Breadth Patterns at Bull Market Highs

1997–2000: A Period of Breadth Transition

Chart 6.4 illustrates the behavior of the advance-decline line and its 21-day rate of change momentum oscillator during periods in which market breadth was essentially favorable in relation to the movement of the Standard & Poor's 500 Index. Favorable internal-external market relationships suggested improving market conditions and a bull market that ensued.

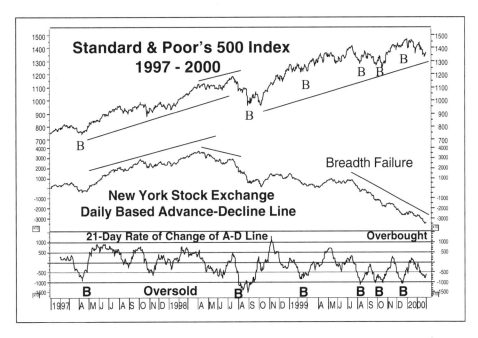

Chart 6.5 Transition in Market Breadth from Bullish to Bearish: The 1997–2000 Period

The New York Stock Exchange advance-decline line kept up with the Standard & Poor's 500 Index during 1997 and into early 1998, when the bull market in market breadth essentially came to an end. Relative weakness in breadth compared to the Standard & Poor's 500 from then into early 2000 presaged the serious bear market that followed.

Chart 6.5 illustrates the reverse, a bull market in both price and breadth that ultimately failed, first in breadth readings and then in price movement. This is a frequent pattern as bull markets come to an end. Let's examine the chart.

The year 1997 started with an intermediate market decline that came to an end as the 21-day rate of change of the advance-decline line declined to the area of –10,000 (not quite falling as low as –10,000), an oversold level that suggested a buying area. The market entry that was indicated proved viable, and prices rose steadily into early 1998. We might take note of the behavior of the 21-day rate of change indicator during the advance of 1997 to early 1998. The indicator spent most of the time above the 0 level, with rates of change generally positive, suggesting favorable breadth throughout the period.

In short, positive breadth confirmed positive price action. All was in harmony.

A Change in Tone

Market breadth and price movement remained in gear until the spring of 1998, when the Standard & Poor's 500 Index drifted down somewhat (not seriously) while the New York Stock Exchange advance-decline line declined sharply. I have marked this period, the beginning of the end of the bull market in breadth, on Chart 6.5. A subsequent recovery to new highs in the Standard & Poor's 500 Index was not confirmed by any real advance in market breadth readings. This breadth failure foretold sharp declines in both breadth measurements and the Standard & Poor's 500 Index that took place during the summer of 1998.

A Major Negative Breadth Divergence Followed

The Standard & Poor's 500 Index developed a bottom during the summer of 1998, indicated, as you can see on Chart 6.5, by the 21-day rate of change of the advance-decline line. The initial market surge from the lows included the internal as well as external markets. The 21-day rate of change of the advance-decline line reached fully overbought levels, usually a sign of strength.

However, market breadth readings quickly failed to keep pace with gains in market indices such as the Standard & Poor's 500 and the Nasdaq Composite indices, both of which surged during 1999 in the final speculative orgy of the bull market. Chart 6.5 reveals the major negative divergence that developed. The advance-decline line fell sharply during 1999 into 2000, even as the Standard & Poor's 500 Index rose to new heights. (You might observe how rate of change readings tracked, for the most part, below the 0 line, and how oversold readings in the −10,000 region were unable to produce more than short-term breadth recoveries.) These negative divergences signaled the major bear market that visibly started in year 2000.

The word *visibly* in the last sentence is employed with purpose. The weakening of market breadth that we see in Chart 6.5 suggests that, for most stocks, the bear market did not begin in 2000. It probably began for most issues as early as 1998, and certainly during 1999.

To sum up, when advances in price levels of various weighted market indices take place without commensurate gains in indicators that reflect market breadth, this warns of a more total breakdown in stock prices shortly down the road.

Conversely, declines in the price levels of weighted market indices that are not accompanied by ongoing weakness in market breadth indicators such as the advance-decline line and new high/new low ratios are not likely to continue. Expect better times ahead.

Look for climactic negative readings in measures of market momentum that could provide highly accurate entry areas very close to serious market lows. I have been suggesting levels in the area of −10,000 for the 21-day rate of change of the advance-decline line. This would represent a number that is approximately three times the number of issues traded on the New York Stock Exchange, about 3,500 in early 2004. A climactic bottom level would be approximately 900–1,000 weekly new lows for the weekly-based new high/new low indicator, which reflects the number of issues that reach new 52-week highs or lows based on full weekly trading ranges. When the number of weekly new lows rises to the 900–1,000 area, stocks are probably ready to stage at least some sort of recovery, possibly a significant advance.

Using a Somewhat More Sensitive Rate of Change Measure of the Advance-Decline Line

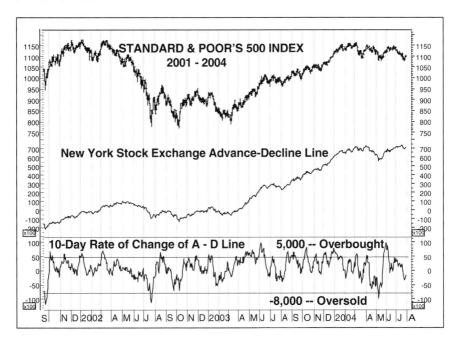

Chart 6.6 The Standard & Poor's 500 Index Advance-Decline Line and Ten-Day Rate of Change, 2002–2004

This chart shows the Standard & Poor's 500 Index and a ten-day rate of change of the NYSE advance-decline line, also shown. The 10-day rate of change seems to change direction more readily than the 21-day rate of change indicator and reflects shorter-term time frames.

The Ten-Day Rate of Change Indicator

Although the 21-day rate of change of the advance-decline line probably represents more significant changes in market momentum, the 10-day rate of change has its uses as well.

As you can see in Chart 6.6, the parameters of the 10-day rate of change tend to be somewhat narrower than the parameters of the 21-day rate of change indicator. Although readings of +/–10,000 sometimes are reached on a ten-day basis, for the most part, rates of change for that time frame tend to vary between +5,000 (overbought) and –5,000 to –8000 and even lower (oversold).

Divergences between the direction of the ten-day rate of change indicator and the direction of the advance-decline line itself frequently indicate imminent changes in shorter- to intermediate-term trends in market breadth. For example, new highs in the advance-decline line that are unconfirmed by new highs in the ten-day rate of change are often suspect, likely to give way to at least a short- and possibly an intermediate-term market decline.

There is a fairly significant six- to seven-week trading cycle in the United States stock market. This cycle can often be tracked with the ten-day advance-decline rate of change indicator, which tends to rise for roughly 15 to 20 trading sessions from cyclical market lows during its six- to seven-week cycle. Caution on at least a short-term basis is often indicated when the ten-day rate of change of the NYSE advance-decline line has risen for three weeks or more.

The Weekly Impulse Continuation Signal

You have already seen the benefits of identifying periods of unusually favorable market breadth and of creating objective parameters to define market climates during which the odds strongly favor the holding of equity positions. New high/new low data was used for this purpose.

Another model employs a similar underlying concept: Achieving certain levels of positive breadth momentum suggests further market advance to come. This model employs advance–decline data rather than new high/new low data. Obviously, there are relationships between these two measures of market breadth, as well as certain overlaps in the periods during which each will produce its positive signals for the stock market. Nonetheless, there are also differences in the frequency of and time frames in which the advance-decline-based impulse signal and in which the NH/(NH + NL) indicator become operative. Each makes its contribution; the concept of synergy suggests that both be employed.

But First, an Introduction to the Exponential Moving Average

The Weekly Impulse Continuation Signal, which is based on weekly advance-decline data, employs in its calculation the exponential moving average (which we have not yet discussed), which is also used when calculating moving average convergence-divergence (MACD) lines (which we will be covering in depth in subsequent chapters).

In their effect, exponential averages are fairly similar to front-weighted moving averages, which are adjusted by weighting so that more recent data assumes more significance in the average than past data. Front-weighting is employed by technicians who believe that recent events carry more significance than older events and want to reflect this in the type of statistical tracking they employ. However, exponential averages are simpler to calculate and maintain than regular moving averages, and are certainly simpler to calculate and maintain than front-weighted moving averages.

The Smoothing Constant of Exponential Averages

Exponential moving averages employ smoothing constants, which are derived by adding 1 to the number of units you want to average and then dividing the result into 2.

For example, to secure the smoothing constant for a ten-day exponential average, you would add 10 (number of units) to +1; the result would be 11. You then would divide 2 by 11 (2 ÷ 11) to secure your smoothing constant, expressed as a decimal—in this case, .1818. For practical purposes, this can be rounded to two decimals, as .18.

If you wanted to maintain a 19-day exponential average, you would divide 19 + 1, or 20, into 2. 2 divided by 20; the result would be .10, the smoothing constant for a 19-day exponential average. If you wanted a 39-day exponential average, you would divide 2 by 39 + 1, or 40, for a smoothing constant of .05 (2 ÷ 40).

This is the formula for calculating exponential moving averages:

New exponential average = Smoothing constant × (Today's data – Yesterday's exponential average) + Yesterday's exponential average

eg Example 1

You are maintaining a ten-day exponential average of daily advance-decline differentials. The previous exponential average stood at +200. The smoothing constant for a ten-day exponential average is .18, as calculated above. Today there are 800 issues up and 500 issues down, for a plurality of +300. The new exponential average would be calculated as follows:

New exponential = .18 (300 – 200) +200

or .18 (100) + 200

or 18 + 200

The new exponential average would, therefore, be +218.

The 300 in the equation is today's advance-decline differential (800 – 500). The 200 is yesterday's exponential average. The smoothing constant is .18.

eg Example 2

Yesterday's .18 exponential average of advance-decline differentials stood at +150. Today there were 600 issues rising and 850 issues declining. What is the new exponential average?

New exponential average = .18 ([600 – 850] – 150) + 150.

New exponential average = .18 (–250 – 150) + 150

= .18 (–400) +150

= –72 + 150

= +78

As you can see, negative numbers often enter into the calculations of exponential averages. You might need to familiarize yourself with the handling of such negative numbers.

eg Example 3

The advance-decline line, a cumulative total of advances-declines on the NYSE, closed yesterday at +60,000 units. Today there were 900 issues rising in price and 600 issued declining. Yesterday's .05 exponential average stood at +59,500. What will the new .05 (39-day) exponential average of the advance-decline line be?

Step 1: Calculate the new level of the advance-decline line. The net plurality today was +300 (900 advances minus 600 declining issues). Add the +300 to the previous level of the advance-decline line (60,000), securing the new reading of the advance-decline line, +60,300.

Step 2: Calculate the new .05 exponential average of the advance-decline line.

New exponential average = .05 (60,300 − 59,500) + 59,500

= .05 (+800) + 59,500

= 40 +59,500 = 59,540 (new exponential average)

Stabilizing the Exponential Average

It is necessary to secure an initial exponential average with which to start your calculations.

There are two relatively easy ways to secure an estimated exponential average close enough for most purposes. As one alternative, you can simply use the first day's price or breadth data as a starting exponential average. In other words, if your first day's close of the Standard & Poor's 500 Index is 1,100, simply use that 1,100 level as your first exponential average. If you are maintaining a ten-day or .18 exponential average, you should plan on at least ten days of posting to consider your exponential average stabilized and at least relatively accurate. Twenty days of stabilization, or double the exponential average time span, would be better. A .05 (39-unit) exponential average should be stabilized for at least 39 days, preferably 78, or double the length of the average.

As a second, preferable alternative, secure a simple moving average of the number of days for which you will be calculating your exponential average, and use that average as the starting exponential average. For example, start your .18 exponential average, which represents ten days, with a simple average of the most recent ten days of data.

Many computer programs that relate to technical analysis have the capability to readily calculate exponential averages, provided that you have sufficient starting data in the database.

Some Special Qualities of Exponential Moving Averages

Exponential averages have certain special qualities that are not characteristic of simple moving averages or even front-weighted moving averages:

- When the latest price or other entry rises from below to above the exponential average, or falls from above to below it, the exponential average has to either turn up or turn down, respectively. This is not the case with other forms of moving average.

- Even the shortest-term exponential average includes within it residues from all past data that have been a part of the history of the particular calculation of that average. Therefore, the exact level of your exponential average depends on the particular date that you started your calculations, although differences are likely to be relatively small if your data stream is fairly long.

- Exponential averages are relatively simple to maintain by hand day by day. The only data that you need to keep is the close of the previous day's exponential average and today's closing data.

Let's move along now to the Weekly Impulse Continuation Signal, our first, but definitely not last, application of exponential moving averages.

The Weekly Impulse Signal

We have been exploring a number of tools based on momentum readings and other market breadth-related data, some of which can be fairly subjective in their interpretation while others are quite objective in their signals. Subjective indicators, usually based on chart pattern recognition and interpretation, have their place in the lexicon of useful market tools, but they also present problems because of their subjectivity and are best employed in conjunction with confirming indicators and cyclical measurements.

In contrast to subjective indicators, objective, mathematically based indicators such as the Weekly Impulse Signal are statistically based, signals objective. Whereas not all signals generated by such indicators are profitable, all are clearly recognizable and subject to back-testing.

The Weekly Impulse Signal, based upon weekly advance-decline data, is fully objective, has a high degree of accuracy, requires just a few minutes each week for calculation, and, between 1970 and 2003, produced 56.4% of the total gain recorded by the Standard & Poor's 500 Index while being invested less than 22% of the time.

The Required Items of Data Each Week

To maintain the Weekly Impulse Signal indicator, you need the following weekly-based items of data, all available in *Barron's* each week, among other sources.

- **The number of issues traded:** This is to accommodate the indicator to changes in the numbers of issues traded on the New York Stock Exchange that have been generally rising over the years. The weekly ratios in the Weekly Impulse Signal are plotted as a percentage of the number of issues traded rather than as a simple numerical differential between the numbers of advancing and declining issues on the senior exchange. Between 3,500 and 3,600 different issues were traded weekly on the New York Stock Exchange in mid-2004.

- **The number of issues that advance and the number that decline each week:** These are not summations of daily advance-decline differentials. These are the differentials based on weekly closing prices of securities compared to their closing prices the previous week. Weekly advance-decline data is frequently more reflective of actual market breadth than daily readings, which often tend to show a downside bias.

No further data is required, although most trackers likely will want to post a table of price levels along with Impulse Signal levels.

Here is the calculation sequence:

1. Secure the number of issues traded each week on the New York Stock Exchange.

2. Secure the number of issues advancing and the number declining on the New York Stock Exchange.

3. Subtract the number declining from the number advancing to secure the net advance-decline reading for the week. For example, if 1,800 issues are advancing and 1,500 issues are declining, the weekly advance-decline differential would be +300.

4. Divide the weekly advance-decline differential into the number of issues traded to secure the net breadth percentage for the week. For example, if the week saw 300 more advancing than declining issues in a given week and 3,500 issues were traded (including unchanged issues), the weekly breadth ratio would be +.0857, or +8.57% (300 net advances ÷ 3,500 issues traded). The number of unchanged issues is included in the total issues column but not in the advance minus decline differential.

5. Maintain a six-week exponential average (.286 smoothing constant) of the weekly net breadth percentages.

Here's an example:

The .286 or six-day exponential average of weekly net breadth percentages closed last week at 25.7%. This week, 3,526 issues were traded on the New York Stock Exchange, of which 1,906 advanced and 1,533 declined. What is the new .286 exponential average of the weekly net breadth percentages?

The weekly advance-decline differential (1906 − 1533) is +373.

Divide +373 by the number of issues traded (3,526) to secure the weekly net breadth percentage. This comes to +10.58% (373 ÷ 3,526).

The new weekly .286 exponential average = .286 (10.58 −25.7) + 25.7

$$= .286 \, (-15.12) + 25.7$$

$$= -4.32 + 25.7$$

$$= + 21.38 \text{ (can be rounded to 21.4)}$$

Now consider this real-time example:

Here is a sequence of weeks between April and May 2003. See if you can define the calculations that produced the various columns of statistics.

Date	NYSE Index	# of Issues	Advancing	Declining	Net	.286 Exponential
4/17	5006.32	3,521	2,701	744	55.58%	24.89%
4/25	5017.62	3,536	2,211	1,227	27.83%	25.73%*
5/02	5201.10	3,533	2,789	668	60.03%	35.53%
5/09	5242.84	3,537	2,443	1,002	40.74%	37.02%

*The weekly reading of 25.73 in the .286 exponential average was sufficient to generate a Weekly Impulse Buy Signal.

Note that the number of issues does *not* equal advances + declines because it also includes unchanged issues.

Buy and Sell Signals

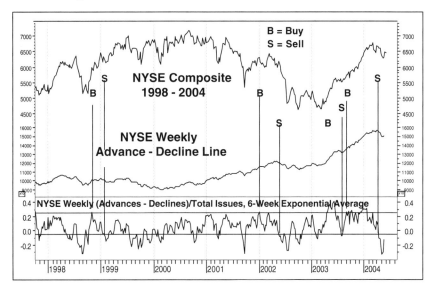

Chart 6.7 The New York Stock Exchange Index: The New York Stock Exchange Weekly Advance-Decline Line and the Weekly Impulse Signal, 1998–2004

This chart shows the weekly impulse signals that developed in the New York Stock Exchange between 1998 and 2004. Signals generated during 2003 proved to be particularly profitable.

Only two signals are associated with the Weekly Impulse Signal: one buy signal and one sell signal.

Buy when the .286 exponential average of weekly net breadth percentages rises to 25% or higher. In the real-time table above, a buy signal took place on April 25, 2003.

Sell when the .286 exponential average of weekly net breadth percentages falls to below –5%. (This is not a sell short signal. It is a sell signal that is operative only if a current buy signal has been in effect, in which case the Weekly Impulse Indicator exits the stock market to a neutral cash position.)

The buy signal that was produced on April 25, 2003 (NYSE Index 5017.62), was cancelled on August 1, 2003, when the .286 exponential average of weekly net breadth percentages declined to –7.26%. The NYSE Index closed the following Monday at 5505.73, so the entry showed a gain of +9.73%. (Calculations of gains and losses for this weekly-based indicator are based on closing prices the first trading day of the week following the week for which data is calculated.

General Concept of the Weekly Breadth Impulse Signal

As you might surmise, the weekly breadth impulse signal is based upon the principle that strong initial impulses in market advances—the rapid development of overbought, or extended to the upside momentum readings—are actually more likely to be the precursor to further advances than to downside market reversals.

In this particular case, we are employing readings of high weekly breadth momentum that are attained only infrequently. The attainment suggests high probabilities of additional advance to come. Rather than discourse in the abstract on this concept further, let us specifically examine the historical performance of the Weekly Impulse Signal.

Table 6.3 *Weekly Impulse Signals 1970–2003*

Signal Date	NYSE Index	Signal Cancelled	NYSE Index	Gain or Loss
09/08/70	45.27	102670	45.40	+ .29%
12/07/70	48.94	051071	56.38	+15.20%
01/10/72	57.17	032772	59.73	+4.48%
10/01/73	58.42	110573	56.71	–2.93%
01/13/75	38.44	040775	42.69	+11.06%
01/12/76	50.99	041276	53.33	+4.59%
12/13/76	56.35	022877	54.23	–3.76%
08/07/78	58.20	092578	57.38	–1.41%
08/20/79	62.02	100179	61.84	–0.29%
05/19/80	61.39	102780	73.82	+20.25%
08/30/82	67.50	071183	97.44	+44.36%
01/21/85	101.12	081285	108.67	+7.47%
11/18/85	114.55	062386	140.71	+22.84%
02/09/87	158.83	041387	162.14	+2.08%
03/07/88	150.53	041888	146.77	–2.50%
02/04/91	190.28	062491	203.50	+6.95%
01/06/92	229.85	033092	222.99	–2.98%

Continued

Table 6.3 *Weekly Impulse Signals 1970–2003* *(Continued)*

Signal Date	NYSE Index	Signal Cancelled	NYSE Index	Gain or Loss
02/08/93	247.07	110893	254.72	+3.10%
06/09/97	450.17	110397	492.63	+9.43%
11/09/98	559.14	012599	586.06	+4.81%
01/07/02	593.15	052002	580.22	−2.18%
04/28/03	485.65	080403	521.56	+7.39%
09/08/03	546.67	120803	568.17	+3.93%

Summary of Results: The Weekly Impulse Signal 1970–2003

Number of trades	23
Number profitable	16 (69.9%)
Points gained	243.77
Points lost	28.38
Gain/loss ratio	8.59 points gained for every point lost
Average percentage gain per trade	+6.62%
Gain per annum	+4.1%
Rate of return while invested	20.3%
Percentage of time invested	21.9%
Maximum closed drawdown	5.4%
Buy-and-hold NYSE index, 1970–2003	7.34% per annum

The Weekly Impulse Signal achieved 56.4% of the stock market's advance while being invested less than 22% of the time, with maximum losses far less than that of the stock market.

Final Comments

Obviously, the Weekly Impulse Signal is not a stand alone timing model, except for very conservative investors who prefer to be invested in the stock market only when the odds are very heavily in their favor (actually, for many investors, this is not the worst of ideas).

The model does miss out on many market advances, although its losses when signals do occur are relatively very low. Is it really worth the trouble to maintain this indicator week after week when it trades less than once each year? Each reader must decide this one for himself or herself, but my staff and I do, in fact, actually post and track the Weekly Impulse Signal each and every week. You might want to review the periods of breadth impulse signals, which were listed trade by trade for this purpose. Approximately one-third of the buy signals took place relatively close to the onset of either new bull markets or very significant intermediate advances, providing significant clues to the strength developing in the stock market. Although other signals proved less significant, some were profitable nonetheless, with losses well contained where they did occur. All in all, the Weekly Impulse Signal has been a profitable tool in and of itself while also providing good indications of greater than average market strength as confirmations of other timing tools you can employ.

The Daily-Based Breadth Impulse Signal

As strong as the Weekly Impulse Signal has been, another breadth impulse signal has provided considerably higher rates of return while invested than the Weekly Impulse Signal, with as high a success rate in terms of the percentage of trades that are profitable as any timing model I have ever seen.

Does a timing model that has produced a 41.6% annualized rate of return while invested over a 34-year period, that has produced profit on 84% of its trades (based on the New York Stock Exchange Index), and that has secured 39 percent of the total buy-and-hold gain of the New York Stock Exchange Index while being invested only 7.4 percent of the time hold any interest? This is the past history of the Daily Based Breadth Impulse Signal, a signal that does not occur all that frequently but that has been extremely powerful when it has taken place, with an average frequency of somewhat less than one signal per year. (I will show you later in this book how to convert the basic version of the Daily Based Breadth Impulse Signal, which is fairly short term in its time frame, to a more intermediate-term version for extended holding periods and expanded returns.)

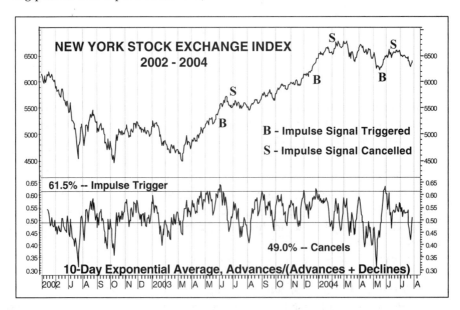

Chart 6.8 The Daily-Based Breadth Impulse Signal

The Daily-Based Breadth Impulse Signal generates buy signals when it rises to or above 61.5%; such signals are cancelled when the indicator declines to or below 49%. Signals occur infrequently but have been very reliable historically.

The Construction and Maintenance of the Daily-Based Breadth Impulse Signal

The Daily-Based Breadth Impulse Signal is based upon a concept similar to the Weekly-Based Impulse Signal, the concept that stock market movements that are initiated with strong initial momentum are likely to continue further than the average stock market swing. The signal utilizes an exponential average of daily market breadth as a measure of breadth pulses. The capability of pulses to achieve defined, unusually high levels signifies well above average market breadth, more often than not the start rather than the end of market advances.

Signals generated by this indicator do not represent a total market timing model. They do isolate limited periods, which occur relatively infrequently, when the odds strongly favor at least short-term profitability in the stock market. Conclusions of entry signals do not, in and of themselves, indicate a stock market decline—only that the immediately positive influences of outstanding market breadth have been ameliorated.

These are the rules of construction and operation:

1. Each day, secure the number of issues that are advancing on the New York Stock Exchange and the number of issues that are declining.

2. Divide the number of issues that advance each day by the sum of the number of issues that advance and the number that decline to secure the ratio, advancing issues divided by the sum of advancing + declining issues.

3. Maintain a ten-day exponential average of the daily ratios secured in Step 2. The ten-day exponential average involves a smoothing constant of .1818, or 2 ÷ 11 (the number of days in the average + 1).

4. The capability of the ten-day exponential average of daily ratios to rise to .615 or higher represents a stock market buy signal.

5. This buy signal remains in effect until the ten-day exponential average of the daily ratios declines to .490 or below, when the model returns to its neutral rating. Sell signals are not generated by the Daily-Based Breadth Impulse Signal.

Now take a look at this sample worksheet:

Number of Day	Number of Advances	Total Declines	(A + D)	Daily Ratio, A (A + D)	10-Day Exponential Average
1	1,500	1,400	2,900	.517*	.517**
2	1,800	1,100	2,900	.621	.536***
3	2,500	425	2,925	.855	.594
4	2,200	650	2,850	.772	.626****

* 1,500 advances ÷ (1,500 advances +1,400 declines) = .517

** .517, the initial entry, is taken as the first exponential average.

*** .1818 (.621 – .517) + .517 = .1818 (.1040) + .517

= .0189 + .517

= .536

**** A breadth impulse buy signal has been generated. The ten-day ratio of advances ÷ (advances + declines) has risen to above .615.

The Performance Record of the Daily Breadth Impulse Signal

The following performance table, derived from hypothetical back-testing, dating back to December 1970, encompasses more than 33 years of stock market history. As you can see, performance has remained consistently reliable over the decades, with only one loss (1974) significant.

Daily Breadth Impulse Signals, 1970–2004

Buy Date	NYSE Index	Cancel Date	NYSE Index	Percent Change
12/29/70	530	02/19/71	562	+6.0%
12/03/71	565	01/24/72	600	+6.2
09/21/73	610	10/16/73	629	+3.1
01/03/74	562	01/10/74	523	−6.9
10/10/74	388	10/24/74	392	+1.0
01/03/75	394	02/25/75	445	+12.9
01/02/76	507	02/27/76	564	+11.2
12/09/76	594	01/12/77	591	−0.5
11/10/77	549	12/06/77	542	−1.3
04/17/78	557	05/23/78	580	+4.1
08/02/78	611	08/29/78	617	+1.0
01/05/79	585	01/31/79	592	+1.2
08/20/82	683	09/29/82	737	+7.9
10/08/82	793	11/16/82	827	+4.3

Continued

Daily Breadth Impulse Signals, 1970–2004   (Continued)

Buy Date	NYSE Index	Cancel Date	NYSE Index	Percent Change
08/02/84	936	09/04/84	1013	+8.2
01/14/85	1040	02/21/85	1105	+6.3
05/20/85	1160	06/12/85	1151	−0.8
11/11/85	1203	12/24/85	1260	+4.7
02/21/86	1368	04/03/86	1421	+3.9
01/12/87	1578	02/23/87	1703	+7.9
01/30/91	1966	03/15/91	2157	+9.7
12/27/91	2365	01/21/92	2391	+1.1
05/05/97	4561	07/21/97	5017	+10.0
05/30/03	5435	06/23/03	5549	+2.1
12/30/03	6444	01/29/04	6556	+1.7
05/25/04	6429	06/14/04	6465	+0.6

Note that price levels of the NYSE Index have been adjusted backward to reflect changes in the composition and pricing of the index that took place at the end of 2003.

Twenty-six signals were generated between December 1970 and May 2004. Twenty-two (84.6%) of these signals proved profitable; four (15.4%) trades were unprofitable.

The average gain per profitable signal was 5.24% per trade. The average loss per unprofitable signal was 2.37%. A total of 115.28% was gained during profitable trades, compared to a total loss of 9.5% during unprofitable trades. All in all, the gain:loss ratio came to 12.13:1.

Signals were in effect only 7.6% of the time between December 1970 and June 14, 2004, when rates of return while invested averaged 40.3% on an annualized basis. This model alone produced gains of 3.07% per year on average, or approximately 39.4% of the average annual gain (+7.8%) of the NYSE Index, while being invested only 7.6% of the time. Potential interest income while in cash is not included in these calculations.

The Application of the Daily-Based Breadth Impulse Signal to Trading the Nasdaq Composite Index

We will not take the space for a trade-by-trade listing of trades of the Nasdaq Composite Index, but the following highlights of signals applied to the Nasdaq Composite between December 3, 1971, and June 14, 2004, should provide a pretty good idea of its performance. Signal dates for this period are the same as for the New York Stock Exchange Index, as listed previously, because signals are based upon the New York Stock Exchange advance-decline ratios. (The Nasdaq Composite Index started on February 5, 1971, so the first trade shown in the NYSE tabulation is not included.)

Twenty-five entry signals were generated between December 3, 1971, and May 2004, the last of which carried into June 2004. Twenty-three (92%) signals proved profitable; only two (8%) proved unprofitable.

The average gain per profitable entry came to +7.76%; the average gain per calendar year was +5.04%. The average loss per unprofitable entry came to 2.28%. The total gain from profitable entries totaled 178.52%. The total loss from unprofitable entries amounted to only 4.57%. The total gain: total loss ratio came to 39.8:1. Over the more than 30-year period, nearly 40% was made for every 1% lost.

Traders who employed this timing model alone for their trading would have been invested only 7.19% of the time and would have achieved 55.4% of the average annual return of 9.1% achieved by a buy-and-hold strategy of being invested 100% in the Nasdaq Composite Index. The annualized rate of return while invested on the model during this period came to 70.15%. Potential interest income while in cash has not been included in these calculations, nor have dividend payouts from stock positions.

Caveat

Although I and my staff have employed variants of this timing device for many years, the calculations going back to the early 1970s should be taken as hypothetical; in any event, similar results might or might not pertain in the future. That said, the Daily-Based Breadth Impulse Signal recorded no losses between late June 1985 and September 2004, the time of this writing.

This long and complex chapter has introduced a new form of moving average, numerous concepts related to market breadth, and several formalized and objective timing models designed to provide insight into the internal as well as external stock market.

We move now to a briefer and less complex discussion of ancillary market indicators that provide insight into the identification of and relationships between buying and selling pressures, as well as other market indicators that reflect public sentiment.

Volume Extremes, Volatility, and VIX: Recognizing Climactic Levels and Buying Opportunities at Market Low Points

We have seen how time and relevant cycles can be used to project when stock market reversals appear likely to take place, and we have reviewed a number of market breadth–based indicators that can indicate when to stay in rising markets, when to exit, and when market declines appear likely to come to an imminent end. In this section, we review a trio of related market timing indicators that reflect buying and selling pressures as well as the emotional tone of the stock market. These indicators also frequently provide timely and significant, frequently major-term, entry and exit signals.

The concepts involved are not complex; the indicators employed for our purposes are rather straightforward. Our discussion starts with a review of certain characteristics of stock market price movement and then moves into the specific construction and interpretation of relevant timing techniques.

Market Tops: Calm Before the Storm; Market Bottoms: Storm Before the Calm

As a general rule, stocks rise approximately 75% of the time and decline just 25% of the time. (Between 1953 and 2003, the Standard & Poor's 500 Index advanced during 38 of the 50 years.) However, stocks generally decline at approximately twice the rate that they advance, so risks in the stock market, particularly for periods of less than a decade, might be greater than we imply by the ratio of the length of the periods of time that prices advance to the periods of time that prices decline.

Significant stock market advances frequently start with strong bursts of energy and thrust. However, upside momentum gradually diminishes as advances continue and ultimately vanishes as bullish trends come to an end. Initial phases of most (not all) bear markets develop in an orderly manner: One by one, industry groups lose strength as price trends of market indices roll over from a rising to a gradually rising, to a gradually falling, to a more accelerated decline as increasing percentages of industry groups simultaneously fall from favor.

As bear markets progress, initial investor perceptions change. Months or years of rising prices tend to create general attitudes of optimism, expectations that stock prices will continue to rise in the foreseeable future. Mutual funds, brokerage houses, and many market analysts trumpet advice to "stay the course," to "have faith in America," or to simply use market declines as "opportunities to buy cheaply" into eternal prosperity.

In due course, pessimism builds—slowly at first and then, as price declines continue, with greater intensity. If investors assume during bull markets that prices will rise forever, eventually, during bear markets, reinforced by increasingly pessimistic media reports, they come to assume that prices will decline forever. (Unfortunately, the greatest percentage of bearish articles and books are published at or near bear market lows, an excellent sentiment indicator in its own right.)

During many bear markets, selling intensifies as final market lows draw near. Price declines become disorderly, and downside volatility increases as complacency gives way to concern and concern surrenders to panic. The process often finally ends in what is called a selling climax, a burst of indiscriminate selling by frightened stock holders to more savvy investors and traders, finally made ready by steeply falling prices to step in and pick up shares at bargain prices.

Our task is to recognize these final stages of bear markets or severe intermediate declines, and to begin to accumulate invested positions before the general public realizes that the worst is over and that a new bull market is underway. This recognition does not take place immediately; delays provide opportunities to observe, process, and act upon the building evidence of emerging transition from major decline to major, or at least intermediate, advance.

TRIN: An All-Purpose Market Mood Indicator

TRIN, also referred to as the Short-Term Trading Index or the Arms Index (after its inventor, Richard W. Arms Jr.), was introduced in *Barron's* by its inventor in 1967. A fuller discussion of the indicator is available in the 1989 book *The Arms Index (TRIN Index): An Introduction to Volume Analysis*, by Richard W. Arms.

TRIN is a popular indicator that many traders use to monitor forces associated with accumulation (buying) and distribution (selling) pressures in the stock market. It can be applied over very short periods of time, even for day-trading purposes, or for longer periods of time, as a measure of buying and selling pressures in the market. In my own experience, I have not found TRIN to be a precise indicator, but have found its patterns to be often useful in reflecting changing market sentiment, particularly periods of extreme pessimism often associated with stock market buying junctures. For the most part, TRIN appears more useful as a bottom-finding tool than a top-defining indicator, which is not unusual for stock market indicators because stock market bottoms tend to be more readily defined than tops.

The Data Required to Compute TRIN

TRIN requires four areas of data:

- The number of issues that have advanced on the New York Stock Exchange that day

- The number of issues that have declined on the New York Stock Exchange that day

- The amount of volume entering into those issues that have advanced (up volume)

- The amount of volume entering into those issues that have declined (down volume)

TRIN also can be calculated for other indices. For example, a Nasdaq TRIN can be calculated using data based on readings of the Nasdaq Composite. TRIN readings also can be calculated midday, based on intraday data compiled for the New York Stock Exchange. Intraday TRIN readings are available on most quotation machines.

Calculating TRIN

This is the formula for TRIN:

$$\frac{\textbf{Number of Issues Advancing}}{\text{Number of Issues Declining}} \div \frac{\textbf{Up Volume}}{\text{Down Volume}}$$

Let's suppose that, at the close today, there were 2,000 issues advancing and 1,000 issues declining on the New York Stock Exchange, and that the up volume (volume entering into advancing shares) was 800 million shares and the down volume (volume entering into declining shares) was 400 million shares. What would the closing level of TRIN be?

$$\frac{\textbf{Number of Issues Advancing (2,000)}}{\text{Number of Issues Declining (1,000)}} \div \frac{\textbf{Up Volume (800 million)}}{\text{Down Volume (400 million)}}$$

$$= \frac{\textbf{2000}}{1000} = 2 \qquad \div \qquad \frac{\textbf{800 million}}{\text{400 million}} = 2 = 1.00$$

As you can see, there were twice as many issues advancing than declining. Advancing issues received their fair share of volume, with twice as much volume entering into rising as declining issues. In this case, TRIN indicated a volume balance between the ratios of rising and declining shares and up and down volume; its reading of 1.00 is a neutral reading as TRIN readings are generally interpreted.

What would the TRIN reading have been if both advancing and declining volume were 400 million shares (instead of 800 million shares for advancing volume), with 2,000 advances and 1,000 declines? Breadth readings are the same as before, but volume ratios have changed.

In this case, you would have divided 2,000/1,000 by 400/400, which would have come to 2.00/1.00, or a TRIN reading of 2.00. Such a reading would imply that rising issues were drawing disproportionately low buying volume and not receiving their fair share of total volume. This sort of reading would generally be considered bearish in terms of volume/accumulation trends, but it might also be considered bullish because it is a very high TRIN reading, suggesting considerable investor pessimism and perhaps even investor panic. (Sometimes things can become confusing.)

Let's suppose now that there 2,000 advances, 1,000 declines, 12 million shares up volume, and 4 million shares down volume. What would the TRIN reading be?

Well, you would divide 2,000/1,000 by 12 million/4 million, or 2/3, for a reading of .67. This reading, well below 1.00, would indicate that advancing shares were receiving a greater than proportionate amount of volume compared to declining shares—evidence of a favorable accumulation pattern for the day.

Interpreting TRIN Levels

For day trading, intraday TRIN readings often provide early notice of trend reversals during the day; TRIN frequently changes direction before changes in the direction of stock prices. Negative and positive divergences that take place between TRIN levels and the price levels of market indices can be significant to day traders.

For example, suppose that the stock market is weak in the early morning, with the Dow down by perhaps 75 points, and 500 more issues declining than advancing. TRIN readings for the morning stand at 1.30, indicating heavy selling pressures (1.00 would be neutral). The stock market recovers a bit and then, during the early afternoon, again declines to a 75-point loss for the Dow, with declines still outnumbering advances by 500 issues. However, in the interim, TRIN readings have improved from 1.30 to 1.00, or even to .90. This could be a significant sign of an impending market recovery. Buying pressures are catching up and have even surpassed selling pressures. There is a good chance that the day will end strongly. TRIN has provided an opportunity to enter before rather than after the stock market changes direction.

The same may well take place in reverse: The stock market opens strongly with very low TRIN readings, such as .65 or even .55. TRIN readings below .70 are very difficult to sustain. Readings below .50 usually indicate intraday buying panics and are generally unsustainable. The ideal is to see strong market breadth, accompanied by strong price gains, accompanied by better than neutral and steadily favorable TRIN readings. In a strong market, this falls in the .70 to .85 area.

For daily- or weekly-based position trading, TRIN is generally interpreted based on daily based price and volume information.

During favorable stock market periods, positive trends appear in price patterns of the various market indices, in breadth readings, and in volume. Accumulation patterns are reflected in relatively and consistently low TRIN readings that average between .80 and .90 on a ten-day moving average basis. In such circumstances, TRIN would be confirming favorable breadth and price trends.

Early warning signs of an impending market reversal might include a weakening of TRIN even as prices advance; negative divergences between TRIN levels that are rising even as stock prices rise would indicate a reduction in buying pressures. (Remember, for TRIN, the lower the reading is, the more intense net buying accumulation is.) However, although many technicians believe that ten-day or somewhat longer TRIN values of .85 or below indicate excessive bullishness and could be dangerous, the evidence in this regard seems scanty. Ongoing low levels of TRIN appear (at least to my jaundiced eye) more indicative of ongoing market strength than do increases in the levels of TRIN.

TRIN as a Bottom Finding Tool

However, TRIN can and often does provide excellent signals of overdone market pessimism and a likelihood of market advance when readings become excessively high, indicating investor panic.

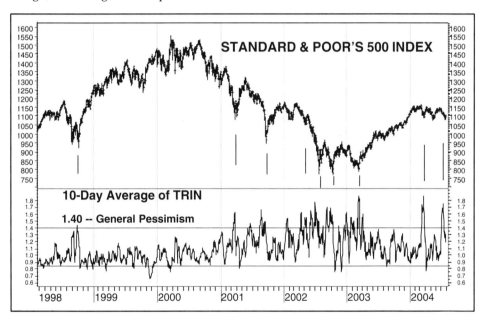

Chart 7.1 The Standard & Poor's 500 Index and the Ten-Day Moving Average of TRIN, 1998–2004

The stock market is usually ready for at least an intermediate and possibly a significant advance when the ten-day average of TRIN rises to levels associated with investor panic. General parameters of TRIN appear to have changed in recent years, with the indicator becoming more volatile. In years past, levels above 1.35 were seen only rarely. In recent years, the indicator has risen to the 1.70 area, with levels of 1.35 or above seen with greater frequency.

Chart 7.1, a ten-day average of TRIN, illustrates this concept. You can readily see spikes in the levels of TRIN at conclusions of selling climaxes during the 2000–2002 bear market and at the market lows of 1998, near where the chart begins.

Like many other market indicators, TRIN readings have tended to become more extreme in recent years, along with rising trading volume and general market volatility. Whereas ten-day average TRIN readings of 1.30 or higher were almost always significant in defining climactic market bottoms in past decades, since 1998 readings of that magnitude have become more common. Ten-day readings in the area of 1.50 or higher in recent years suggested selling climaxes and the imminent likelihood of upside market reversals.

Chart 7.1 illustrates this concept with the ten-day moving average of TRIN. Chart 7.2 illustrates the concept with the 35-day moving average of TRIN, for which levels of 1.30–1.35 represent a climactic extreme.

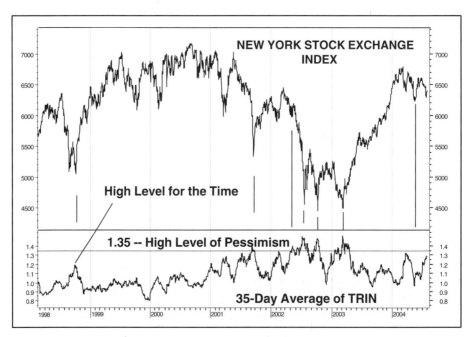

Chart 7.2 The 35-Day Moving Average of TRIN and Its Climactic Areas, 1998–2004

The 35-day moving average of TRIN has moved into bullish territory when it rises to 1.30 or higher on the New York Stock Exchange. It might be safer to await a turndown before entering when the level of TRIN has become this overbought.

The 35-day moving average of TRIN tends to signal at approximately the same times as the 10-day average of TRIN, but there is less "noise" in its patterns, which are more readily identifiable. You can follow the 10-day average or the 35-day average, or your own choice of moving average, initiating market positions as TRIN moves into areas associated with bear market low points. Or, you can wait for TRIN to peak and then diminish a bit before taking positions, which is probably safer.

Used in this manner, TRIN has had an excellent record of confirming significant market low areas. There has been a tendency of peak TRIN readings to take place at progressively higher levels in recent years. This makes it difficult to set a permanent objective target level that would clearly indicate excessive investor pessimism and a high-percentage, low-risk entry level for investors. The 35-day moving average of TRIN provided entries a decade or so ago when it reached levels of 1.05 to 1.10. This is no longer the case. Again, the 10-day moving average of TRIN used to top out in the area of 1.20–1.30. This is also no longer the case. Recent peak readings have been above 1.50—even as high as 1.70 or so.

It might be necessary for users of this indicator to re-evaluate buying parameters from time to time, but the effort is likely to prove worthwhile. Climactic TRIN levels have produced many fine indications for and entries into the stock market when most investors have been frightened and overly pessimistic. If you can think in terms of contrary opinion (betting against the general crowd) when the stock market seems the very worst, you should find TRIN very helpful.

The Volatility Index (VIX) and Significant Stock Market Buying Zones

Periods of very high and rising stock market volatility, the rate at which stocks change in price, usually accompany stock market price declines. Stock market bottoms are often accompanied by a reduction in volatility, which usually runs higher during market declines than market advances. Chart 7.3 and others in this series of charts illustrate historical relationships between volatility levels and price movement over the decades.

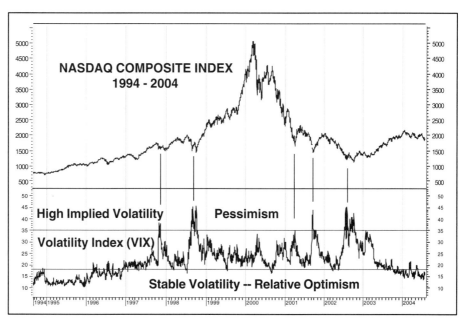

Chart 7.3 The Nasdaq Composite and VIX, 1990–2004

VIX, an indirect measure of stock market volatility and investor sentiment, reaches a level of 35 only infrequently. Such levels generally represent excellent buying opportunities. Investors have been safe from market declines of any significance until VIX has fallen from above 35 to 18 or below, although readings below 18 do not constitute sell signals in and of themselves. Vertical lines indicate areas in which VIX has risen to above 35. You can see periods when VIX subsequently declined to below 18.

The Volatility Index

The Volatility Index is a measure of the implied volatility of the stock market as it might be derived from the prices of options of stocks related to the Standard & Poor's 500 Index (SPX). Before 2003, the calculations of VIX were based on options related to the smaller Standard & Poor's 100 Index (OEX). The old VIX is still being maintained under the symbol VOX. The older VIX is slightly more volatile in its movements than the new VIX, but essential patterns and methods of interpretation appear little changed.

The theoretical value or price of stock options is based on the length of time remaining in the life of the option (the further in time the expiration date is, the more value in the option there is), current levels of interest rates (the higher the prevailing interest rates are, the higher the options will be priced), the relationship of the current stock price to the strike price of the option, and the volatility of the stocks involved with the options.

Options on more volatile stocks or during more volatile market periods are, understandably, higher priced than options on less volatile stocks or during quieter market periods. For example, if a stock generally carries low volatility, the value of a call that would represent a bet on a price rise, would be less than the value of a call on a more volatile issue that would have a greater chance of achieving an equal amount of advance because of higher intrinsic volatility. The seller of a call on a low-volatility stock likely would settle for less of a premium than the seller of a call on a higher-volatility issue because holding the lower-volatility issue carries less risk to the call seller.

Both sellers and buyers of options on less volatile vehicles generally agree to lower prices and values of options than if they were pricing options on vehicles with more volatility.

Theoretical Pricing of Options

Options traders use certain formulas (such as the Black-Scholes formula) that are designed to provide theoretical fair values of options. Of course, sellers will try to sell at above fair value, and buyers will try to buy at below fair value. These formulas are based on data that include measures of stock or general market volatility, interest rates, time of life remaining in the option, and the relationship of the strike price of the put or call option to the current level of the stock price or market level (for market index options).

In theory, you enter these variables into the formula and calculate the theoretical values as derived by the formula. In practice, options sometimes sell at or close to their theoretical values—and sometimes do not.

Implied Volatility

Given the fact that current interest rates, time to expiration, and the relationship of stock or market price to strike price of the option are all known, why would the actual prices of options deviate from their theoretical values? Well, this deviation occurs because option traders are employing in their willingness to buy and sell their estimates of future volatility in the stock market rather than past volatility. If option traders anticipate a future increase in market volatility, they are likely to raise option prices. If option players anticipate a future decrease in market volatility, they are likely to decrease option prices.

It is possible to employ option-pricing formulas to derive the anticipated or implied volatility of the stock market or of an individual stock if you know all the other variables involved, including, this time, the actual prices of the options involved.

The level of actual option prices, therefore, can often be taken as a wager on anticipated market volatility: The higher the option pricing is, the greater the anticipated market movement is. Periods of higher volatility are usually associated with stock market weakness, so periods in which implied volatility ratings are high are also periods in which option (and probably other) traders tend to be the most pessimistic.

Periods of the greatest investor pessimism are largely the best periods in which to accumulate shares of stock. It follows, then, that high levels of VIX, which imply broad investor pessimism, are likely to accompany favorable buying junctures.

Ranges of VIX

VIX readings, available weekly in *Barron's* and elsewhere, tend to range between roughly 15 at the low end (expectations of low risk and volatility) to as high as 35–50 or so (expectations of high risk and volatility).

Since 1990, when VIX was introduced, the stock market has generally proven to be a good buy when VIX has risen to above 35. You can purchase as VIX rises through that area, or you can make purchases as soon as VIX reaches its peak and starts to turn down.

When VIX has risen to its buy zone, it has been safe in the past to hold stocks at least until VIX declines to 18 or lower. A decline in VIX from above to below 18 does not constitute a sell signal in and of itself; it simply indicates the end of the almost automatic safe period for holding stock.

Chart 7.3 shows signals that were generated between 1990 and mid-2004. Interpreted in accordance with the previous parameters, VIX produced highly profitable entries into the stock market during 1990, 1991, 1997, 1998, 2001, and 2002— including even signals that occurred during bear markets, which proved profitable from buy parameters to the end of the safe period. The period from 2000–mid-2002 proved more difficult for this indicator, which did seem to resume its winning ways with signals that developed late in the bear market.

Bullish Vibes from VIX

I know of no reliable sell signals that can be developed from VIX—just the signals that signify an end to the very safe period that follows upon buy signals.

As a matter of fact, low VIX readings (like low TRIN readings) actually tend to develop during relatively stable market periods, with their continuation accompanied by steadily rising and consistent bull markets. VIX readings remained low throughout most of the 1990s, a very favorable period for the stock market, although readings much below 18 are often taken to imply some excess bullishness.

Summing Up

You will probably not want to calculate VIX yourself, but you might find it very helpful to keep track of VIX as it is published in *Barron's* or on the Internet. Be prepared to enter the stock market as VIX readings cross from below to above 35, with the intention of holding positions until VIX declines to at least 18–20 and possibly longer than that.

Of course, VIX and TRIN levels should be interpreted in the context of other timing tools that you might use, but, over the years, they have produced some excellent bottom-finding indications on their own.

The Major Reversal Volatility Model

As we have seen, stock market volatility usually increases as market declines proceed along, ultimately reaching climactic levels as price breakdowns carry through to their ultimate conclusion.

Climactic levels of TRIN tend to develop at such times, so peak TRIN levels can be used as indirect measures of stock market volatility, with a likelihood of imminent reversals of market weakness. Maximum VIX readings, which suggest high levels of projected market volatility and perceived risk from option pricing, act as another indirect measure of such volatility.

Both TRIN and VIX indirectly reflect volatility, so they tend to produce market entry signals in roughly the same time frames, which is to be expected.

We have one final arrow in our quiver of bear market bottom-buy weapons, this one a direct measure of stock market volatility. The Major Reversal Volatility Model is based on the following premises, which should be no surprise by this time:

- Volatility tends to increase during weaker market climates.

- During the transition from weak market climates to improving market climates, volatility levels are likely to peak and then to turn down.

- The stock market is likely to advance for as long as volatility remains stable or decreasing.

Although the underlying concepts are familiar, the Major Reversal Volatility Model employs direct measurements of stock market volatility rather than employing indirect indications of the type seen in VIX and TRIN.

Calculating the Major Reversal Volatility Model

1. At the end of each week, calculate the weekly percentage change in the Nasdaq Composite Index. It does not matter whether the week produces rising prices or declining prices; the absolute percentage change is being measured.

2. Maintain a ten-week moving average of the absolute weekly percentage changes. Use weekly closing prices for this purpose.

Major Market-Reversal Buy Signals

Market entry levels do not take place all that frequently and require two conditions to be met:

- The ten-week average of weekly percentage changes on Nasdaq must rise to 3% or above, but not to above 6%, which would indicate a very unstable market climate.

- A buy signal is generated when the ten-week average declines by at least half of 1% from its peak reading. For example, if the ten-week average of weekly percentage changes rises to 4.5%, a decline in the average to 4% or below would create a buy signal. If the ten-week average of weekly percentage changes rises to above 6%, no buy signal can take place until it has first fallen to below 3%, risen to above 3% (but not as high as 6%), and then fallen by half of 1% from its peak.

There are no sell rules. The Major Reversal Volatility Model identifies stock market buying junctures but does not provide an exit strategy.

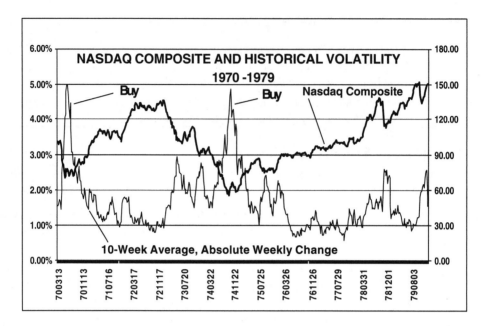

Chart 7.4 Major Reversal Volatility Signals, 1970–1979

There were only two Major Reversal Volatility Signals between 1970 and 1979. The first took place in July 1970, and the second occurred in September 1974. Both were extremely fine entries right at the lows of the two most serious bear markets of the decade.

The 1970–1979 Decade

Only two major buy signals were generated during the 1970s, each providing just about as fine a market entry as an investor might expect. These signals are shown in Chart 7.4, above.

The first signal took place in July 1970, as the conclusion of the 1969–1970 bear market was taking place. Within 40 weeks of the signal, the Nasdaq Composite had gained more than 50% in value.

The second entry took place in September 1974, very shortly before the final lows of the 1973–1974 bear market, which, at the time, was the worst bear market since the 1929 market crash. Forty weeks following the entry, the Nasdaq Composite showed a gain of 37%.

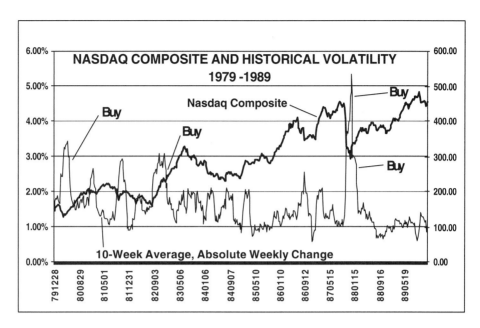

Chart 7.5 Major Market-Reversal Signals, 1979–1989

Chart 7.5 shows major volatility-based reversal signals that took place between 1979 and 1989. All signals during this period proved profitable for longer-term holding periods.

The 1979–1989 Decade

Four major market-reversal signals based on market volatility were produced during this period. They may be seen in Chart 7.5.

A major buy signal was produced in June 1980, developing more than two months after the actual market lows that took place in March of that year. Despite the somewhat delayed market entry, the Nasdaq Composite was 32% higher 40 weeks after the generation of the signal and 45% higher one year following the signal.

Another major buy signal, generated in December 1982, produced gains in the Nasdaq Composite of 28% over the subsequent 40 weeks. This gain was reduced to 20% if measured to the conclusion of the 52-week period following the entry.

A third entry took place a few weeks after the October 19, 1987, stock market crash, on December 1987. The entry proved to be well-timed: The Nasdaq Composite Index advanced by 16% over the subsequent 40 weeks and advanced by 13% over the subsequent 52 weeks.

A final entry signal took place in February 1988. This was actually a secondary signal during the period following the 1987 crash, created by a short-term blip upward and then a rapid reduction in volatility. The stock market gained 4% over the 40 weeks subsequent to the signal, and 14% over the subsequent 52 weeks.

A rapid volatility spike occurred during the summer of 1986, which suggested a timely market entry, but this is not included in the formal array of entry signals because the full parameters for a major-term reversal signal were not quite present.

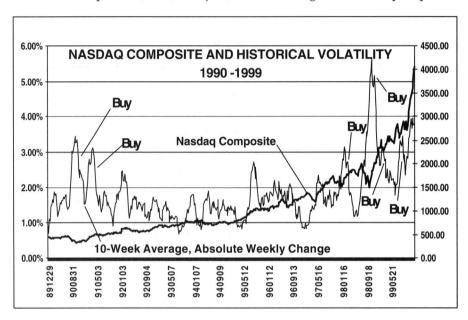

Chart 7.6 Major Term Market-Reversal Signals, 1989–1999

Six signals generated between 1989 and 1999 proved very to be well-timed. Stock market volatility as a whole increased during the late 1990s, ushering in what seem to have become new paradigms of price movement in the stock market.

The 1989–1999 Decade

Six major buy signals (Chart 7.6) were generated during this decade, with the frequency of signals increasing again from the decade previous. The winning streak of the indicator remained intact, and all signals proved profitable.

A superb buy signal in November 1990 produced gains of 51% for the 40-week period and 61% for the 52-week period.

A signal that took place in April 1991 resulted in a 40-week gain of 25% for the Nasdaq Composite. This gain was reduced over the subsequent 12 weeks, and the 52-week period ended with a gain of 16%.

February 1998 saw another major entry, this one resulting in a 40-week profit of 17%, which increased to 32% at the conclusion of the 52-week time frame.

The stock market sold off strongly later in 1998 before staging a recovery starting in October that year. The entry of that period proved to be among the very best, generating a 40-week gain of 43% and a 52-week gain of 74%.

The best entry signal of all was produced in March 1999, with the major buy followed by a gain in the Nasdaq of 64% over the subsequent 40 weeks and a gain of 92% over the full 52-week post-signal period.

A final signal in September 1999 produced gains of 34% over the subsequent four weeks and 38% over the 52-week period following the signal.

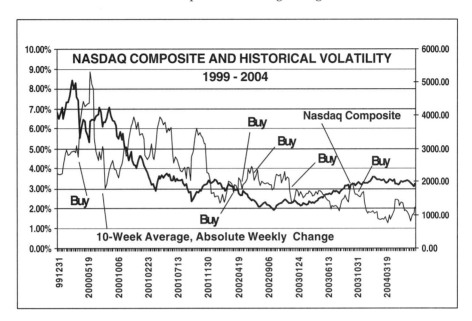

Chart 7.7 *Major-Term Market-Reversal Signals, 2000–2004: For the First Time, Failing Signals Appear*

This chart shows six volatility-based entry signals that developed between the end of 1999 and mid-2004, as well as volatility peaks that were high enough to preclude the generation of signals. The performance of entry signals was not as positive during this period as in previous decades.

Post-1999: Mixed Results

Between 1970 and 1999, the Major Reversal Volatility Model produced 12 consecutive profitable entries. However, the 2000–2002 bear market, which witnessed the worst decline in the history of the Nasdaq Composite, accompanied with the highest volatility seen in the stock market since the early 1930s, finally proved too much even for this previously unvanquished indicator. Chart 7.7 shows the 2000–2004 period involved.

The first mishap took place with a buy signal generated relatively early in the bear market, in April 2000. The Nasdaq Composite declined by 41% over the 40 weeks following that ill-timed entry and by 61% over the full 52-week post entry period.

You might notice in Chart 7.7 a series of four additional volatility spikes between May 2000 and November 2001 that *did not* precede buy signals because of maximum volatility readings above 6, indicating too high a level of general volatility and stock market instability for safe entry. Volatility readings did not decline to below 3.0 until early 2002. A series of entry signals developed thereafter during 2002 and 2003. The first proved premature, the latter proving increasingly profitable as the bear market drew to a close.

The four-and-one-half-year period from the end of 1999 to mid-2004 witnessed six major entry signals, as many as during any full decade since 1970. This is a reflection, it would seem, of the gradual rise in stock market volatility that has taken place over the years. It would appear that the concepts underlying the Major Reversal Volatility Model remain valid, if not guaranteed on a trade-by-trade basis, but parameters might have to be altered in time if trends toward higher stock market volatility levels continue.

Table 7.1 shows all Major Reversal Volatility Model signals and their outcome between 1970 and mid-2004.

Table 7.1 *Major Reversal Volatility Model Signals, Subsequent Market Movement, 1970–2004*

Entry Date	Nasdaq Level	5 Weeks Later	10 Weeks Later	20 Weeks Later	40 Weeks Later	52 Weeks Later
07/02/70	72.21	+4.5%	+10.4%	+14.0%	+50.1%	+50.6%
09/06/74	60.70	−0.5%	+6.1%	+7.7%	+37.5%	+28.1%
06/06/80	152.68	+8.0%	+17.8%	+28.5%	+32.4%	+44.9%
12/31/82	232.41	+8.3%	+14.5%	+30.6%	+28.0%	+19.9%
12/24/87	333.19	+3.4%	+12.1%	+11.8%	+16.4%	+13.3%
02/12/88	353.27	+8.0%	+5.9%	+11.7%	+4.1%	+13.9%
11/02/90	336.45	+10.4%	+7.5%	+38.0%	+51.1%	+60.8%
04/12/91	501.62	−4.0%	−3.2%	+4.8%	+25.0%	+16.5%
02/20/98	1728.13	+5.5%	+8.4%	+12.4%	+16.7%	+32.1%
11/13/98	1847.98	+12.9%	+26.6%	+34.9%	+43.3%	+74.3%
03/19/99	2421.27	+7.0%	+2.0%	+5.2%	+63.9%	+98.2%
09/10/99	2887.03	−5.4%	+16.7%	+34.6%	+33.7%	+37.8%
04/07/00	4465.45	−20.6%	−13.2%	−9.1%	−40.9%	−61.31%
03/28/02	1845.35	−12.6%	−16.8%	−26.3%	−24.8%	−25.8%
05/10/02	1600.80	−6.0%	−17.6%	−25.1%	−18.2%	−8.4%
07/05/02	1448.30	−9.8%	−10.8%	+1.4%	−6.2%	+14.9%
12/20/02	1363.10	−1.5%	−1.9%	+11.5%	+31.5%	+43.1%
10/24/03	1865.59	+5.1%	+7.6%	+6.4%	+2.3%	Incomplete
Number of gains:		10	12	15	14	14
Number of losses:		8	6	3	4	3
Percentage profitable:		55.6%	66.7%	83.3%	77.8%	82.4%
Average change:		+0.7%	+4.0%	+10.7%	+20.2%	+26.6%

Although 18 signals might be too few to meet data length standards of statistical purists, the ratio of winning to losing entries, particularly for holding periods of between 20 and 52 weeks, appears to be rather striking: Approximately 80% of entries proved profitable if held for periods of 20 weeks or longer. The model also shows clearly positive past results if positions were held for ten weeks. (Hopefully, failures between 2000 and 2002, the most volatile period for stocks since the very early 1930s, will prove more an aberration than the norm in the future.)

The model also provides a secondary benefit from the average lead time between the generation of entry signals and the time required for the stock market to respond favorably. Five-week holding periods, on average, produce rather minimal profits following the generation of signals, which allows investors time to gradually assume positions, perhaps during short-term market weakness, in anticipation of more favorable action to come. There is even time, again, on average, up to ten weeks past the generation of buy signals, to accumulate long positions. In general, major gains develop after the initial ten-week period following buy signals.

The Ideal Scenario

In ideal situations, synergistic and confirming signals will develop between early entry signals that employ extremes in market sentiment (TRIN and VIX), volatility, and market momentum and continuation signals that suggest much stronger than average upside momentum in the stock market (such as very favorable new high/new low and advancing issues/declining issues ratios). The one set of models might place you into the stock market in a timely manner. The other set might keep you in the stock market for as long as trends show above-average strength. Coupling such signal sets with long-term cyclical patterns and with market mood indicators (interest rate trends and Nasdaq/NYSE Index relative strength) might well add further dimension to your long- and intermediate-term timing models and investment results.

Next we move to what is widely considered to be one of the best, if not the very best, indicators of change in market momentum, the Moving Average Convergence-Divergence (MACD) indicator, which often provides excellent advance notice of impending changes in market trend.

8

Advanced Moving Average Convergence-Divergence (MACD): The Ultimate Market Timing Indicator?

The Moving Average Convergence-Divergence (MACD) timing model, which I invented during the late 1970s, has become one of the most popular of technical tools, used by short- and longer-term investors in the stock, bond, and other investment markets. It is a featured indicator on virtually every computer-based technical trading program and trading platform.

MACD is an indicator for all seasons. If monthly data is maintained, MACD can be used in the analysis of longer-term trends. It can be applied to somewhat shorter time periods, reflected perhaps by weekly or daily data, in the analysis of intermediate- and shorter-term market trends. It can be applied on an intraday basis for time frames as short as hours or minutes, which makes it suitable for short-term day-trading purposes. The indicator is frequently capable of producing precise entry and exit signals: One of its strongest features is its ability to detect the conclusions of and favorable market entry junctures following serious intermediate market declines.

Strangely enough, in spite of its widespread use, relatively little has been written regarding MACD or of some of the best ways in which MACD patterns can be maintained, approached, and interpreted. We consider many of these in this chapter.

Scope of Discussion

Our discussion of MACD covers many areas. First, we review the underlying concepts and construction of the MACD indicator. The charts reviewed represent varying periods of market history, varying periods of time, various MACD combinations, and varying market climates. You will receive suggestions on the best buying, holding, and selling MACD patterns; how to establish stop-loss orders; and, of course, how to apply MACD in synergy with other market tools that you have learned. Although our discussions focus on MACD in particular, the concepts involved are almost certainly applicable to other measures of market momentum as well.

The Basic Construction of the Moving Average Convergence-Divergence Indicator

Chart 8.1 illustrates the construction and the basic underlying concepts of MACD.

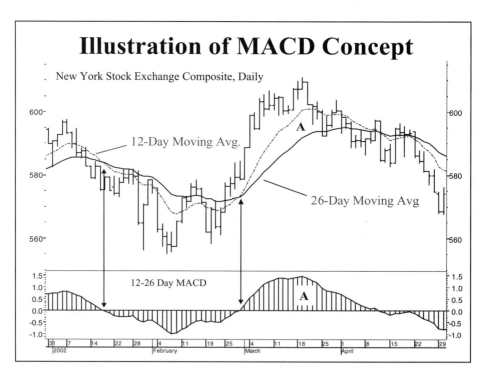

Chart 8.1 The New York Stock Exchange Index 2002: Introducing the MACD Concept

The MACD indicator is created by subtracting a longer-term exponential moving average from a shorter-term exponential moving average of prices or other measures of the vehicle that you are tracking. MACD generally rises if shorter-term trends are gaining strength and generally declines if shorter-term trends are losing strength. The lower scale on the chart is a histogram that measures the difference, a 12-day exponential minus a 26-day exponential average of the New York Stock Exchange Index.

The price scale is of the New York Stock Exchange Index, daily based. Overlaying the price scale are two exponential moving averages: a 12-day exponential moving average and a 26-day exponential moving average. Straight moving averages can be employed as an alternative, but exponential averages are easier to maintain and track trends more closely. (You might want to review the construction of exponential averages in Chapter 6, "Bottom Fishing, Top Spotting, Staying the Course: Power Tools That Combine Momentum Oscillators with Market Breadth Measurements for Improved Market Timing.")

As you can see in the chart, the shorter-term exponential average, tracking more closely with actual price movement, is more sensitive to changes in price trend than the longer-term average. As the market declines, the shorter-term average declines more quickly than the longer-term average. If previous trends have been rising, the shorter-term moving average might decline from above to below the longer-term average. As declines continue, the shorter-term average will decline further below the longer-term average.

As declines come to an end, the shorter-term average will flatten, usually before the longer-term average, and will then move upward with rising prices, crossing and then moving above the longer-term moving average.

The MACD indicator is calculated by subtracting the longer-term exponential average from the shorter-term exponential average. MACD can be expressed as a set of bars or as a line curve, both illustrated in Chart 8.1. The level at which the short- and longer-term moving average cross, where they are equal, is the 0 line on the chart. At this point, shorter- and longer-term trends are in probably temporary balance, and relative strength relationships between short- and longer-term trends often reverse. The greater the positive distance is between the short-term exponential average and the longer-term exponential average, the more positive the MACD readings will be. The greater the negative distance (short – long) between the shorter- and longer-term exponential averages is, the more negative the MACD readings will be. Area A in the top and lower scales of Chart 8.1 indicates the differential: the 12-day short-term moving average minus the 26-day longer-term moving average.

Basic Concepts

- MACD represents the difference of the short-term exponential moving average minus the long-term exponential average.

- When market trends are improving, short-term averages will rise more quickly than long-term averages. MACD lines will turn up.

- When market trends are losing strength, shorter-term averages will tend to flatten, ultimately falling below longer-term averages if declines continue. MACD lines will fall below 0.

- Weakening trends are reflected in changes of direction of MACD readings, but clear trend reversals are not usually considered as confirmed until other indications (discussed shortly) take place.

- During the course of price movements, short-term moving averages will move apart (diverge) and move together (converge) with longer-term moving averages—hence, the indicator name moving average convergence-divergence.

What length moving averages should be employed for MACD? There are no hard and fast rules, although illustrations herein will show possible combinations. As a general rule, the longer-term moving average will be two to three times the length of the shorter-term average. The shorter the shorter-term average is, the more sensitive the MACD will be to short-term market fluctuations. The 12-26 combination shown in Chart 8.1 is widely employed but is hardly the only possibility. Illustrative charts in this chapter include various MACD combinations.

Trend Confirmation

MACD signals are more likely to prove reliable if shorter-term MACD signals are confirmed by longer-term trends in the stock market, perhaps reflected by longer-term MACD patterns. For example, purchases made based on daily MACD lines are more likely to succeed if weekly or monthly MACD patterns are favorable, indicating strength in the primary market cycle. Short-term short sales are more likely to prove profitable if longer-term market trends are down. The maintenance of multiple MACD charts, reflecting varying length of market cycle, is recommended.

Chart 8.2 illustrates a further component of MACD: the signal line.

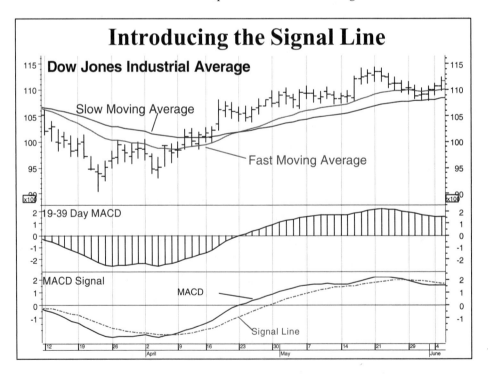

Chart 8.2 Dow Industrials: 2000 Introducing the Signal Line

As illustrated in Chart 8.2, the signal line is an exponential average of MACD levels, not of the price of the investment vehicle or index that is being tracked. Signal lines are usually created employing three-day to nine-day exponential averages of MACD lines. The shorter the average is, the more sensitive the signal line will be.

This chart employs MACD lines based on differentials between 19-day and 39-day exponential averages of the price levels of the Dow Industrials, and a signal line that employs a nine-day exponential average of the MACD line.

The Signal Line

Although changes in MACD direction (from down to up, and vice versa) and crossings of MACD lines above and below 0 carry significance, crosses of MACD from below to above its signal line (an exponential average of MACD readings) and from above to below its signal line carry additional significance of their own.

As a general rule, crossings of MACD from below to above its signal line can be taken as confirmations of buy signals originally indicated when changes in direction have taken place in MACD from down to up.

The previous buy and sell signals are subject to further conditions, reviewed shortly. However, as a basic rule, reversals in the direction of MACD carry significance, which is confirmed when MACD crosses its signal lines.

MACD buy signals, confirmed by signal line crossings, are illustrated in Chart 8.3. Notice that signal line crossings take place after MACD lines change direction but usually before MACD lines have crossed the 0 line.

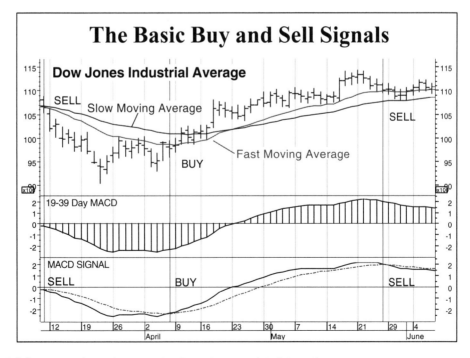

Chart 8.3 Dow Industrials: 2000 Confirmed Buy and Sell Signals

Chart 8.3 displays basic buy and sell signal confirmations generated as MACD crosses from below to above and from above to below its signal line.

My research over the years has suggested that greater net gains generally occur if reversals in MACD (especially slower-moving combinations) are employed for buying and selling rather than crossings of signal lines. However, using changes in the direction of MACD without signal line confirmation produces larger numbers of trades, with attendant extra expenses. You might notice in Chart 8.3 that you would have secured slightly more favorable entries and exits during the period shown if you had acted on changes in the MACD direction rather than awaiting signal line crossings, but that crossings of the signal line produced more immediately productive signals than simple changes in MACD direction.

Very Important Supplementary Buy and Sell Rules

The following are very significant supplementary additions to the basic rules relating to MACD buy/sell signals:

- Buy signals are much more reliable when the MACD has crossed from above to below 0 at some time since the most recent sell signal. The MACD does not have to be below 0 at the time of the buy signal, but it should have been below 0 at some time since the start of the recent decline.

- Sell signals are more reliable when the MACD has crossed from below to above 0 at some time since the most recent buy signal. The MACD does not have to be above 0 at the time of the sell signal, but it should have been above 0 at some time since the start of the most recent advance.

- During very strong market periods, usually during the early and best stages of bull markets, the MACD will retreat during market reactions to a level just above 0. In this case, you can shade the previous rules a bit as you might if the MACD tops out just below 0 during a bear market or severe intermediate decline. Most often, however, the 0 crossing condition should be respected.

Rationale for Supplementary Rules

Charts in this chapter illustrate many occasions when MACD lines change direction or cross above and below their signal lines in the process of tracing out declines from above to below 0 and from below to above 0. Such crossings are frequently of little significance.

As a general rule, it is best to sell positions following market movements that take prices from oversold to overbought levels, and to buy new positions when the market has become oversold, or at least somewhat extended to the downside. By waiting for the MACD to fall below 0 for buying and to rise above 0 for selling, you are setting up procedures by which you "buy weakness" and "sell strength" rather than buying and selling on every change in minor trend.

The supplementary rules, described above, are likely to both reduce the frequency of trading (with its attendant transaction costs) as well as reduce the numbers of unproductive whipsaws. These are pre-conditions that are worthy of respect.

Using Divergences to Recognize the Most Reliable Signals

Negative divergences are said to take place when price levels of the investment in question reach new highs, but measures that reflect upside market momentum fail to reach new positive areas.

Positive divergences are said to take place when price levels of the investment in question fall to new lows for the cycle, but measures that reflect downside market momentum fail to decline to more negative areas.

The failure of measures of momentum to confirm new highs or new lows in price by failing to concurrently achieve new peaks or new lows, respectively, indicates a diminishing of market thrust in its current direction. Divergences suggest a more or less imminent market reversal ahead, often of at least intermediate significance.

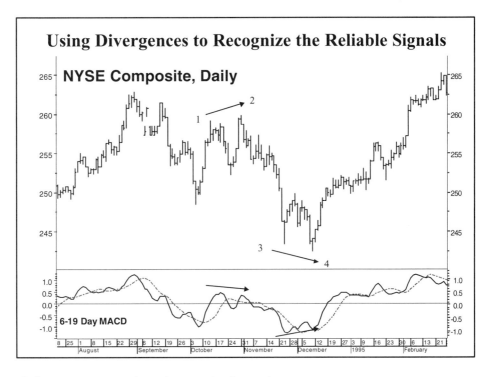

Chart 8.4 Divergence-Confirmed Buy and Sell Signals

Buy and sell signals that are accompanied by divergences in direction between MACD and price trends are usually more significant than buy and sell signals that are not accompanied by such divergences.

In Chart 8.4, you can see two peaks in the stock market between October and November. At the first peak, Area 1, in October, levels of price and MACD reached new recovery peaks simultaneously. MACD, a measure of momentum, confirmed the rise in price. The price level of the New York Stock Exchange Index declined along with the MACD, but the decline did not carry very far and was quickly reversed.

But what happened at Area 2? The price level of the NYSE Composite Index advanced to a higher recovery high, but this high in price was unconfirmed by the MACD, which failed to reach a new high along with price. This failure of the MACD to confirm the new price high was a negative divergence, suggesting a more serious decline, which, in fact, did take place.

The decline continued into Area 3. (You might notice the angle change, not marked on the chart, that took place during the decline, providing an almost perfect projection of its ultimate extent.) An initial buy signal took place at the end of November, following declines in both price and momentum to new MACD-price confirmed lows. The stock market then declined to Area 4, when the NYSE Composite reached a new low area. What about the MACD? When the price was falling to a new low, MACD patterns failed to do so! A positive divergence had developed, suggesting conditions that favored a more extended market recovery, which, in fact, did take place.

Additional Examples

Chart 8.5 provides additional examples of positive and then negative divergence between price movement and market momentum.

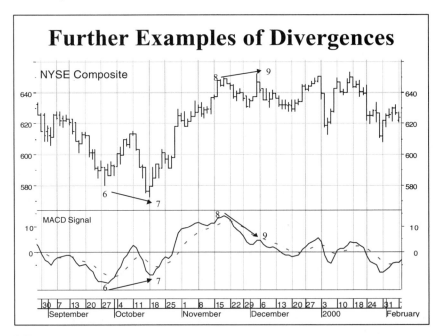

Chart 8.5 Further Examples of Divergences

In Chart 8.5, the area between 6 and 7 represented a strong positive divergence between the MACD and price movement. The area between 8 and 9 represented a strong negative divergence, which correctly foretold the end of a market advance. In this case, however, this was not followed by an immediate decline of significance. A 6- to 19-day exponential MACD is employed in this chart. (Different MACD parameters are employed in this chapter to illustrate the appearance of short-term, intermediate-term, and longer-term MACD combinations. To some extent, this might appear to contradict some of the rules of operation that I suggest be followed, but as a general rule, differentials in entry and exit levels are not considerable.)

An MACD buy signal at Area 6 was unaccompanied by a positive divergence, so the failure of the subsequent advance to catch was not all that unusual. However, a secondary buy signal at Area 7 was accompanied by a positive divergence—note the conflicting trends between price and momentum in the area—and, therefore, was better grounded. The subsequent advance proved very tradeable.

The advance essentially ended in Area 8 when the MACD produced a well-timed sell signal. However, a double top in price at Area 9 (slight new high) accompanied by a negative divergence (clear declining top in the MACD) reinforced the likelihood of more significant market weakness. The implications of this negative divergence, however, were not actualized for several weeks. The bearish portents of the negative divergence were perhaps a bit premature, but it should be kept in mind that the onset of the year 2000 bear market was only weeks away.

Improving MACD Signals by Using Different MACD Combinations for Buying and Selling

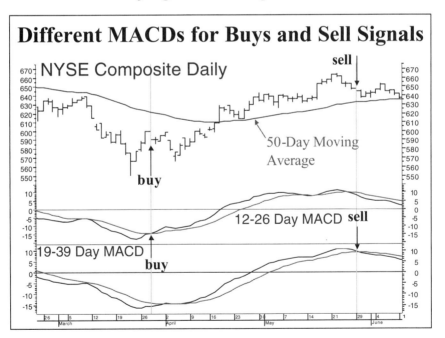

Chart 8.6 Different MACD Combinations for Buying and Selling

Chart 8.6 illustrates how more accurate MACD buy and sell signals can often be secured by using more sensitive MACD combinations for buying purposes and less sensitive MACD combinations for selling purposes.

Two MACD Combinations Are Often Better Than One

Stock prices decline at more rapid rates than they rise, so it is generally good practice to employ at least two, and perhaps even three, MACD combinations. Different combinations are useful for buying and for selling. For example, let's review Chart 8.6.

Chart 8.6 employs three elements new to our discussion of the MACD. First, there is a straight, not exponential, 50-day moving average, which we will employ to define market trend (actually, a somewhat subjective exercise). As a general rule, we shall presume that the prevailing market trend is at least neutral and possibly bullish if the 50-day moving average is either rising or essentially flat. If the 50-day average is clearly declining, we will assume that the market trend is down.

The chart has two scales in its lower half. The upper scale represents an MACD line created with differentials between a 12-day and a 26-day exponential moving average, along with a signal line created via a nine-day exponential average of the MACD line.

The lower scale represents an MACD line created from the differential between a 19- and a 39-day exponential moving average. This MACD is less sensitive to minor market fluctuations than the faster-moving 12- to 26-day MACD combination.

It is feasible to use other MACD combinations, of course, but I have found that using the 12- to 26-day MACD combination is generally fine for generating buying signals and that using the 19- to 39-day MACD combination is generally fine for generating MACD sell signals, as long as the general market climate is favorable to just moderately negative.

If market trends are very strong, a very sensitive MACD combination, perhaps of 6 to 19 days, can be used for buying, providing more rapid entries than the 12- to 26-day combination. The 19- to 39-day combination remains as the selling signal.

If market trends are very weak, you would continue to buy on the 12- to 26-day combination, but you might also use that combination for selling.

A review of Chart 8.6 should clarify the rationales behind these rules.

A stock market decline carried prices down to oversold levels in March, when both the 12–26 and 19–39 MACD patterns started to firm. As you can see, however, the more sensitive 12–26 MACD combination traced out both a rising double-bottom formation (bullish) and a crossing from below to above the 0 line in advance of the slower moving 19- to 39-day MACD combination. In this particular case, there was probably not much benefit to buying earlier than a few days later, but as a general rule, the earlier the buy signal at a market low is, the better, particularly when market trends are favorable. Remember, however, to confirm that the MACD combination employed for buying has crossed below 0 since the most recent MACD sell signal.

Moving into May, you can see that the 12- to 26-day combination crossed below its signal line in mid-May, producing a premature sell signal compared to the slower-moving 19- to 39-day combination. In this particular case, again, differentials of price levels were not significant between the faster and slower signals, but the slower-moving 19- to 39-day combination did better in allowing the market advance to run its full course. We review additional charts later that illustrate these concepts. Remember, however, that the MACD line that you are using for selling must have crossed above 0 before generating a valid sell signal.

Other sell signals that are possible are discussed shortly.

To sum up the golden rules just one more time:

• You should maintain at least two MACD combinations: a faster one for buying and a slower one for selling.

• When market trends are very positive, buy very fast and sell very slow. You can employ the 6–19 combination for buying, or you can employ the somewhat more reliable 12–26 combination. The 19- to 39-day combination is used for selling.

• When market trends are neutral to somewhat positive, buy fast and sell slow. Use the 12–26 combination for buying. Use the 19–39 combination for selling.

• When market trends are clearly negative, buy fast and sell fast. You can use the 12–26 MACD combination for both buying and selling, in which case you will sometimes be selling before the slower-moving 19- to 39-day MACD has crossed from below to above 0. However, unless a stop-out takes place, the 12–26 MACD lines should generally rise above 0 as a precondition for a sell.

MACD During Strong Market Uptrends

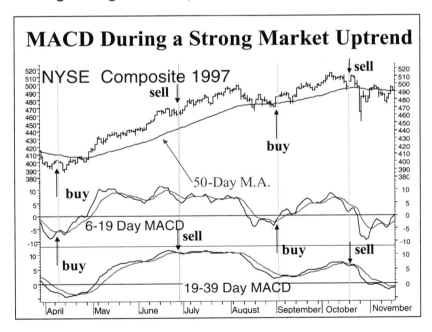

Chart 8.7 MACD During Strong Market Uptrends

The MACD is an excellent timing indicator, but it is not perfect. As shown in Chart 8.7, sometimes during strong stock market uptrends, the MACD will produce premature sell signals. You might notice, however, that the use of a slower MACD combination produced more timely sell signals than if the more rapid MACD combination, excellent for buying during this period, was used for selling as well. Signal lines in the chart reflect nine-day exponential averages of MACD levels.

Chart 8.7, the New York Composite Index from April to November 1997, illustrates an occasional pitfall of MACD: the generation of sell signals too early during strong and lasting market advances. This does not always take place, but it does sometimes.

The chart also illustrates the benefits of employing multiple MACD combinations, rapid combinations for buying and slower combinations for selling.

The sensitive 6- to 19-day MACD combination generated an excellent entry during April 1997 well in advance of a buy entry that might have been generated by the slower 19–39 MACD combination. However, sell signals based on this rapid combination would have developed rapidly. The slower 19- to 39-day MACD combination did not produce a sell signal until the end of June. The stock market advanced further into the end of July, but a new buy signal (based on the more rapid 6–19 combination) produced a re-entry just slightly above the level of the June exit. The sell signal that took place in October was well enough timed, reflecting again the benefit of using slower MACD combinations for selling.

MACD During Market Downtrends

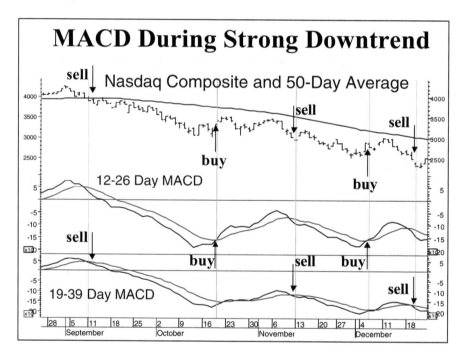

Chart 8.8 MACD During a Market Downtrend

MACD often has difficulty producing profits on the long side during market downtrends, but because sell signals tend to be more accurate during market downtrends, it can often produce favorable results for short-sellers.

Chart 8.8 shows the performance of MACD during a market downtrend. Buy signals during this period were not particularly productive, trading against the trend. On the other hand, they did not result in losses of consequence. Sell signals (which also can be used for short-selling) were productive.

Two MACD combinations are shown on the chart: a 12- to 26-day combination that is being used for buying, and a 19- to 39-day combination used for selling. During market downtrends, it is often preferable to employ a more rapid exit or sell strategy, which can be implemented by using a more sensitive MACD combination for selling. If you review the chart carefully, you might be able to identify all the areas in which a more rapid sell, based upon the 12- to 26-day MACD combination, would have outperformed slower-developing sell signals that were based upon the 19- to 39-day MACD combination.

Remember, during downtrends, it is advisable to use parameters that make it harder to buy and easier to sell!

All in all, the MACD indicator neither gains nor loses much, on balance, when you trade against prevailing market trends, but does tend to be quite profitable when you trade in the direction of prevailing trends. This quality enables investors to take positions with a certain assurance that losses likely will be well contained even if price trends are unfavorable, and that they will be properly positioned as market trends change.

Modifying MACD Rules to Secure the Most from Strong Market Advances

We have already seen one instance in which MACD patterns have produced premature sell signals when basic buy/sell rules are followed. A sell rule modification can be applied during favorable market climates that frequently provides superior exit levels during strongly uptrended market periods, while still containing risk levels. The conditions below are required for a delayed sell signal to be placed in effect:

- The stock market must be in an uptrend that can be defined by a rising 50-day moving average. A slow MACD combination is employed for selling.

- At the time that the first crossing of the sell MACD line from above to below its signal line takes place, check whether there have been any negative divergences, either in the MACD that is being used for buying or in the MACD that is being used for selling.

- If there are no divergences—MACD lines and price lines are moving in conjunction—and trends of the market are favorable, with prices above a rising 50-day moving average, you can ignore the first sell signal generated by MACD. *You should, however, take a second sell signal.*

- As a back-up exit strategy, you can use a crossing of the price of your investment from above to below the 50-day moving average, which would probably take place after the MACD sell signal that you did not follow.

Reviewing Chart 8.9

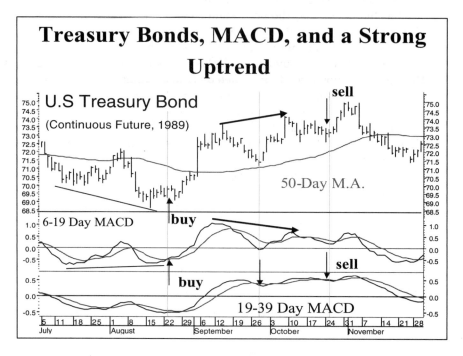

Chart 8.9 Treasury Bonds, MACD, and a Strong Uptrend

During favorable market climates, if no negative divergences are present, you often can bypass the first sell signal that develops following a market rally. However, you definitely should follow the second sell signal. In the situation illustrated, the rule modification set back the sell signal from late September to late October.

We will now review Chart 8.9 to illustrate the conditions under which a first MACD sell signal can be bypassed. Starting on the left of the chart, at July 1989, we can see that the MACD recently generated a sell signal. Bond trends were generally favorable at the time, so a 6- to 19-day MACD combination was used for buying, and the familiar 19- to 39-day combination was used for selling.

Market Entry Supported by Positive Divergence

An initial buy signal was actually generated in mid-July but was aborted in early August—neither a buy nor a sell was noted on the chart. A second buy signal in mid-August was well supported by a positive divergence in the buying, 6- to 19-day MACD, by a rising double bottom in the indicator, and by a crossing of the signal line. The 19- to 39-day MACD combination shortly confirmed the buy signal.

Moving Averages, MACD Patterns Confirm Advance

Bond prices advanced into September, with the 50-day moving average turning up and reconfirming the generally bullish climate. Both the 6- to 19-day and the 19- to 39-day MACD combinations reached peak areas along with the price of bonds, and both turned down as the price decline got underway. A turndown of the MACD along with prices does not constitute a negative divergence; this takes place only when new price highs are unconfirmed by the MACD.

Initial Sell Signal Not Reinforced by Any Negative Divergence

The price turndown was sufficient to produce an initial sell signal in late September when the slower MACD combination, which had risen above 0 (remember the stipulation?), crossed from above to below its signal line. However, this was the first sell signal after the MACD buy, the trend was up, and there had been no negative divergences, so this sell signal might well have been ignored.

Secondary Sell Signal Confirmed by Negative Divergence

As matters turned out, the bond market did rapidly recover, rising to a new high in October. Was the situation different at that time? Yes, indeed. The new highs in October were not confirmed by the MACD, which did not make a new high along with price; this was a clear-cut negative divergence. Therefore, the second sell signal in October was followed (as are all second sells). As you can see, the initial delay in selling proved beneficial. In this case, prices did rise to new highs following the sell signal that would have been followed, but, in the end, this did not result in any missed profit of significance.

Use Moving Average as Back-Up Stop Signal

What if prices had not turned up quickly following that initial sell signal? Well, the 50-day moving average would have represented a court of last resort. You could have sold on a penetration of that average, as a back-up stop loss, reverting then to the fast MACD as your re-entry trigger.

As you might surmise, this modification of sell rules draws upon the concept that sell signals that take place in the absence of negative divergences tend to be less serious than sell signals that take place following negative divergences—hence, the assumption of some risk while still maintaining a stop-loss strategy as damage control.

In the absence of any negative divergence, and with the market in a general uptrend, short-selling in this situation would probably carry too high a level of risk to be warranted even if the 50-day moving average had been violated.

The Stop-Loss When Trades Prove Unsuccessful

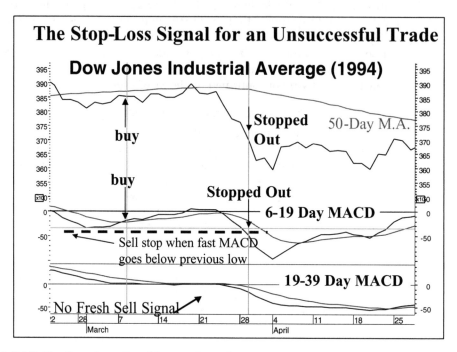

The Stop-Loss Signal for an Unsuccessful Trade

Dow Jones Industrial Average (1994)

buy

Stopped Out   50-Day M.A.

buy

Stopped Out

6-19 Day MACD

Sell stop when fast MACD goes below previous low

19-39 Day MACD

No Fresh Sell Signal

Chart 8.10 The Stop-Loss Signal Dow Industrials, 1994

The 19- to 39-day MACD selling combination did not rise above 0, so no sell signal could be generated based upon that MACD line. Therefore, we make use of a secondary sell rule that is triggered when the buying MACD combination declines following a buy signal to a low that is below the low that preceded the buy. The sell-stop is not based upon price falling to below a previous low point. It is based upon momentum readings (MACD) falling to below a previous low point.

The MACD is a strong timing indicator but is, of course, imperfect. Sometimes MACD entries will fail to produce any followthrough in the stock market and other markets.

Chart 8.10 illustrates an MACD stop that can be employed if a rise following buy signals fails to bring the slower, selling MACD to above 0, a prerequisite for more common sell signals.

The buy signal in early March was accompanied by basic criteria signifying a favorable market climate, with a rising 50-day average at the time justifying the use of the very fast 6–19 combination as the buy trigger. Prices moved up slowly following the entry, not sufficiently enough to bring the slower 19- to 39-day MACD combination above 0. A downturn in prices as March moved along brought prices below support levels (often taken as a stop-loss signal, but one that we do not use with the MACD). As the decline continued, the rapid 6–19 MACD combination fell to below the lows of late February/early March, indicating that downside momentum had increased to new high levels for the swing. This violation of support in the MACD indicator that had been employed as the buy trigger, not the price pattern, created the stop-loss sell.

MACD stop-loss signals and exits are often followed by rather rapid recoveries in the MACD, with new buy signals frequently taking place at roughly the same level as the sell signal. This is the case in the example shown.

As a key point, again, MACD stop-loss signals are created by violations of support areas in the MACD indicator, not by violations of price support. This modification of usual stop-loss strategies often prevents premature selling that frequently takes place when slower basing and bottom formations develop.

Synergy: MACD Confirmed by Other Technical Tools

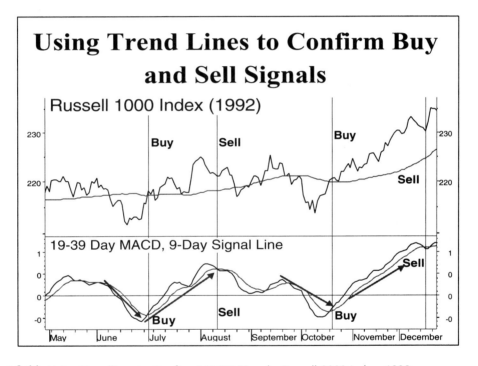

Chart 8.11 Using Trendlines to Confirm MACD Signals: Russell 2000 Index, 1992

Signal line crossings that are confirmed by trendline penetrations of MACD lines as shown on the chart tend to be quite reliable.

MACD patterns are frequently very suitable for trendline analysis.

Chart 8.11 illustrates situations in which buy signals took place right in the area at which downward sloping trendlines were penetrated, and situations in which MACD sell signals were confirmed by declines in the MACD down and through rising uptrend lines.

The combination of trendline violation and MACD penetration of signal lines is more powerful than either element alone.

MACD Patterns Confirmed by Cyclical Studies

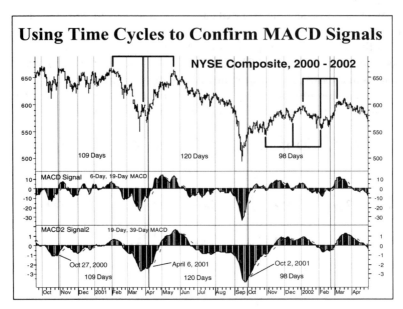

Chart 8.12 Time Cycles and MACD Signals: NYSE Composite, 2000–2002

The stock market followed an intermediate cycle averaging approximately 110 days during the period shown. MACD buy signals were nicely confirmed by cyclical projections, which can be based on momentum indicators such as the MACD rather than price. T-formations matched very well with MACD sell signals during the spring of 2001 but were premature in their projections later that year.

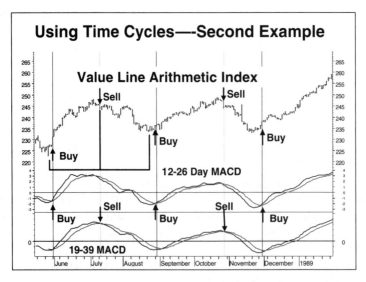

Chart 8.13 Time Cycles, A Second Example: Value Line Composite Index, 1989

Time cycle projections as well as T-formations confirmed actual MACD signals that developed during the second half of 1989.

Charts 8.12 and 8.13 illustrate the use of cyclical projections as confirmations of MACD buy and sell signals. As you can see, MACD buy signals were well confirmed by cyclical projections during both periods, 1989 and 2000–2002.

The sell signal in May 2001 fit the relevant T-formation (see Chart 8.12) almost exactly, but not the exact workout of the sell of March 2002, which developed a week after the projection made by the T-formation.

Timing oscillators frequently reflect market cycles very well, as you can see on these charts.

Market cycles exert their most apparent influence during periods of neutral price movement. Chart 8.13 is an excellent example.

If a market cycle takes longer than normal to complete, the next cycle will frequently be shorter, with the average of the two defining the basic cyclical length of the cyclical wave. This concept is illustrated in Chart 8.12: You can see how the development of a longer cycle between April and September was followed by the development of a relatively shorter market cyclical workout.

When the MACD Does Not Provide the Most Timely Signals

MACD is a very powerful timing indicator, but, like any indicator, it does have its Achilles's heel. In this regard, it does encounter occasional difficulty in dealing with steadily trending, narrow-channeled market advances or declines.

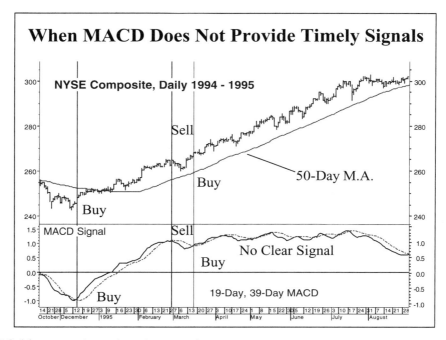

Chart 8.14 New York Stock Exchange Index, 1994–1995

As shown in Chart 8.14, the MACD provided a fine market entry in December 1994 and carried through well into March 1995, but then, along with many other technical indicators, produced a premature sell signal. The advance continued thereafter without providing a formal opportunity for MACD re-entry.

Buy signals shown are based upon the 19- to 39-day MACD combination for purposes of chart clarity. Normally, a somewhat more rapid MACD combination would be employed for this purpose.

Chart 8.14 illustrates the type of formation that produces problems. MACD did a fine job of entering the stock market as 1994 drew to a close. The initial sell signal at the end of February 1995 might have been bypassed—there were no negative divergences between the MACD and price movement—but subsequent sell signals, particularly those generated in June (which were accompanied by a negative divergence), would generally be followed.

Sometimes such patterns take place during market declines. Prices decline steadily, quietly and persistently, even as MACD rises; the stock market is very slow to respond to the favorable implications of diminishing downside momentum.

I know of no ready way to deal with such situations, if decisions are based upon MACD patterns alone. However, we have already reviewed a number of tools that might well have identified strength in the stock market and counteracted daily-based MACD sell signals at certain times. For example, the 10-day ratio of new highs to the sum of new highs and new lows might be tracking above the 90% level, or weekly ratios of advances in relationship to the number of issues traded on the New York Stock Exchange could be producing their own signals to remain in the stock market.

Money Management with the MACD (and Other Indicators)

The stock market advances approximately 75% of the time, with shorter-term sell signals, particularly during bull markets, more often than not just as well ignored as followed, on average. This applies to daily-based MACD sell signals as well, which are often followed by relatively minor market declines and by re-entry buy signals that take place in the general area of previous sell signals.

In this regard, it is often better money-management practice to develop approaches that phase capital into and out of the stock market rather than attempt to take massive action on every buy or sell signal. Given the general upside bias to the stock market, there are relatively few periods each year during which you are likely to want to be fully out of the stock market, particularly if your portfolio includes a relatively large portion of lower-volatility mutual funds that are leading in relative strength.

An MACD Configuration That Suggests More Active Selling

One MACD configuration carries clearly bearish implications—not on every signal, but based on extensive research into the history of the stock market, in the aggregate. These are the parameters:

- The 19- to 39-day MACD combination is employed for the signal to stay out.

- The 19- to 39-day MACD combination must be falling. If it turns up, the bearish implications are cancelled.

- The 19- to 39-day MACD combination must also be below 0. Although the most dangerous periods for the stock market develop when the 19- to 39-day MACD combination is still falling and has declined to slightly above 0, for practical purposes, you can view the 0 line as the crucial level that defines the completion of the most reliable MACD sell signals.

To restate, a "full-fledged" MACD sell signal takes place when the 19–39 day MACD line is in decline and has fallen to below 0. It is cancelled when the MACD line turns up, even below 0, although you might await buy signals from more rapid MACD combinations before actually re-entering the market.

- Even given the previous conditions, not every decline will graduate into serious market damage. However, on average, the sell signals described are followed by further market decline and should be respected.

- Total timing results likely will prove slightly more efficient if all MACD sell signals are followed when they occur, rather than waiting for the 19- to 39-unit MACD to decline to below 0. However, this comes at the cost of more frequent trading, with its attendant expenses and greater numbers of whipsaws.

- One recommended money-management strategy involves lightening up more rapidly with some long positions on initial sell signals, but maintaining at least some holdings until full-scale MACD sell signals take place.

MACD Through the Years: Long Term, Short Term, and Intraday

We have pretty well covered the basic operating principles of MACD and have discussed some ways that MACD patterns can be integrated with other technical tools and approaches. In this portion of our discussion of MACD, we review the performance of MACD over decades of stock market history, employing weekly and monthly MACD patterns as well as daily and even intraday patterns. This is truly an indicator that can be applied to virtually all timeframes.

The Start of a Bull Market

Weekly charts are often very useful in tracking longer intermediate and/or major trends in the stock market. Chart 8.15 carries through the first two years following the onset of the great bull market that started in 1982.

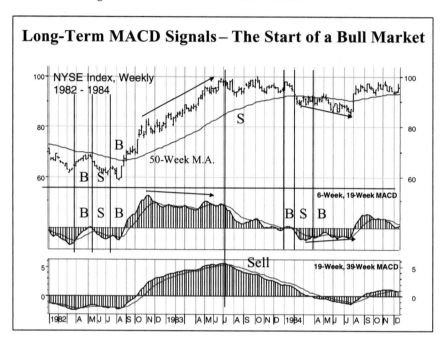

Chart 8.15 The First Years of the Great 1982–2000 Bull Market: New York Stock Exchange Index, 1982–1984

This is a weekly chart of the NYSE Index, 1982–1984.

Familiar parameters are employed, translated from daily to weekly data: a 50-unit moving average, a 6–19 MACD combination for buying, and a slower 19–39 MACD combination for selling. (A 12–26 MACD combination might well have been employed at different times during this period as the buy trigger.)

Following an aborted but still profitable buy signal during the spring of 1982, a weekly MACD-based buy signal was generated in July 1982. Prices fell to below the purchase level in August, with the MACD falling right to its previous lows at the time (which could have been taken as a sell signal), but repeat buy entries rapidly developed.

From August 1982 on, the MACD performed flawlessly. Both shorter-term and longer-term MACD combinations rapidly rose through the 0 level. Negative divergences and crosses from above to below the signal line that took place in the short-term 6- to 19-week MACD combination did not produce sell signals because the slower-moving, longer-term MACD line advanced smoothly until it generated a sell signal in July 1983. This finally signaled an end to a market advance that had lasted for nearly a full year. This is an excellent example of the benefits of using shorter-term MACD combinations for buy signals and longer-term MACD combinations for sell signals.

An Example of the MACD Stop–Loss Signal in Action

The patterns of the MACD and the price movement of the stock market during 1984 are instructive. Following the buy signal of March 1984, stock prices drifted downward until the start of August, moving to new lows as the spring and summer moved along. However, MACD levels did not make a new low in the interim, therefore forestalling a stop-loss sell signal; the holding of positions ultimately was well vindicated by the late summer market rally.

MACD Employed for Day-Trading Purposes

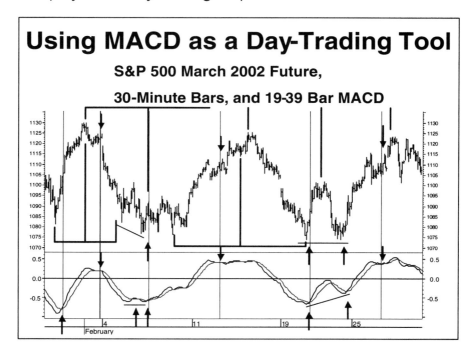

Chart 8.16 Thirty-Minute MACD Patterns and Day Trading: S&P 500: March 2002 Futures Contract

This chart is a 30-minute bar chart of the S&P 500 futures contract, along with a 19- to 39-unit MACD combination, used in this illustration for both buying and selling. Notice the use of T-formations to confirm MACD signals.

It is quite a jump from long-term weekly-based charts to 30-minute charts employed for day-trading purposes, but, as you can see in Chart 8.16, MACD patterns remain very much the same (as do T-formations, which really come into their own during neutral market periods).

A number of angle change formations on this chart have not been marked off—you might want to try to identify some of them. Two very fine positive divergences, which have been marked, provided excellent confirmations of favorable entry points. Intraday price ranges are often fairly narrow, so it is more important in day trading than in position trading to establish positions as early as possible.

MACD and Major Market Trends

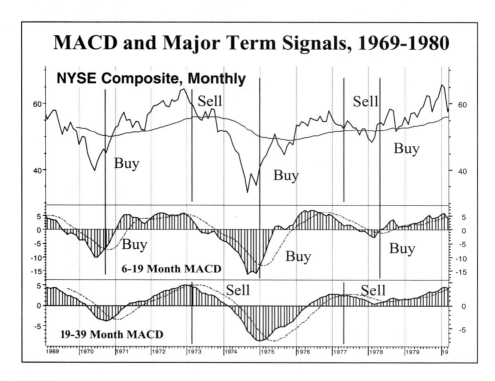

Chart 8.17 MACD and Major-Term Signals: New York Stock Exchange Composite, 1969–1980

Monthly-based MACD patterns have had a fine, if imperfect, history of confirming reversals in major market trends, as a general rule generating buy and sell signals approximately three months after actual major term peaks and lows in the stock market. (During some of the period shown, the 12- to 26-month MACD combination would have been more usually employed as the buy trigger than the 6- to 19-month combination illustrated.)

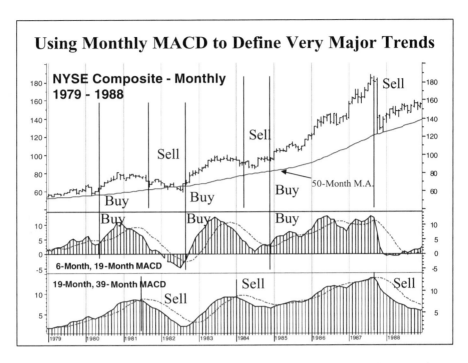

Chart 8.18 Monthly MACD and Major Market Trends: New York Stock Exchange Index, 1979–1988

Monthly-based, major-term price and MACD charts generally reflect the usefulness of shorter-term MACD combinations for buying purposes and longer-term MACD combinations for selling purposes. The 19- to 39-day MACD combination did cross from above to below its signal line late in 1986, but without any negative divergences in either the shorter-term 6- to 19-day MACD pattern or the longer-term 19- to 39-day pattern, the first penetration might have been bypassed as a sell signal. It was actually touch and go as to whether the monthly MACD was able to avoid the 1987 crash, although weekly MACD patterns clearly did so.

Monthly MACD patterns (Charts 8.17 and 8.18) reflected the secular change that developed in the stock market from the late 1960s into the 1970s and then into the 1980s. The stock market was essentially neutral in its major trend throughout the 1970s, ending the decade pretty much where the 1968 bull market came to an end. Peaks in MACD patterns actually declined as the decade moved along, with the nadir for MACD taking place late in 1974 along with the lows of the stock market.

The stock market clearly strengthened as the 1970s came to an end, into the 1980s and ultimately the 1990s. The increasing strength was reflected in the ability of even the shortest-term monthly MACDs to remain above the 0 level between 1982 and 1987, a nearly six-year period. In fact, a certain liberty has been taken in the assumption of a 1984 buy signal because the 6- to 19-month MACD combination never declined to below the 0 level, generally a required precondition to buy signals.

At times, stock market indicators, including the general principles involved in using MACD, produce conflicting signals. Decisions then have to be made based on what appears to be the weight of evidence. In this case, the rising double bottom in

MACD, coupled with a cross of the MACD line above its signal line and just a narrow miss of reaching the 0 line, all within the context of a rising 50-month moving average, would seem to have suggested sufficient justification for re-entering the stock market during the last quarter of 1984.

Weekly-based MACD patterns, as well as monthly MACD patterns, provide meaningful information regarding longer-term stock market trends. It is often beneficial to track a number of time frames simultaneously. Periods at which lows and highs of shorter- and longer-term MACDs coalesce often carry particular significance.

The Amazing Ability of the MACD to Identify Significant Market Low Points Following Severe Stock Market Declines

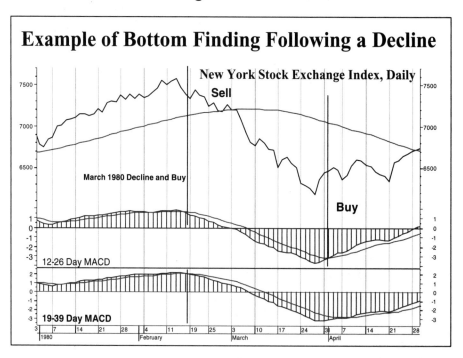

Chart 8.19 New York Stock Exchange Index: The February–March 1980 Stock Market Decline

After producing a sell signal only three days after the significant market high in February 1980, the MACD remained out of the stock market throughout the decline, re-entering only three days after the final lows had been established as March came to a close.

The MACD would be worth following even if only one of its capabilities existed: its ability to define market re-entry junctures following serious intermediate- and long-term market declines. We have already seen this ability as it relates to longer-term market trends in the ability of monthly-based MACD charts to identify major bear market lows. Chart 8.19 illustrates the ability of the MACD to identify with considerable reliability the conclusions of intermediate stock market declines. I, myself, know of no indicator that surpasses the MACD in this regard.

The stock market decline that took place during the late winter of 1980 is a fine example. Strong enough during most of 1979, the stock market encountered a second successive "October crash" (actually, not severe enough to qualify as a crash). The decline, followed by a period of base building, was reversed by a strong advance into February 1980. In mid-February of that year, high interest rates and rates of inflation, coupled with high levels of speculation in the precious metals sector, resulted in a severe stock market decline that took the normally placid New York Stock Exchange Index down by approximately 20% in just six weeks.

And how well did the MACD cope with these market gyrations? Actually, rather well. The sell signal did not occur at the very highs of the stock market in mid-February, but it took place only three days following the ultimate peak. Thereafter, the MACD remained out of the stock market until late March. MACD lines turned upward on the first day of the recovery and crossed the signal line only three days after the final market bottom.

It goes without saying that not every market cycle is so well tracked. That said, it should also be observed that the success of MACD during this February cycle was not unusual.

MACD Patterns and Significant Market Bottoms

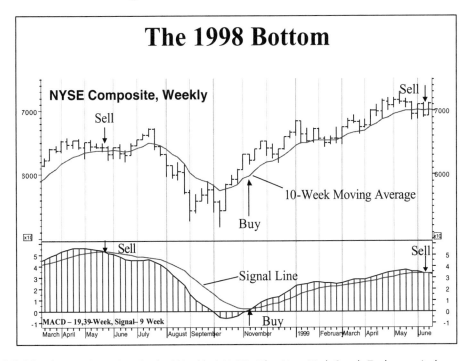

Chart 8.20 The 1998 Market Cycle, Weekly MACD: The New York Stock Exchange Index

A longer-term weekly MACD turned up just one week after the final lows of a very serious market 1998 market decline, although the 19- to 39-week MACD did not cross its signal line until five weeks from those lows. A sell signal in May 1998 was somewhat premature, but the sell signal in June 1999 proved well-timed.

Chart 8.20 illustrates the application of MACD, this time weekly based, to another intermediate market cycle. The chart shows a longer-term 19- to 39-week MACD combination, normally used for selling. The use of the 12- to 26-week MACD instead of the 19- to 39-week MACD for selling would have produced a market re-entry one week sooner than the entry shown.

After a somewhat premature sell signal in May 1998, the 19- to 39-week MACD remained out of the stock market through the final leg of the market advance and through the very severe summer decline of 1998, finally producing a buy signal in November, five weeks from the lows of the market decline. (During this period, daily-based MACD patterns produced one unusually poor and ultimately stopped-out buy signal in August 1998 and, subsequently, excellent repeat buy signals in September and October, both just days after low points of a final double-bottom formation that can be seen on the weekly chart as well.)

Weekly MACD patterns would have kept investors in the stock market for seven months, capturing the best part of the market advance.

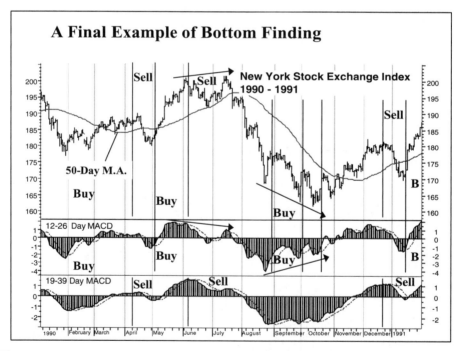

Chart 8.21 A Final Example of Bottom Finding: The New York Stock Exchange Index, 1990–1991

A successful sequence of MACD buy and sell signals took place during 1990 and early 1991. This detailed chart illustrates many concepts relating to MACD, including positive and negative divergences, rising bottom formations, wedges, and T-formations. Readers might want to make copies of this chart and draw in chart formations that have not been marked.

The 1990–1991 period (Chart 8.21) presented many opportunities for active market trading. As a final review of the operating principles of MACD, we examine the price movement and MACD patterns of the period.

Initial Rally at Start of Year

The stock market declined during January 1990, an excellent 12- to 26-day MACD buy signal developing in early February. MACD patterns started strongly with the advance, and rising bottoms developed in both shorter- and longer-term MACD lines. However, between March and April, negative divergences developed in the 12- to 26-day MACD pattern, warning of incipient market weakness. Because negative divergences were in place, the sell signal produced in April by the longer-term 19- to 39-day combination would be followed.

Brief Decline and Well-Timed Market Re-Entry

The sell signal was, indeed, followed by a relatively short-term though very tradeable market decline, sufficient to draw the 12- to 26-day buying MACD line to below 0 and establishing a prerequisite for a new buy signal, which took place early in May.

Rally and Topping Formation

Prices advanced sharply immediately following the early May entry, but by the end of May, slackening momentum created negative divergences in the 12- to 26-day MACD, establishing the prerequisites for the sell signal that developed in early June. There was a quick MACD re-entry in mid-June (not shown on the chart) and a secondary sell signal in mid-July (not marked); by that time, more serious negative divergences (marked on the chart) had developed.

The time span between the tops in early June and mid-July, approximately seven weeks, during which upside momentum clearly diminished, is usually significant if negative divergences take place during the period. MACD peaks for both shorter- and longer-term MACD patterns were clearly lower at the highs of July than of June, although prices reached new highs in July. In any event, the mid-July MACD sell signal proved to be extremely well timed.

Waterfall Decline, and Then Bottoming Process

The stock market broke down sharply following the July sell signals. The MACD did reach its lows in late August, producing initially a premature buy signal that was not stopped out even though prices declined in September to new lows because the MACD failed to confirm those new price lows.

Subsequent market action produced increasingly favorable patterns in both price movement and the development of favorable MACD configurations. Between September and October, prices traced out a declining wedge formation with its bullish implications. (See if you can draw the lines.) At the same time, the MACD, both short and long term, traced out a series of higher lows; positive divergences developed between lower lows in price and higher lows in MACD.

The market recovery ultimately took hold, with prices moving up and out of the base formation.

Final Shakeout and Recovery

An MACD sell signal took place in December as the 12- to 26-day MACD combination produced negative divergences, and the slower 19- to 39-day MACD crossed from above to below its signal line.

A successful scalp was possible between this sell signal and a fresh buy signal in January 1991. The faster 12–26 MACD first fell below 0, achieving this precondition and then turning up and crossing its signal line thereafter.

All in all, the MACD produced very accurate signals throughout the 1990–1991 period, with the exception, perhaps, of that early buy signal in August—when all was said and done, even that ultimately proved profitable.

MACD and the Four Stages of the Market Cycle

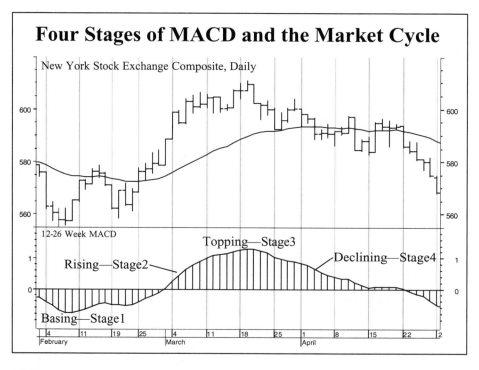

Chart 8.22 New York Stock Exchange Index: 2002 MACD and the Four Stages of the Market Cycle

The smooth patterns of the MACD frequently provide clear indications of the four stages of the market cycle.

As a final note regarding the MACD, we might observe that its patterns, which are relatively smooth compared to most market indicators, provide suggestions relating to the four stages of market cycles. Chart 8.22 illustrates the related concepts.

As we know, the accumulation of long positions takes place generally during the latter half of Stage 1 or at the onset of Stage 2. Positions are held throughout Stage 2 into Stage 3, during which stage holdings are reduced in anticipation of the declines anticipated in Stage 4.

This daily chart reflects a relatively short-term market cycle. Weekly- and monthly-based charts will reflect the stages of more significant market cycles.

Reviewing Rules and Procedures Associated with the MACD Indicator

A lot of ground has been covered in this section, so we conclude with a summary of the rules and procedures that can be associated with the MACD indicator.

Creating and Maintaining Your MACD Indicator

You should calculate and maintain sets of three MACD combinations: one daily-based set for shorter-term trading, one weekly-based set for longer-term trends, and, if you want, one monthly-based set to reflect major long-term trends. The MACD indicator can be followed for day trading as well, in which case 5-minute, 30-minute, and 60-minute sets are likely to prove very useful.

Each set should employ a short-, medium-, and longer-term MACD combination. These might include, for example, a 6- to 19-unit MACD for rapid buy signals during more favorable market climates, a 12- to 26-unit MACD for buy signals during neutral market periods and for sell signals during very weak market periods, and a 19- to 39-unit MACD combination for sell signals. Signal lines will usually be six- to nine-unit exponential moving averages of the MACD lines. Shorter-term signal lines will often produce more timely signals but will also be more prone to false signals and whipsaws.

In addition to the MACD, it is recommended that you maintain an appropriate trend-defining moving average. The 50-unit moving average tends to work well in this regard.

Buy Signals

First, test for a trend with the 50-unit moving average.

Second, test for positive divergences in your buy MACD indicators.

Third, test for market cycles, T-formations, bullish wedges, angle change projections, and potential violations of downtrends in MACD.

If market trends (measured by the direction of the 50-unit moving average) are at least neutral, positive divergences are in place, or favorable cycles or chart patterns are present, you might use the rapid 6–19 MACD combination for entry. As a general rule, the medium 12- to 26-day combination is somewhat less likely to create whipsaws.

If market trends are negative, the medium MACD is generally used for buying.

Prerequisite

Unless longer-term market trends are very favorable, a clear positive divergence is in place, or a significant downtrend has been violated, no buy signal can take place until the MACD combination employed for buying has first fallen to below 0 since the last sell signal. The waiver of the 0 penetration requirement takes place infrequently.

Sell Signals

If there are negative divergences in the MACD, even if long-term trends are neutral to bullish, sell on signals generated by the 19- to 39-unit MACD combination. Sell indications take place when the MACD turns down in an area above 0 and are confirmed when the MACD line crosses from above to below the signal line.

If there are no negative divergences in either the medium or slow MACD combinations, you can bypass the first sell signal that takes place.

If you do bypass this signal, use the 50-unit moving average as your stop, and sell if that average is penetrated to the downside. Sell stops also take place if, following a purchase, the buying MACD level falls to below its previous low point, even if the area above 0 has not been reached.

Always take the second sell signal generated by the 19- to 39-unit MACD combination.

If longer-term trends are clearly negative, you can use the 12- to 26-unit MACD for selling as well as for buying, selling on a turndown and cross from above to below its signal line, in the area above 0.

The more confirmations you secure of the timeliness of your MACD positions, the more positions you should take. Remember the concept of synergy.

Oh, yes, just in case you thought I forgot....

Converting the Daily Breadth Thrust Model into an Intermediate Entry

I promised at the end of Chapter 6 to show you how to employ the MACD to convert the shorter-term daily-based Breadth Thrust timing model into a more intermediate version that is capable of remaining in the stock market for longer periods of time. Incidentally, you can employ this method to extend the lives of other shorter-term timing models that you use. There is a very good chance that you will find yourself extending profit while reducing trades with their attendant whipsaws and transaction costs.

The rule changes are actually rather straightforward. Here are the rules for the intermediate version of Breadth Thrust.

Buy Signals

As before, you buy when the 10-day exponential average of the ratio, advancing issues/advancing + declining issues, rises to 61.5% or higher. There are no other buy entries.

Sell Signals

As before, you sell when the 10-day exponential average of advancing issues/advancing + declining issues falls to 49% or lower.

Providing That...

The 19- to 39-day MACD of prices on the New York Stock Exchange must not lie above 1%.

Both conditions must exist simultaneously, with Breadth Thrust levels at 49% or below, and MACD levels below +1%. Otherwise, no sell signal takes place.

The 1% level is calculated by subtracting the slower 39-day exponential average of daily closing prices of the New York Stock Exchange Index from the faster 19-day exponential average of daily closing prices, and then dividing the result by the level of the faster 19-day exponential average.

For example, if the 19-day exponential average of the New York Stock Exchange Index stood at 6,500 and the 39-day exponential average of the New York Stock Exchange Index stood at 6,400, you first would subtract 6,400 from 6,500 (6,500 −6,400). The result is +100.

You would then divide 100 by 6400 (100 ÷ 6,400). The result is +.0156. Multiply by 100 to convert this into a percentage: +1.56%. Because the MACD lies above 1%, no sell would take place at this time. You would sell only after the MACD has fallen below 1%, *as long as* Breadth Thrust readings stood at or below 49% at that time.

Again, both conditions must exist simultaneously.

Table 8.1 *The MACD Filtered Version of Breadth Thrust: New York Stock Exchange Index, 1970–2004 (The method of calculating levels of the NYSE Index was changed as of December 31, 2002. Data before that date has been rescaled to conform to current pricing procedures.)*

Buy Date	Price	Sell Date	Price	Gain/Loss
12/29/70	530	05/18/71	587	+10.7%
12/03/71	565	04/28/72	634	+12.2
09/21/73	610	11/06/73	595	−2.5
01/03/74	562	01/10/74	523	−6.9
10/10/74	388	10/24/74	392	+1.0
01/03/75	394	07/28/75	502	+27.4
01/02/76	507	04/14/76	564	+11.2

Continued

Table 8.1 *(Continued)*

Buy Date	Price	Sell Date	Price	Gain/Loss
12/09/76	594	01/27/77	586	–1.3%
11/10/77	549	12/06/77	542	–1.3
04/17/78	557	06/27/78	564	+1.3
08/02/78	611	09/26/78	611	0
01/05/79	585	02/08/79	578	–1.2
08/20/82	683	07/19/83	1009	+47.7
08/02/84	936	10/09/84	989	+5.7
01/14/85	1040	03/25/85	1089	+4.7
05/20/85	1160	08/05/85	1165	+0.4
11/11/85	1203	05/19/86	1423	+18.3
01/12/87	1578	04/20/87	1714	+8.6
01/30/91	1966	05/15/91	2136	+8.6
12/27/91	2365	03/04/92	2396	+1.3
05/05/97	4561	10/27/97	4897	+7.4
05/30/03	5435	08/04/03	5516	+1.5
12/30/03	6444	03/15/04	6445	+0.0
05/25/04	6429	06/14/04	6465	+0.6

Summary of Results

Eighteen of 24 (75%) trades were profitable, with one breakeven. Profitable trades produced average gains of 9.4%; losing trades produced an average loss of –2.6%. Total percentage profits were 12.76 times the total percentage losses. The model, invested only 18.3% of the time, produced annual returns of +4.23%, or more than half the total gain recorded through 100% investment in the New York Stock Exchange over this period. Dividend payments and interest while in cash are not included.

MACD Filtered Breadth Thrust Applied to the Nasdaq Composite Index

The Nasdaq Composite began its existence on February 5, 1971. The following summary is based on data from May 1971, with the first buy signal taking place on December 3 of that year. Apart from the initial trade, the model, applied to the Nasdaq Composite but based on NYSE Index data, would have had the same dates as in Table 8.1.

Table 8.2 *The MACD Filtered Version of Breadth Thrust: Nasdaq Composite Index, 1971–2004*

Buy Date	Price	Sell Date	Price	Gain/Loss
12/03/71	107.26	04/28/72	131.33	+22.44%
09/21/73	109.46	11/06/73	106.29	−2.90
01/03/74	94.18	01/10/74	91.42	−2.93
10/10/74	58.54	10/24/74	62.60	+6.94
01/03/75	61.23	07/28/75	83.09	+35.70
01/02/76	78.06	04/14/76	88.75	+13.70
12/09/76	94.10	01/27/77	96.04	+2.06
11/10/77	99.98	12/06/77	102.97	+2.99
04/17/78	111.93	06/27/78	119.18	+6.48
08/02/78	128.16	09/26/78	132.92	+3.71
01/05/79	122.05	02/08/79	123.41	+1.11
08/20/82	166.96	07/19/83	311.17	+86.37
08/02/84	238.87	10/09/84	244.09	+2.19
01/14/85	255.46	03/25/85	276.26	+8.14
05/20/85	294.48	08/05/85	302.14	+2.60
11/11/85	302.31	05/19/86	383.74	+26.94
01/12/87	385.46	04/20/87	417.73	+8.37
01/30/91	408.53	05/15/91	478.08	+17.02
12/27/91	565.71	03/04/92	630.29	+11.42
05/05/97	1339.24	10/27/97	1535.09	+14.62
05/30/03	1595.91	08/04/03	1714.06	+7.40
12/30/03	2009.88	03/15/04	1939.20	−3.52
05/25/04	1964.65	06/14/04	1969.99	+0.27

Twenty of 23 (87%) trades were profitable; the average gain of profitable trades was 14%, and the average loss on losing trades was −3.1%. The total percentage gain came to +280.47%, and the total percentage loss was −9.35%; the total percentage gain:loss ratio was a very high 30.0:1. For every 1% loss shown by the model, there was a 30% gain. The MACD-filtered Breadth Thrust model was invested 17.2% of the time, producing an annualized rate of return of 41.53% while invested. If you were invested only when this model was favorable, your annual rate of return would have come to 7.19% plus interest while in cash, although, again, you would have been invested only 17.2% of the time.

It goes without saying that past performance does not ensure future performance in any way. Many timing models have gone by the wayside over the years, performing well for periods of various length and then losing efficiency. In its short and intermediate forms, the Breadth Thrust model appears to have maintained its efficiency for more than 30 years now and has had an excellent record of identifying the onsets of significant stock market advances. Students of past stock market behavior and those of us who have lived with the stock market over the decades will recognize the significance of the market launching pads that developed in December 1971, January 1975, January 1976, August 1982, November 1985, and January 1991, for example. However, the model was somewhat later than usual in finding its way into the stock market in 2003.

9

Moving Average Trading Channels: Using Yesterday's Action to Call Tomorrow's Turns

I trust that you are finding this guide to technical analysis both useful and helpful. My staff and I employ the tools we have discussed each day as we make trading and investment decisions. In this chapter, you will learn what I consider to be among the most practical of the practical power tools in our decision-making arsenal: the moving average trading channel. Like the MACD, another of our favorite practical power tools, the moving average trading channel can be employed in virtually any timeframe, its application extending from day trading to long-term investment.

As usual, this chapter works through how to construct the necessary data and charts into an array of concepts and rules for interpreting the chart patterns observed. The underlying concepts are actually quite straightforward, very much in keeping with concepts already discussed in this book. There are elements of subjectivity, of course, in the analysis of moving average trading channels. Chart reading, unlike statistically based timing models, often involve somewhat subjective judgment—but in the case of moving average trading channels, the subjective elements are frequently well-informed. Along with the MACD, the moving average trading channel (or band) is a technical tool I respect highly.

The moving average trading channel can be employed for time frames ranging from the short term to the major term. Patterns of price movement within the channel can help determine the following:

- Whether the markets are showing increasing strength or are losing upside momentum

- Where forthcoming support and resistance levels are likely to develop

- Whether initial attempts to rally appear likely to develop a good follow-through

- When it is safe to buy market weakness

- Where and when market retracements are likely to occur, and whether the odds favor subsequent recovery

The Basic Ingredients of the Moving Average Trading Channel

A moving average reflects the trend of the stock market for the timeframe in which you are operating. There might be definite benefits to maintaining multiple channels that reflect, among them, longer- and shorter-term market periods and trends.

As you know by now, moving averages are tools for smoothing price data that clarify the direction and strength of underlying market trends by removing noise associated with short-term price fluctuations. The longer the term of the moving average is, the longer the trend it will reflect, and the smoother and slower changes will be in direction of the average.

Moving averages employed in moving average trading channels might vary in length from 5 to 50 units based upon five-minute readings of the stock market or individual securities, bonds, or commodities, to moving averages of 50 units or longer based on daily, weekly, or even monthly postings. The 21-day moving average tends to reflect market trends based upon a seven- to eight-week market cycle, roughly twice the length of the moving average employed. The ten-day moving average reflects short-term trends and tends to reflect a three- to four-week market cycle.

There are probably no hard and fast rules regarding the selection of moving averages to employ, which can vary not only by market climate, but also by the volatility of the particular investments that you are tracking. I have found that moving averages ranging from 21 days to 50 days (or weeks, for longer-term charts) to be generally useful.

To review, moving averages are constructed by adding the most recent closings for the number of days you want to track and then dividing by the number of entries. For example, if you are maintaining a ten-day moving average of the Nasdaq Composite Index, you would secure and total the closing prices of the most recent ten days, and then divide that total by 10. On the eleventh day, you would add in that eleventh day and remove the farthest day back of the previous total so that you are always averaging the most recent ten-day closing total. Almost any computer program that relates to technical analysis will have the facility to provide moving averages of various user-selected lengths, as well as the boundaries of moving average trading channels.

Again, the shorter the moving average is, the more closely it will follow shorter-term market fluctuations. The longer the moving average is, the longer the trends it will track. We will be seeing charts that reflect moving averages of varying lengths. It is probably not crucial if you employ, for example, a 10-day average in lieu of a 12-day average, or vice versa.

It is advisable to create channels that reflect longer-term trends, centered on longer-term moving averages, as well as channels that reflect shorter-term trends, centered on shorter-term moving averages, for your analyses of interactions between shorter-term and longer-term market trends.

Creating the Channel

Create a channel around the moving averages that you employ by drawing lines based on offsets by a defined percentage above and below the level of the moving averages being used. The lines created thereby become the upper and lower boundaries of your moving average channel. A line representing the level of the moving average itself becomes the center line of the channel.

For example, suppose that the 21-day moving average of the closings of the Standard & Poor's 500 Index stands at 1,000 and that we want to create a channel with boundaries 4% above and 4% below the moving average (actually, a pretty normal configuration for this index). The 21-day average, 1,000, would lie at the center of your channel. A line 4% above the 21-day average (1,000 + 4% of 1,000 = 1,040) would designate the upper boundary of the 21-day channel, and a line 4% below the 21-day average (1,000 − 4% of 1,000 = 960) would designate the lower boundary of the 21-day channel.

What Length of Offset Should Be Used?

Mathematical formulas can be employed to determine amounts of offset that might be used in moving average trading bands, to encompass definite percentages of price movement but, for practical purposes, the exact amount of offset employed is probably not critical.

The more volatile the underlying market being tracked is, the wider the channel should be and the greater your offsets will be for any given length of moving average. As a general rule, you should employ offsets to your moving averages so that approximately 85–90% of price movement of the data that you are tracking lies within the boundaries of the trading channel. The exact percentage is not crucial. The bands can generally be set by eye if you have a computer program that allows you to experiment with varying channel widths.

Some analysts suggest that bands be set so that 95% of activity takes place within the channel. I find it useful to allow a little more frequency in excursions outside the moving average channel, but this is almost certainly not a crucial differentiation.

The amount of offset from the moving average is influenced by two factors: the volatility of the market index or investment vehicle that you are tracking and the length of the moving average. The more volatile the data is, the more the fluctuation is and the wider the moving average channel is. The longer the moving average is, the wider the channel is because longer-term market swings encompass larger ranges of movement than shorter-term market swings. If you have access to a technical computer program, you can experiment and set your channels to what you believe to be a best fit for your investment vehicle.

Many users of moving average trading bands adjust band width as market volatilities rise and fall, using statistical devices such as standard deviations over various periods of time to track changing volatility. Band widths narrow as market volatility decreases and expand as market volatility increases. John Bollinger developed Bollinger bands for this purpose, which definitely provide certain beneficial information. I prefer constant-width moving average trading channels that provide certain information in a form that I find most useful. Readers might want to explore the use of Bollinger bands on John Bollinger's Web site, www.bollingerbands.com.

Remember synergy! Maintain confirming indicators and time cycles to go along with your trading channels. Remain alert to bullish and bearish chart formations. Moving average trading channels are powerful tools in and of themselves, but, like MACD, they benefit from outside confirmation when such confirmation is available.

Moving Average Trading Channels in Operation

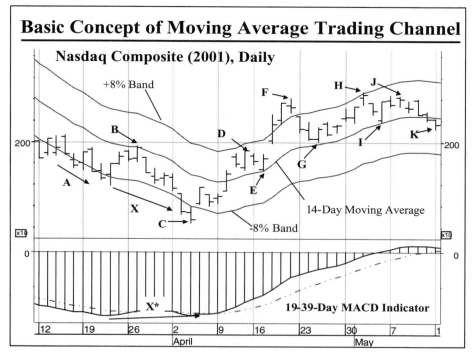

Chart 9.1 Basic Concepts: The Nasdaq Composite, 2001

Chart 9.1 shows daily price movement of the Nasdaq Composite Index during the spring of 2001, a particularly volatile period for the stock market. A 14-day moving average is employed as the center line, and upper and lower boundaries are offset by +/–8% of the moving average, a higher than normal offset because of the extent of market volatility at the time.

In addition to a 14-day moving average line, around which are upper and lower band boundaries (8% above and below the moving average), the chart shows the 19- to 39-day MACD indicator. Its patterns interact well with patterns that can be observed in the relationships between daily levels of the Nasdaq Composite and its moving average trading channel.

Area A: The Chart Opens with a Market Downtrend

As Chart 9.1 starts in March 2001, a serious stock market downtrend is underway. Price levels of the Nasdaq Composite are declining, tracking along the lower boundary of the moving average trading channel, which, itself, is in a clear downtrend. In addition, the declines in price trend and channel direction are confirmed by the 19- to 39-day MACD indicator, in its most negative configuration, declining below its signal line and below 0. This confluence of negative price trends, negative longer moving average trend, and negative MACD patterns suggests lower prices ahead.

However, as prices in Area A on the chart trail down, they straddle the lower boundary of the moving average trading channel, reflecting an oversold condition in the stock market; the downward momentum of the decline is high. As a general rule, **(Rule 1): the stock market usually (not always) can be purchased for at least a short-term upswing when prices decline to below the lower boundaries of a significant moving average trading channel.** There is a strong likelihood of some sort of a recovery when prices get this far extended to the downside. Sure enough, although a buy at the left of the chart, when all of a daily range lay below the lower trading band, obviously would have been premature, it could have been closed out with a slight profit or break-even at Area B, when prices next rallied to the area of the downtrended moving average.

By and large, however, such scalping attempts are best avoided when virtually all trends and measures of price momentum remain in a state of deterioration. It is usually a better policy to await some improvement in the technical structure.

Area B: The First Recovery Rally

The first recovery rally takes place at Area B, and we come to our second trading rule relating to moving average trading channels:

Rule 2: As a general rule, the first rally following a downside penetration of the lower boundary of a moving average trading channel is likely to fail, frequently stalling at the moving average line in the center of the channel, which normally acts as resistance to initial rallies from very oversold positions.

If the penetration through and below the lower boundary of the trading channel has been considerable, perhaps as wide as half of the moving average trading channel itself, the first area of resistance might lie at the lower band of the channel rather than at the center band moving average line.

In fact, the Nasdaq Composite at Area B did recover to the center line of the trading channel, the 14-day moving average, where it met what could have been anticipated resistance. This was the first serious attempt at recovery following a series of downside penetrations through the lower boundary of the moving average trading channel. As per Rule 2, the failure of the rally at the center band was to be expected.

Area X: The Technical Picture Improves

At C, prices have again fallen to below the lower boundary of the trading channel. However, certain changes have taken place in a number of indicators, suggesting an improving technical picture.

For one thing, the MACD is no longer in decline and is creating a positive divergence: lower prices, rising MACD. A double bottom in the MACD has developed, as shown in Area X. In addition, the pattern of price decline from B to C appears to be taking the form of a declining wedge, a bullish formation. (The downside slopes that can be drawn from B–C and A–C are converging.)

In light of these developments, aggressive investors might be justified in assuming long positions during the periods around Area C when prices lie at or below the lower band of the trading channel (remember Rule 1). The general pattern suggests a market recovery to at least the middle band of the trading channel, with at least fair possibilities of an attack on the upper band because this is the second, not the first, attempt at rally from the lower band.

Area D: The Upper Trading Band Is Reached

As matters turned out, prices moved through the middle band of the trading channel to the upper boundary (Area D). This brings us to Rule 3 of moving average channels:

Rule 3: Rallies that originate from the lower band boundary of the moving average trading channel usually meet resistance at the center line, especially if such rallies are the first attempt at rally from the lower band. However, if the center line of the channel is penetrated, the next area of resistance will often be the upper boundary line of the moving average trading channel.

Area E: Prices Retrace to the Center Channel

At Area D, prices reach the upper boundary of the moving average trading channel, retreating thereafter to E, the center line of the moving average trading channel.

Rule 4: If prices reach the upper boundary of the trading channel, unless technical conditions are unusually weak, the first areas of support during initial downside corrections are likely to develop at the center line of the channel, or at the moving average line.

Again, prices have advanced and reached the upper boundary of the trading channel. Technical indicators are improving. The MACD has turned up, rising above its signal line. The moving average channel itself has turned up. Stage 1 of MACD (basing) has given way to Stage 2 (rising). Although the stock market is clearly showing improving strength, it can still be dangerous to buy near or above the upper boundaries of moving average trading channels. It is generally safer to wait for a market pullback to the first area of support, the moving average line of the trading channel. This area usually represents an excellent buying zone if you missed the initial phase of the rally or want to add to positions. The initial retracement from the upper boundary of the channel (D) finds support at the center line of the channel (E).

Area F: Improving Market Momentum Confirmed

The stock market again follows through. Prices not only rise from Area E to the upper boundary of the trading channel, but they break through to above the upper band boundary.

Bullish Indications

Compare the slope of the advance from C to D (Chart 9.1) with the slope of the advance from E to F. The advance from E to F is taking place with a greater vertical slope, indicating an increase in positive momentum. Bullish! The moving average channel is also rising at an increasing rate. Bullish! The rising slope of the MACD is increasing as well.

Improving slopes, a rising MACD, and upside penetration of the channel are all positive indications. The odds are high that the next market reaction will find support at no lower than the midline of the moving average trading channel.

Area G: The Center Line of the Moving Average Trading Channel

As expected, prices find support at G, the center line of the moving average trading channel. The trading swing has aged a bit, but with upside momentum still on the rise, the decline to G provides one more opportunity to take a relatively low-risk entry into the stock market.

Area H: Warning Signs

Prices advance to the upper boundary of the channel (H), but warning signs are beginning to appear. The slope of advance from G to H is not as sharp as the slope of advance from E to F. Upside momentum is declining.

Prices at H are unable to penetrate the upper band as they did at F. This is another sign of weakening momentum, which introduces our next rule:

Rule 5: If a market advance does not carry prices as far above or as close to the upper moving average channel boundary as the previous advance, this is a sign of weakening market momentum and a weakening market. In terms of moving average channel theory, this failure to carry as far above or to the upper band boundary, even if prices reach new recovery highs, represents a negative divergence with bearish implications.

Areas I to J: One Final Attempt That Fails

There was just enough impetus to the market advance for prices to support one last time at the center line of the moving average trading channel (I), where the market staged one final rally attempt to J. However, this failed to reach the upper band of the trading channel before it came to a conclusion.

There is now a succession of three market peaks, which have developed at progressively lower levels in relation to the upper band boundary of the moving average trading channel. Although the peak at H was actually higher in terms of price than the peak at F, it was not higher in terms of the relationship of price to the boundaries of the moving average trading channel. The peak at J failed on all counts to match previous peaks. This progression of weakening peaks—F, H, J—implies a weakening of the stock market.

The failure at H of the stock market to penetrate the upper boundary of the moving average trading channel provided a warning of weakening strength. Traders would have been well-advised to lighten up on short-term market strength, for example, near H, and definitely in the area of J.

(It goes without saying that peaks are more obvious after they have occurred than at the time they are actually taking place. At J, you might have been helped by a minor T-formation, H–I–J, that developed from a diminishing slope to the advance from I to J, with the peak at J ultimately receiving confirmation the next day when prices established lower highs and lower lows on a daily basis. As we know, a certain amount of subjectivity always is involved in chart analysis.)

The subsequent decline to K brought prices down to below the center moving average line, which, at E, G, and I, had been able to contain market declines.

Rule 6: If a market advance fails to carry to the upper band of a trading channel, the next decline will probably penetrate the moving average or center line support.

The Basic Concept

With each swing of the stock market (and other markets), compare the power of its impulse with the power of the impulse of the market swing that preceded. If prices are falling, you might want to check out some pertinent issues. Is the MACD losing or gaining downside momentum? Are declines carrying lower in relation to the moving average line and to the bottom boundary of the moving average trading channel? Are slopes to declines increasing or moderating? Is the channel itself declining with greater or lesser momentum?

With each swing of the market to the upside, question the reverse. Are upswings gaining or losing momentum? Slopes? MACD patterns? Relationships of price to the upper boundaries of the moving average trading channel? You will often be able to gain insight into future developments by comparing the present to the past.

The Evolution of Phases Within the Moving Average Trading Channel

A Classic Topping Formation to End a Major Bull Market

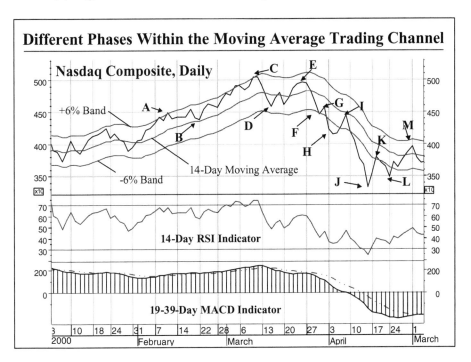

Chart 9.2 The Final Transition from a Bull to Bear Market: The Nasdaq Composite, 2000

The Nasdaq Composite traced out a classic topping pattern as the bull market underwent a dramatic transformation during March 2000.

Of course, many signs of incipient danger emerged as the speculative bull market of the 1990s drew to an end during 1999 and 2000. We have reviewed breadth failures that took place during this period. Fundamental valuations indicated gross over-pricing of stocks based upon dividend payout, earnings, and book value relationships to stock prices. Investors, both amateur and professional, had become highly speculative, with interest centering largely on technology and Internet issues. Many, if not most, students of the stock market recognized the excesses of the day, but many were afraid to leave the party too soon.

Moving average trading channels, however, provided excellent signals to exit the fray, as fine an array of exit warnings as we might ever expect. Let's turn now to Chart 9.2.

Chart 9.2: The Ingredients

Chart 9.2 shows a 14-day moving average of the Nasdaq Composite, and a moving average trading channel created with trading bands 6% above and 6% below the 14-day moving average. Beneath the price and moving average chart is a chart of the 14-day Relative Strength Indicator (RSI), a measure of market momentum. Below that is the now-familiar 19- to 39-day MACD Indicator, the combination most often employed for selling purposes.

In addition to examining relationships between the movement of price and the movement of the moving average trading channel, we will be considering relationships among price, the moving average trading channel, and these two popular measures of market momentum, the RSI and MACD. The RSI was developed by Welles Wilder (author of *New Concepts in Technical Analysis*) during the late 1970s, and it remains among the most popular technical indicators.

Our analysis of the first months of year 2000 begins with a new rule regarding trading channels:

Rule 7: If a market top or market low indicated by the action of price movement within the moving average trading channel is confirmed by supporting technical indicators, the odds of a trend reversal taking place increase. A synergistic approach to trading bands is definitely useful.

Let's now see the application of this rule.

January 2000: The Bull Market in Nasdaq Moves Along Steadily

The Nasdaq started the year 2000 in a quiet but steady uptrend, with prices rising quietly, neither reaching the upper band of the trading channel nor declining to as low as the lower band. The moving average itself was uptrended. Supporting technical indicators reflected the quiet strength of the Nasdaq Composite: The RSI was moving within a bullish range between 50 (neutral) and 70 (strong upside momentum). MACD patterns also traveled in a flat but positive area, clearly above 0.

An improvement in strength developed in February as prices reached the upper boundary of the trading channel (Area A), an accomplishment reflected by improvements in both the RSI and the MACD. Sure enough, the decline from A found support at the center line of the moving average trading channel, B, (Rule 4) before starting upward again.

The advance to the final peak at C was fairly gradual but steady. Although the slope of the advance from B to C was moderate, the final high point (C) was confirmed by both the RSI and the MACD, so there was no really clear warning of the initial bear market decline that directly took prices below the moving average line of the moving average trading channel to D, not quite to the lower band, but below the moving average center line, a penetration warning that something might be going amiss.

Area E: The Fun and Games of the Bull Market Come to an End

Prices traced out a double-bottom formation before they rose again, this time to E, an area close to but not at the upper band of the moving average trading channel. The failure of the Nasdaq Composite to reach the upper band at E after accomplishing this task at Area C was, in itself, a serious warning of trouble to come.

Rule 8: If a market peak fails to carry as high as a previous market peak, the odds are good that the next decline will carry to a level beneath the level of the low area between the two peaks. If a market low is followed by a lower low, the odds are that a following rally will not rise above the peak level of the rally that took place between the two lows.

Moreover, as per Rule 7, supporting technical indicators provided further warning of incipient problems to come. For example, the RSI indicator failed, at E, to reach recent peak levels, indicating diminishing upside momentum. Notice the divergence between price and RSI. Price levels were nearly as high at E as at C; however, RSI levels clearly diminished between price peaks Similarly, MACD patterns turned down even as the price highs of early March were being approached. The 19- to 39-day MACD line fell below its signal line, tracing out a declining double-top formation as the stock market declined from Area E.

A decline to below the lows of Area D, probably to the lower boundary of the trading channel, and possibly a significant trend reversal was to be expected for these reasons:

- The rally to E failed to reach the levels of the rally to C. This suggested that the ensuing market decline would carry to below the lows of Area D, the lows that followed upon the rally to C (Rule 8).

- Supporting technical indicators (RSI and MACD) had both traced out declining highs (Rule 7).

- Selling action would be indicated and undertaken as the price level of the Nasdaq Composite, RSI, and MACD readings turned down during the third week of March.

Area F: Trend Reversal Is Confirmed and Completed

The Nasdaq Composite did decline to below Area D, to the bottom band of the moving average trading channel, Area F. This decline confirmed that at least an intermediate reversal in trend had taken place: lower highs of C–E, and lower lows of D–F.

According to Rules 2 and 3, we might have expected perhaps a recovery to the center line of the moving average channel, but the attempt at recovery from F to G produced virtually nothing in the way of upside retracement before prices declined through the bottom band of the moving average trading channel to Area H, well below the moving average lower boundary. This indicated increasing downside momentum.

Area H produced a short-term market advance (Rule 1) that stopped, as expected, at the center line of the moving average trading channel. That was good enough, possibly, for an aggressive short-term trader, not nearly enough to confirm a reversal of what was becoming a serious downtrend.

The short-lived recovery to the center line (I) was followed by a renewed market decline to Area J, far below the lower boundary of the moving average trading channel. The decline produced very oversold readings, as far as price relationships to moving averages were concerned (prices very far below), in the RSI (the 30 level is a highly oversold level), and in the MACD (now quite extended in negative territory). However, downside momentum remained very high.

The Development of a Bottom Formation

The Nasdaq Composite finally found support at Area J and advanced rapidly to K, where it met resistance at the lower boundary of the moving average trading channel (Rule 2).

Prices dipped a little from Area K to Area L, with technical patterns improving considerably in the process. Between J and L, the RSI traced out a bullish rising double-bottom formation. The gap between the MACD and its signal line narrowed during this period, with the MACD turning up as prices rallied from Area L. The slope of the moving average channel, which had been sharply downtrended, moderated, confirming a weakening of downside momentum. Finally, the Nasdaq Composite itself did not decline as far below the moving average band at L as it had at J.

With Area L developing at a higher level than Area J, it was not surprising to see the rally from L rise to M, above the levels of Area K, which had followed upon the advance from J. A pattern of higher lows, J–L, and higher highs, K–M, was now in place, reversing the intermediate decline that had been in place.

We can learn these lessons from Chart 9.2:

- The locations of previous market turning points in relation to the moving average trading channel often provide roadmaps to subsequent market action.

- As a general rule, again, advances to or above the upper boundaries of moving average trading channels are likely to be followed by reactions that will find support at the center of the moving average trading channel.

- Similarly, declines to or especially below the lower boundaries of the moving average trading channel are likely to meet initial resistance at the center line of the moving average channel.

- Advances to well above or declines to well below the moving average boundaries might meet support or resistance (respectively) at the boundaries of the channel.

- Market advances that cross the center lines of the channel in either direction have at least a fair chance of following through to the channel boundary.

- Confirm moving average channel patterns with other technical indicators.

Moving Average Channels and the Major Trend

Like the MACD, moving average trading channels can be employed to reflect major- as well as intermediate- and short-term market trends. Monthly based charts can be employed for this purpose.

Market indices such as the Standard & Poor's 500 Index and the NYSE Index (shown here, adjusted to reflect changes in its calculation) performed strongly between 1995 and early 1999. We will track the major perambulations that appear in Chart 9.3.

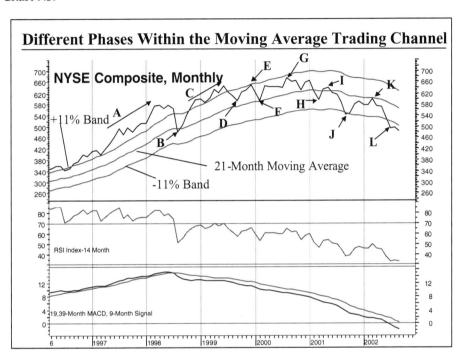

Different Phases Within the Moving Average Trading Channel

Chart 9.3 A Long-Term Moving Average Trading Channel: The NYSE Index, Monthly Based, 1996–2002

Moving average channels did a fine job in defining major-term trends between 1996 and 2002. This chart employs a 21-month moving average, with band boundaries set 11% above and below the moving average. A 14-month RSI indicator and 19- to 39-month MACD are employed to confirm the major trend.

1996–1998: Strong Bullish Upthrust

The stock market was strongly uptrended between 1996 and mid-1998. Prices tracked well above the upper boundary of the 21-month moving average trading channel, declines found support at the upper boundary, and strength improved through Area A until a final double-top formation developed.

The First Correction Stops at the Center Channel Line

A more serious market correction developed during the summer of 1998. Interestingly enough, this stopped right at the center channel line (B) of the major-term chart, an example of the benefit of maintaining longer-term as well as shorter-term moving average channel calculations and charts.

Resurgence of Market Advance

Prices recovered from B, the center channel line, moving back upward to C, and tracking again above the upper band of the moving average trading channel—but not as far above the channel as they had tracked in Area A. Again, price declines initially were supported at the upper band, and a decline in late 1999 found support at the midchannel line (D).

Technical Warnings Develop

Although price levels reached new highs in Area C, a number of negative divergences that had developed, suggesting increasing danger to the major uptrend:

- In Area C, price levels of the NYSE Index did not rise as far above the upper boundary of the moving average trading channel as they had risen in Area A. This failure constitutes a moving average trading channel negative divergence.

- The 14-month RSI traced out a declining double top as Area C developed, reflecting diminishing upside price momentum.

- The 19- to 39-month MACD failed to confirm new market highs as well. The general picture suggested that the market advance was maturing, the start of a Stage 3 distribution period.

The Top Formation Moves Along

The decline from Area C again found support at the 21-month moving average line (D). Prices then rose to E, the upper channel boundary; declined to F, the center channel line; and recovered to G, not quite at the upper boundary.

The failure of the stock market to reach the upper band suggested that the next decline would penetrate the center or midchannel line; this was the case during the subsequent decline from G to H.

Major Downtrend Gets Seriously Underway

The long-term moving average trading channel had provided investors with many warnings of an incipient bear market.

Peaks at Areas A, C, E, and G had all taken place at successively lower levels, measured by the distance between price level of the NYSE Index and the upper boundaries of the moving average trading channel. Market declines at D, F, and H had carried prices both lower and deeper within the channel. The RSI and the MACD both developed clear downtrends and ultimately fell into negative territory.

Patterns Suggest a Phasing-Out of Long Positions

The gradual weakening of moving average channel patterns, coupled with declining MACD patterns and reductions in RSI momentum, suggested some initial caution as Area C developed, further confirmed by a weakening of momentum indicators at the peak, E, and especially at G.

As patterns of this nature emerge, the strategy is generally to gradually phase out long positions, to place closer stops on remaining positions, and to increase selling activity as early warnings of a weakening market become confirmed.

We are looking not so much for a one-day signal to exit all long positions as much as for a general area in which to shift emphasis from buying and then to holding and then to gradually selling positions as Stage 3 (topping) of the stock market moves along to the start of Stage 4 (declining).

Significant Downturn Is Confirmed

By Area H, the NYSE Index had shown a sequence of lower highs and lower lows (between G and H). The failure of the stock market to penetrate the midchannel line with any significance (I) simply confirmed the warning signals that were being generated.

The Stage 3 distribution period moved into a Stage 4 decline as the New York Stock Exchange Index declined from I to J, the lower boundary of the moving average trading channel. During this process, the moving average channel itself turned more clearly downward.

As we have come to expect, the *first* rally from the lower boundary met with resistance at the center channel line (K) before declining again to L, below the lower boundary of the moving average trading channel.

The stock market ultimately found support later in 2002, where the Stage 4 decline gave way to a new Stage 1 period of accumulation.

Price action does not always follow moving average trading band rules with the precision that we have been seeing, but we can certainly see many occasions when price movements have followed the implications of moving average trading channel patterns.

How to Construct a Price/Moving Average Differential Oscillator

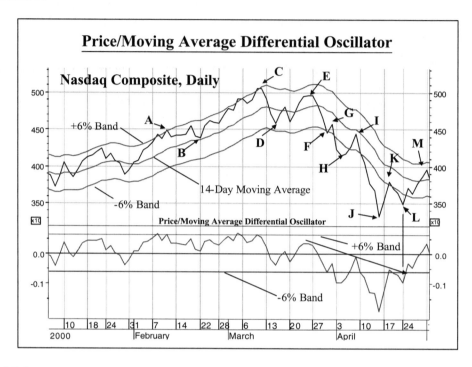

Chart 9.4 Constructing a Moving Average Price Oscillator: The Nasdaq Composite, January–April 2000

Chart 9.4 illustrates the conversion of moving average channel data to a more familiar price oscillator chart.

Although patterns that develop within moving average trading channels tell their own story, sometimes relationships between price and moving average become clearer if the data that is reflected in the moving average trading channel is converted to a more familiar oscillator format.

As illustrated in Chart 9.4, the conversion is readily accomplished. This chart includes the Nasdaq Composite Index (daily based), with a 14-day moving average with band boundaries placed 6% above and below the 14-day moving average.

The lower scale of the chart is an oscillator that can be created from moving average channel data. The 0 line on the lower scale represents the level of the 14-day moving average, wherever that might lie. The upper line of the oscillator represents the upper boundary of the channel and is set 6% above the 0 or moving average line. The lower line of the oscillator represents the lower boundary of the channel, set 6% below the 0 or moving average line. Postings to the oscillator are made each day, reflect the differential between the price close and the moving average.

The oscillator defined the consistent strength of the Nasdaq Composite during February and early March 2000. The price level of the Nasdaq tracked between the center line and the upper boundary of the moving average trading channel, with the oscillator moving between the 0 level and the +6.00 level.

The gradual weakening of market momentum that developed after the market peak at C was reflected in the oscillator, which showed steadily declining peaks and lower lows as the Nasdaq Composite first flattened and then declined.

An upside violation of the declining trendline in late April confirmed the bullish implications of the improving moving average channel patterns that developed at Area L as the Nasdaq Composite found an intermediate bottom.

A Review of the Key Rules Associated with Moving Average Trading Band Trading

Calculate and maintain moving average trading band channels that use different moving average lengths and different time frames to reflect major-, intermediate-, and short-term trends of the stock market. Set boundaries to encompass between approximately 85–90% of stock market movement.

- As a general rule, it is safe to buy penetrations of the lower bands of moving average trading channels with the expectation that, in the not-too-distant future, the market will recover at least to your buying level and probably some what higher.

- As a general rule, the first rally following a downward penetration of the lower boundary of the moving average trading channel stops at the moving average, which will act as resistance. If the penetration of the lower boundary has been considerable, the first rally attempt might stop at the lower boundary line.

- Rallies that originate from the lower band of the moving average trading channel often meet resistance at the center line of the channel. If the center line of the channel is penetrated, the next area of resistance is likely to develop at the upper boundary of the trading channel.

- If the upper band is reached and confirming indicators are positive, the first area of support will generally be no lower than the center line or area of the moving average.

- If a market advance fails to carry prices as far above the moving average as the previous market advance, this is a sign of weakening upside momentum and possibly a weakening stock market. This pattern suggests a market downturn in the relatively near future. A reverse of this pattern during market decline suggests a forthcoming upside reversal.

- If a market advance fails to carry to the upper band of the trading channel, the next decline will probably penetrate the center line of the channel.

- If a market top (or market low) indicated by moving average trading channel patterns is confirmed by supporting technical indicators, the odds of a trend reversal taking place increase.

- If a market peak fails to carry as high as a previous market peak, the odds are that the next decline will carry to a level beneath the level of the low area between the two peaks. If a market low is followed by a lower low, the odds are good that an immediate rally will not carry above the level of the rally that took place between the two lows.

Putting It All Together: Organizing Your Market Strategies

Now that you have a collection of practical power tools, the time has come to organize your array of trading weapons into an orderly approach to the selection and the timing of stock market investments. Without further ado, we move into this process.

The First Step: Define the Major Trend and Major Term Cycles of the Stock Market

Trend-defining tools: Employ the tools and procedures below to define significant trends in the stock market.

- The direction of major term moving averages—the 40-week or approximately 200-day moving average—is very useful for this purpose. Consider not only the direction, but also changes in the slope of the moving average. It is less significant if prices lie above or below the moving average on an absolute basis. Trends in the relationship of price to moving average are more significant. (See Chapter 3, "Moving Averages and Rates of Change: Tracking Trend and Momentum.")

- Study the direction of longer-term moving average channels and the patterns of price movement within these channels. (See Chapter 9, "Moving Average Trading Channels: Using Yesterday's Action to Call Tomorrow's Turns.")

- Maintain monthly and weekly, in addition to daily, MACD charts. (See Chapter 8, "Advanced Moving Average Convergence-Divergence (MACD): The Ultimate Market Timing Indicator?") Look for monthly and weekly MACD patterns for indications of strength in the longer-term market trend.

- Employing the previously mentioned tools, try to define and establish the position of the stock market in terms of its four stages. These include Stage 1, basing and accumulation; Stage 2, rising, the most positively dynamic stage; Stage 3, topping and distribution; and Stage 4, dynamic decline, the weakest stage. (See Chapters 3 and 8.)

- Keep track of longer-term indicators that have had a good record in the past of defining major-term market low areas. For example, review the Major Term Volatility Model (see Chapter 7, "Volume Extremes, Volatility, and VIX: Recognizing Climactic Levels and Buying Opportunities at Market Low Points"), and check for reversal patterns, climactic readings of new high and new low data (see Chapter 6, "Bottom Fishing, Top Spotting, Staying the Course: Power Tools That Combine Momentum Oscillators with Market Breadth Measurements for Improved Market Timing"), and TRIN (see Chapter 7), as well as for major bottom formations in the stock market.

- Do not neglect stock market time and political cycles. The 48-month or approximate four-year stock market cycle has been significant for decades. (See Chapter 5, "Political, Seasonal, and Time Cycles: Riding the Tides of Market Wave Movements.") *A favorite!* Pre-election years have shown gains in the Standard & Poor's 500 Index during 16 of 19 four-year cycles since 1931. Only two years, 1931 and 1939, actually showed losses; 1947 was a break-even. The pre-election year cycle produced 14 consecutive winning years between 1951 and 2003. (See Chapter 5.)

The Second Step: Check Out Market Mood Indicators and Seasonal Cycles

- Maintain and keep track of the Nasdaq/New York Stock Exchange Relative Strength Indicator. (See Chapter 2, "Two Quick-and-Dirty Stock Market Mood Indicators.") The stock market has generally produced superior rates of return in virtually all market sectors during periods when the Nasdaq Composite has led the NYSE Index in relative strength. In addition to the formal techniques for defining the position of this indicator described in Chapter 2, you might maintain MACD readings and moving average trading channels based upon weekly levels of this relative strength indicator.

- Maintain and keep track of the Intermediate Monetary Filter, described in Chapter 2, which, like the Nasdaq/NYSE Index Relative Strength Indicator, can be employed to separate investment climates during which stocks are most likely to thrive from investment climates during which stocks generally show relatively small gain.

- Seasonal influences as well as cyclical forces (see Chapter 5) provide their own market mood suggestions. *A favorite!* The three-month period between November and January has a strong bias to the upside. October historically has been a month that sees the completion of market declines.

The Third Step: Establish the Direction and Strength of the Current Intermediate Trend and Try to Project the Time and Place of the Next Intermediate-Term Reversal Area

Useful tools for this purpose include these:

- **MACD (Chapter 8):** Maintain weekly and daily MACD calculations. Look for trends in MACD, positive and negative divergences, slopes of rises and declines in MACD, and particularly trendline breaks in the slopes of moving average lines. Slow MACD is very useful in this regard.

- **Moving average trading channels (Chapter 9):** These work well in conjunction with MACD and also on their own for intermediate trend as well as shorter-term and longer-term trend analysis.

- **Rate of change indicators:** Ten-day rate of change measurements, 21-day rate of change measurements, and others (see Chapter 3) provide perspective on whether trends are gaining or losing momentum. Look for positive and negative divergences between market momentum and price for early notice of stock market reversal.

- **Market breadth indicators:** Advance-decline lines of major exchanges, as well as the numbers of issues rising to new highs or falling to new lows (see Chapter 6), should be followed for indications of the strength of breadth during market advances and declines. It is unusual for the stock market to undergo significant decline during periods of strong and improving breadth. Look for improvements in new high/low relationships as a precursor to the completion of market declines, to slippage in these areas as an early warning of market decline to follow.

To project likely time frames and locations of turning points, use these tools:

- Intermediate-term time cycles and T-formations (see Chapter 5).

- Chart patterns—Angle changes, reversal formations, wedges, trendline support, and resistance areas (see Chapter 4, "More Than Just Pretty Pictures: Power Tool Chart Patterns").

- Seasonal considerations.

- Sentiment indications, such as VIX (see Chapter 7).

These special statistical timing models are useful for intermediate traders:

- The Triple Momentum Nasdaq Index Trading Model (see Chapter 4) provides statistically derived buy and sell signals that can be followed on a purely objective basis.

- The MACD Filtered Breadth Impulse Model (see Chapter 8) employs a combination of trends in MACD levels and measurements that define unusually strong upside breadth impulses to produce a powerful intermediate term buy/sell indicator.

- The 90–80 New High–New Low Indicator and the Weekly Impulse Continuation Signal both indicate periods of above average market strength. For as long as these indicators are tracking in favorable territory, the stock market is rated at least a hold. (See Chapter 6.)

The Fourth Step: Fine-Tune Your Intermediate-Term Studies with Studies Based on Shorter-Term Daily—or Even Hourly—Market Readings

The following tools and tactics should help you develop more precise entries and exits, even if you are an intermediate term trader.

- Check out daily and/or hourly data for short-term market trends and momentum. MACD, rates of change, chart patterns, and shorter-term hourly and/or daily market cycles might be useful.

- Here's a special short term buy/sell timing model: The short-term version of the Daily Based Breadth Impulse Signal triggers infrequently but very reliably to indicate shorter-term, high-momentum market advances. This indicator can be employed with MACD as a sell filter, in which case it can graduate into a full-scale intermediate-term hold indicator. (See Chapters 6 and 8.)

Remember Our Favorite Mutual Fund Selection Strategy!

Of course, many measures of intrinsic value, current momentum, and other tools might go into the selection of vehicles in which to invest, which are beyond the scope of this study of tools of technical analysis.

The method of selecting mutual funds based on relative strength (see Chapter 1, "The No-Frills Investment Strategy") is among our favorite strategies for selecting and rotating your investments. This method features, within its structure, concepts related to relative strength and the benefits of lower volatility and true value. It is highly recommended!

Lessons I Have Learned During 40 Years as a Trader

These are hardly original, which makes them no less valid. As you might notice, many, if not most, are associated not so much with the stock market as with our own attitudes as traders. Unfortunately, most investors pay for what they learn over the years in some way. I have certainly paid in bad experiences for much of what I have learned. Maybe you can save yourself some money by considering the price of this book your payment and go directly on from there. Here they are, in no particular order:

- The news media, including the stock market TV channels, tend to be the last to know and almost always tend to follow stock market trends rather than to lead them. As a general rule, a good time to buy stocks is when the popular magazines and front pages of major newspapers are featuring stories dealing with bear markets and investor doom. In a similar vein, stock market newsletters and advisory services have not had the very best of records in terms of market forecasting. The greater "gurus" have often tended not to be more correct than others.

- There might be many benefits in attending lectures, meetings, and technical classes regarding trading tactics and investing, but it is probably best to operate alone in making and implementing actual trading decisions and to assume, within yourself, the responsibilities of poor trades and the credit for good ones.

- Similarly, it is best to keep your results and performance private. The temptation to boast of your successes and fears of reporting failures will almost certainly not help your performance.

- Human nature operates against good trading practices. We enjoy taking profits and hate taking losses. As a result, traders often tend to close out their strongest positions too early (locking up the profit) and maintain their weakest positions for too long ("not a loss until I take it") instead of letting their strongest positions run and closing out their weakest with small losses.

  Keep in mind that even the best timing models tend to be profitable only a certain percentage of the time, but their winning trades are much larger, on average, than their losing trades.

- The name of the game is to make a good (but not unreasonably good) return for your time and capital, not to feel "smart." I know many, many people who overextended their welcome in the stock market as 1999 moved into 2000, not because they failed to recognize the dangers of the stock market, but because they were having such a good time feeling smart during the bull market that they hated to leave the party.

- Don't confuse rising stock prices with being a financial genius.

- For most people, in-and-out trading will not be as profitable as well-considered intermediate-term trading. It is not easy to overcome the additional costs in transaction expenses and bid-ask spreads involved in day trading and very short-term trading, although there are, no doubt, successful traders in this regard.

- It is better to miss a profit than to take a loss. Go back to Chapter 1 regarding this subject.

- For the most part, it is probably best not to operate at the market opening. There are pauses during the day, usually at around 10:30 a.m. Eastern time and around 1:15 to 1:30 p.m., when the stock market is quieter and when you can act with relative calm.

- Do not enter into an invested position without an exit plan.

- It is much better to trade with no more capital than you can comfortably risk.

- One successful trade makes us feel good. Two successful trades in a row make us feel pretty smart. Three consecutive successful trades makes us feel like a genius. That's when they get us....

- Make note of your losing transactions. Have you violated some basic rules of trading or investing because of some emotional reason? There will be losses.

  Not every losing trade is a mistake. The stock market, at best, is a game of probabilities.

- Finally, we have reviewed in this book many techniques and tools that are designed to help you identify market conditions that most favor profitable investing. There is no need to be invested in the stock market at all times. If matters appear unclear or if you are less certain than usual (there's no such thing as certainty regarding stocks), be free to simply stand aside until matters clarify.

Recommended Reading and Resources

The following is by no means an all-inclusive list of useful literature, but it does include many of my favorite resources.

Charting Resources

Metastock: Equis International, 90 South 400 West, Suite 620, Salt Lake City, UT, 84101 (*http://www.equis.com*).

This technical charting service provides historical data that you can download, as well as the capacity to create longer- and shorter-term charts that include price levels as well as various indicators and cyclical data. The majority of charts in this work were created with this program.

TradeStation: TradeStation Securities, Inc., TradeStation Building, 8050 SW 10th Street, Suite 2000, Plantation, FL, 33324 (*http://www.TradestationWorld.com*).

This real-time online quotation service provided by a brokerage firm can be employed to track the movement of the stock market and individual securities during the day. The program also provides historical data as far back as 1981, along with the capacity to chart and to conduct research via a built-in program and language facility. You can find charts at a relatively low price, compared to many such services. Rates are reduced further if you become a client of the brokerage firm.

Sources for Research

Formula Research, by Nelson F. Freeburg, Editor, 4646 Poplar Avenue, Suite 401, Memphis, TN, 38117 (1-800–720–8607).

This is a highly regarded source of research and suggested timing models relating to the stock, bond, and other markets. Research studies, usually based upon statistical studies of long-term market history, are objective and reasonable in their promise and description. The mathematical bases require some statistical savvy, but not more than is required in this book. It is unlikely that you will find get-rich schemes—the editors are too realistic for that—but you will learn things about stock market behavior in general, in addition to specific timing models.

Technical Analysis of Stocks & Commodities, 4757 California Ave. S.W., Seattle, WA, 98116 (*http://www.traders.com*).

This monthly publication publishes often highly sophisticated articles relating to stock and commodity market charting, research, trading strategies, money management, and other topics. Articles often require familiarity with advanced mathematical concepts and computer programming. It's a favorite among research-oriented technicians, with interesting concepts even for relatively inexperienced technical analysts.

Books Relating to Technical Analysis

Trading for a Living, by Dr. Alexander Elder (John Wiley & Sons, 1993).

This is a fine general introduction to technical analysis, the psychology of investing, and money management by Dr. Alexander Elder, a well-known educator on matters involving trading and a psychiatrist. Also recommended by the same author is *Come into My Trading Room* (2002), a more detailed work on the same subjects, also published by Wiley. Dr. Elder provides educational programs in stock market trading at special investor seminars. Further information may be secured at *www.elder.com*.

Bollinger on Bollinger Bands, **by John Bollinger (McGraw-Hill, 2002).**

This is John Bollinger's definitive book on the creation and use of moving average trading bands that are adjusted for market volatility. It includes many suggestions on the use of trading bands and an education into technical analysis in general. This book is a fine supplement to Chapter 9 of this book, which discusses moving average trading channels.

The Stock Trader's Almanac, **by the Hirsch Organization (Wiley & Co., 2005).**

An annual publication since 1966, originally edited by Yale Hirsch and now by Jeffrey Hirsch. Formerly distributed by the Hirsch Organization, it is now published by Wiley & Co. This is the ultimate seasonal publication, with articles regarding stock market investment in general and seasonal influences upon the stock market in particular. Yale Hirsch has been a well-known pioneer in seasonal investing. The Almanac contains excellent historical data along with reports regarding changes in seasonal influences and trends.

Investment Newsletters

NoLoad Fund*X, **235 Montgomery St., Suite 1049, San Francisco, CA, 94104** (*http://www.fundx.com*).

This investment newsletter maintains and recommends mutual fund portfolios that fit strategies discussed in Chapter 1 related to the maintenance of mutual fund portfolios on the basis of relative strength. The Hulbert Financial Digest has awarded high marks to this newsletter for its performance over the years.

The Value Line Investment Survey, **220 E. 42nd St., New York, NY, 10017** (*http://www.valueline.com*).

This venerable newsletter has secured above-average performance over the decades with portfolios of selections from more than 1,700 monitored stocks ranked for timeliness and safety. It is suited more for investors than short-term traders. For best results, sufficient assets are required to support a diversified portfolio. The performance of this report has been monitored by the Hulbert Financial Digest, which has rated the newsletter highly.

The Chartist, **P.O. Box 758, Seal Beach, CA, 90740.**

In publication since 1969, *The Chartist*, edited by Dan Sullivan, has been among the longest-lasting investor newsletters, joined by *The Chartist Mutual Fund Letter*, since 1988. *The Chartist* is a technically oriented newsletter with a major focus on intermediate market trends and relatively infrequent trading. Portfolios recommended in the newsletter are maintained by the editors in real time with real capital.

Ned Davis Research Investment Strategy, **2100 RiverEdge Parkway, Suite 750, Atlanta, GA, 30328 (*www.ndr.com*).**

A highly regarded publication, widely employed by institutional portfolio and money managers. Includes a variety of printed and online reports including economic data, technical indicators, timing models, industry, individual stock analysis and market outlooks and more. Periodic conference calls to subscribers supplement the publication.

One final word:

You have learned what I believe you will find to be a number of useful practical power tools. If you have gotten this far along, I believe that you have the will. There will be winners. And there will be losers. Hope for the one, but do expect the other. Keep at it. With my very best for good trading....

Gerald Appel

Index

Symbols

A

B

N

O

P

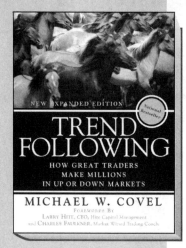
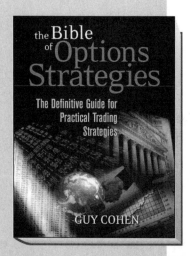